D1029006

THE LIFE OF
ARTEMAS WARD

ARTEMAS WARD

At the age of Sixty-Seven

From the portrait by Charles Willson Peale in Independence Hall.

THE LIFE

OF

ARTEMAS WARD

THE FIRST COMMANDER-IN-CHIEF
OF THE AMERICAN REVOLUTION

A man "universally esteemed, beloved and confided in by his army and their country."—*John Adams.*

BY

CHARLES MARTYN

NEW YORK
ARTEMAS WARD
1921

CONTENTS

ILLUSTRATIONS

PUBLISHER'S PREFACE

FROM my childhood I had hoped to write the biography of my great-grandfather, Artemas Ward, the first commander-in-chief of the American Revolution, and I have always promised myself that some day I would publish a life story that would give him his rightful place among Revolutionary leaders.

I have not been alone in my uneasy conviction that Artemas Ward's memory has been unjustly neglected. Others, though lacking the impulse of relationship, have felt that in the history of the founding of the United States there is a blank that should be filled with the story of his life. Even so long as eighty-one years ago, Emory Washburn expressed a hope that some one would "yet" prepare a biography of General Ward that would "do justice to the memory of one of the earliest and bravest of the patriots of the Revolution."

If a commonplace biography would have contented me, it could have been produced very easily by interweaving some of the original material in the Artemas Ward Manuscripts with a conventional account of the American Revolution and the establishment of the United States, but I had no desire to write or publish such a biography.

To accomplish what I desired involved a great amount of research—it was plainly a labor of years. I continually hoped to be able to set aside all other claims upon my time and to devote my whole attention to the task, but the opportunity always evaded me, and, finally, I turned to Mr. Charles Martyn and commissioned him to do the research for me. I knew that he would spare no effort in the hunt for original pertinent material, and, further, that there was not the slightest danger that he would gild a point or dodge an issue for the sake of making a palatable story.

In giving this commission, my intention had been to write the biography myself on the foundation of the material that Mr. Martyn should gather, but as he progressed and turned up record after record that threw new light on the ancestor whom I so greatly admire, and from these records presented me with a living portrait of Artemas Ward as his contemporaries knew him, I increasingly felt that his memory would be better served if his biography were written by the man who had made so intensive a study of his career.

Therefore I finally decided to entrust the entire work to Mr. Martyn, and I feel that this volume is both my justification and reward. Its accuracy, its completeness, and its many newly presented points will, I am confident, win for it a permanent place among standard histories. I do not think that any reader will take exception to the statement that no one can obtain a correct understanding of the siege of Boston unless he supplements other authorities with a perusal of the several chapters devoted to it in this biography.

ARTEMAS WARD.

INTRODUCTION

THIS volume, modest though its size, represents a great deal of labor. It has involved a personal scrutiny of the original official records of half a century, and of a great quantity of other material, printed and manuscript, in scores of public and private depositories.

Its story is of the high elevation of an eighteenth-century Massachusetts country-township leader. In Artemas Ward it presents a type as clear-cut and distinct as that of the Samuel Adams of the Boston town-meeting and the wealthy Washington of Virginia; and it tells of a life lived in the strength of an unquestioning faith in the Puritan religion, of an intelligence of high order "directed chiefly to the practical interests of mankind," of a character distinguished by industry, and patience, and forgetfulness of self, by tenacity of conviction and complete integrity.

I have worked throughout with the intent to produce a biography faithful to accuracy. I have kept ever in mind the title of historians and students to the full evidence without interpolation, omission, or evasion; and I have ruthlessly discarded pleasing family traditions except when I have found them to be supported by impartial authorities.

I gratefully acknowledge the invaluable assistance of many individuals.

Chief among them is Mr. Artemas Ward of New York, publisher of the biography, whose whole-hearted coöperation has been extended every step of the way, who stimulated enthusiasm when the task grew wearisome—who never begrudged expense, and who sturdily agreed with me on an unswerving policy of the *truth,—only the truth*,—and the *whole truth.*

Next came Miss Clara Denny Ward of Shrewsbury, Mass., custodian of the Artemas Ward Manuscripts. It is my one regret that she did not survive to read the story in which she was so keenly interested.

Lengthening the list are the other descendants of General Ward who opened family collections for my use, and officers of archives, historical societies, and libraries.

A great deal of my material was obtained from the rich store of manuscripts in the Massachusetts Archives. Most of my research there was done while Mr. James J. Tracy was Chief, and he accorded me every possible aid and facility. I found the same earnest effort to be of service when Mr. John H. Edmonds succeeded Mr. Tracy. A special tribute is due to Miss Alice R. Farnum, First Assistant, for much long-continued painstaking investigation.

I have frequently delved also in the collections of the Massachusetts Historical Society and the American Antiquarian Society; and Mr. Julius H. Tuttle, librarian of the former, and Mr. Clarence S. Brigham, librarian of the latter, have always met me with most kindly helpfulness.

I have, in addition, spent months in the New York Public Library and have enjoyed the consistent courtesy of its officials; and I have been the recipient of many favors from the Manuscript Division of the Library of Congress, from the Boston Public Library, and from Mr. William C. Lane, librarian of Harvard College.

Finally, I acknowledge my indebtedness to Lord Dartmouth, great-great-grandson of the Lord Dartmouth of this biography, for generously free access to the famous Dartmouth Manuscripts; and to Mrs. Harriette M. Forbes for having placed at my service the manuscript of her forthcoming Bibliography of Early New England Diaries.

For the convenience of students and in support of statements, I have given copious references, except that I have omitted all references to executive and legislative journals. Every statement made of the proceedings of the Massachusetts General Court, the Provincial Congresses, the Continental Congress, and the United States Congress has—unless otherwise especially noted—been taken from the official journals, and, being dated, can be found almost as easily without, as with, page numbers. To have given references for all such statements would have greatly increased the number of foot-notes, and would have been of only trifling assistance to students.

CHARLES MARTYN.

ARTEMAS WARD

CHAPTER I

The Birth of Artemas Ward. His Boyhood

MASSACHUSETTS was in the throes of a religious awakening when on Sunday, November 26,[1] 1727, in the new settlement of Shrewsbury, a boy was born "unto Nahum Ward and Martha, his wife." They christened him "Artemas," having drawn the name from the Bible in the old New England way. This book is his biography.

In 1727 we are still but a little way beyond our first century in North America.

The English colonies have waxed strong despite their losses and tribulations in conflict with nature, the French, and the Indians; despite their struggles with fiscal problems; despite the mixed blessings of the imperial control of the seventeenth (and eighteenth) centuries. Their farms and plantations are productive, their ships and boats are many, and their commerce has steadily grown.

Their dominion comprises, however, a mere ribbon of territory along the Atlantic seaboard. And if one add to it the French settlements and outposts to the north and west, and the Spanish efforts to the south and southwest, the total thus attained of all the works of European hands and brains on the North American continent is still utterly overshadowed by the immensity of the unconquered spaces—the millions of miles of wild land peopled by savages. The French and English bloodily disputed the ownership of a continent upon whose surface all their forces were but as toy soldiers on a prairie.

[1] *Shrewsbury Town Meeting Records,* I, 300. Not November *27,* as generally stated.

This was less than two hundred years ago—yet there are today within the United States a number of cities which have each a greater population than the total, then, of *all* the white people in North America.

The house in which Artemas Ward was born, and in which he grew to manhood, stood back from the Connecticut Road—later known as the Great Country Road (frequently abbreviated to the Great Road or the Country Road), the Post Road, the County Road, and (now) the State Road—nearly opposite the present Artemas Ward House. It was a square frame structure, with a big stone chimney and home-hewn oaken timbers.[2]

His father—known generally at that time as "Lieutenant Ward" from his militia rank—was a man of importance in the little group of farmers which constituted the Shrewsbury community. He had been one of the founders of the township—as, early in the history of New England, *his* grandfather, William Ward, a Puritan exodist, had shared in the founding of Sudbury and Marlboro. He was Shrewsbury's first moderator and its first selectman, and, as years went by, he filled every other town office—sometimes several of them simultaneously. On the incorporation of Worcester County, he became a justice of the peace and was admitted to the bar. Later, he was commissioned as a colonel in the colony service and a judge of the Court of Common Pleas. As a youth he had followed the sea, and as a young man in his early twenties he had been master of a merchantman in the West Indian service.

Lieutenant Ward's wife, Martha, was a daughter of Captain Daniel How and Elizabeth Kerley. She was his first cousin, once removed: a great-granddaughter of William Ward, the exodist, through his daughter Hannah, and a granddaughter of Abraham How, another of the early "proprietors" of Marlboro.

[2] After the death (1754) of Nahum Ward, the house was sold to Henry Baldwin and achieved local fame as the Baldwin Tavern.

The child life of little Artemas was that of the average eighteenth-century Massachusetts country boy in a family of comfortable circumstances. He was one of six children: four of them older, one of them younger. He attended school during the short periods that "school kept" in Shrewsbury, and supplemented this instruction by home studies under the supervision of the minister, the Reverend Job Cushing; he did his share of the farm chores; he got into a moderate amount of boyish mischief. He rode to the neighboring towns on his father's errands: with greatest frequency to the little county-town, Worcester. As his penmanship acquired neatness and steadiness, he helped his father in the filling out of writs and other legal papers—an apprenticeship to the judicial career which later so well became him. And on the Sabbath he sat and stood through the long sermons and long prayers which consumed the greater part of the day.

Nor, for their influence on an imaginative young mind, let us forget the evenings of the New England winters as the family sat within the glow of the big log fire, and Lieutenant Ward (or *Colonel* Ward, as his father became while Artemas was still a small boy) told of the dangers and adventures and hardships encountered and overcome during the first century of the history of Massachusetts: dwelling much on the early Puritan days, and what had been lost, and what had been saved, of their works and faith; and recounting tales of the French and Indian wars which had blazed and devastated.

He told of his grandfather's house in Marlboro, garrisoned as a fort in King Philip's War; and of his uncle, Eleazer, who in the same conflict was killed by Indians on the highway between Marlboro and Sudbury. Of the township of Worcester, only five miles away, twice abandoned because of the redskin danger: Lieutenant Ward was twenty-nine years of age when it was finally resettled in 1713, and for yet another dozen years it was intermittently in peril of being again blotted out. Of the slaying or capture of his brother Elisha by Indians, and how his mother never gave up hope of

Elisha's return: when she died, eleven years later, her will contained a remembrance for him if he "shall ever come again." Of other relatives and many friends who had lost their lives in frontier skirmishes or along the Indian trail.

Thus the boy grew up, the history of an eventful century strong in his ears and mind, and blending therein with the lore of township and provincial politics universally and perpetually discussed by those around him.

As he passed into his teens the development of his character set him somewhat apart from his brothers, and suggested and justified his father's decision to send him to Harvard College. So to the Reverend Cushing was assigned the duty of preparing him for entrance.

For home reading, he had the benefit of his father's library —twoscore books and several dozen pamphlets, chiefly on religious subjects and the law; a very small library by modern standards, but much above the average of the time.

CHAPTER II

1744–1763: Age 16–35

Enters Harvard College 1744. Is graduated, A.B., 1748. Goes to Groton to "teach school." Returns to Shrewsbury and opens a general store. Marries Sarah Trowbridge. Elected to various township offices. Commissioned as Justice of the Peace. A.M., 1751. Captain and Major in the county militia. Elected Representative for Shrewsbury, and repeatedly reëlected. Marches on the alarm after the capture of Fort William Henry by the French. Major in a regiment raised for the Ticonderoga campaign. Promoted to Lieutenant-Colonel. The Battle of Ticonderoga. Commissioned as Colonel. Appointed Judge of the Court of Common Pleas for Worcester County. Moves his family into the "Old Part" of the present Artemas Ward House.

THE full chronicle of the life of Artemas Ward commences with his admission to Harvard College in 1744. He was then sixteen years old. Prior to that time, testimony is scant; after it, his footsteps may be clearly followed.

The tutor for Ward's class was Thomas Marsh, a graduate of 1731. From 1737 to 1741 he had been college librarian and in 1755 he became a Fellow of the Corporation.

Marsh, as was then the custom at Harvard, took his class through the entire course from freshman to senior, excepting divinity, Hebrew, higher mathematics, astronomy, and natural philosophy. It was not until 1767 that the four tutors began to divide the subjects instead of the pupils they taught.

Much time was spent on theology and the classics, and Hebrew was an important item of the curriculum.

The Professor of Divinity was the Reverend Edward Wigglesworth, of the class of 1710 and S.T.D. Edinburgh

University, 1730. Higher mathematics, natural philosophy, and astronomy were taught by Professor John Winthrop, 1732, a man of broad acquirements who became an authority on astronomy and seismology. Hebrew classes were conducted by Judah Monis, a converted Jew of Italian birth who served as a Harvard instructor for nearly forty years.

In Ward's day the number of students at Harvard averaged about a hundred, against the several thousands of recent years.

Customs differed also—the breakfast served at Commons then consisted of bread and a "cue of beer"! Equally distinctive was the "placing" of students by the social rank of their families—a custom closely related to the New England practice of "dignifying" the meeting-house. The stations thus assigned held good everywhere within college jurisdiction: in chapel, at recitations, at Commons, etc. Of the twenty-nine freshmen of 1744, Ward was "placed" as seventh.

Ward's record at college is very clean. During his term a number of the students were brought before the faculty on various charges,—for not returning on time at the close of vacations, for drinking liquors, for being absent from Commons without leave, and for disorderly conduct of various degrees,—but Ward's name never appears among the delinquents.

In 1747 (November 21), a senior sophister, he is second on the list of twenty-two students who volunteered to assist the president of the college in a crusade against "swearing and cursing."

Profanity was a common failing of the times. In later years, as justice of the peace, Ward individually supplemented this students' crusade by fines freely and frequently laid upon offenders!

Those twenty-two student volunteers held no conception of profanity as merely "disorderly speech" or "vulgarity." For them, it held its original significance in the fullest force: it was a sinful taking in vain of "the great and holy name of God"; a breach of one of the Commandments on which their forefathers had founded the laws of a new country; a crime against their supreme Sovereign, the dread Ruler of the universe. The Puritan religion had lost its earlier harsh inhumanity and had dropped much of its bigotry, but it remained a very virile creed, not at all given to euphemistic glossing.

Ward was between twenty and twenty-one years of age when he was graduated on July 6, 1748. A great occasion for him and his classmates when they marched, two abreast, to the meeting-house to receive their Bachelor degrees.[1] And the little town of Cambridge echoed the thought, for it overflowed with dignitaries and lesser visitors from far and near, Commencement Day being then the chief of Massachusetts holidays.

Four of Ward's classmates were to achieve political prominence in the province. Two of them took their stand on the patriot side when the break came; two of them adhered to the tory, or prerogative, party.

After graduation Ward went to Groton, Mass., to "teach school."

He boarded with the Groton minister, the Reverend Caleb Trowbridge, well known in his own right and with a wife who represented a line of famous Massachusetts theologians: she was a daughter of the Reverend Nehemiah Walter, a granddaughter of the Reverend Increase Mather, and a great-granddaughter of the Reverend John Cotton.

[1] Because no names are attached to the theses by the candidates for the Bachelor's degree, it is impossible to determine which was Ward's, but in 1751 when he came up for his Master's degree he was Affirmat Respondens on the *Quaestio*, "An conscientia constituat Identitatem personalem."

The defense of theses by A.B. candidates, and of the positions assumed on quaestiones by A.M. candidates, had descended as a custom from previous generations. Each candidate was supposed to be ready to uphold his proposition or standpoint, but in the course of time it had come about that in most cases the listing was both the beginning and the end of the subject: he was an exceptional candidate who spoke at the commencement exercises. Ward was one of the exceptions in 1751—he was one of the three candidates for the Master's degree who actually defended their standpoints. The other two were Perez Marsh and Thomas Sanders.

The Trowbridge house, a square two-story building, then stood on the site of the present High School.

Young Ward's room was on the second floor rear, overlooking the meadow which stretched away from the base of the high ground of the house location. Within easy range was a pond which attracted wild ducks on their migrations. The tradition is that the young school-teacher—at a future year to be the first commander-in-chief of the American Revolution—used to amuse himself by "potting" ducks from his chamber window.

Not all of his spare moments were, however, devoted to duck shooting, or otherwise spent in the privacy of his own room. Some were given to courtship, for it was not long before he found himself attracted to the minister's oldest daughter, Sarah, a young woman of twenty-five years, three years his senior.

There remains no description of Sarah Trowbridge as a girl, but as remembered in later life she was a "calm, self-possessed woman." Family tradition has it that she "inherited some of the firm characteristics of her Mather ancestors." Her strength of mind was probably pleasing to Artemas Ward, for there was nothing light or frivolous in his composition!

With matrimony in prospect Ward resigned his position as schoolmaster and returned to Shrewsbury early in 1750 to establish himself in the house known to tradition both as the Yellow House and the (first) Sumner House, standing westerly of the meeting-house and facing toward the Great Country Road.

The boundaries of the property, of inverted-L shape, enclosed about thirty-four acres of farm-land, fronting about five hundred feet on the road.[2]

[2] The Yellow House and farm were purchased by his father, Colonel Nahum Ward, in three lots on April 4 and 7, 1750: the house, two acres of land, and a barn on the adjoining "meeting-house land," from Moses Hastings; about nine acres to the west and north of the Hastings plot, from Asa Bowker; and twenty-three acres adjoining the

QUESTIONES

Pro Modulo Diſcutiendæ,

SUB REVERENDO

D. Edvardo Holyoke,

COLLEGII-HARVARDINI,

Quod eſt, Divinâ Providentiâ

Cantabrigiæ Nov-Anglorum,

PRÆSIDE.

In Comitiis Publicis à Laureæ Magiſtralis Candidatis, *Quinto Nonarum Quintilis.*

M D C C L I.

I. AN Bellum, ſeu Continuatio Belli, Pace dubiâ tutior ſit.
Affirmat Reſpondens EDVARDUS HUTCHINSON.

II. An in Mercaturâ, Commodum immutabile, Juſtitia poſtulet.
Negat Reſpondens DUDLÆUS ATKINS.

III. An ulla Occupatio ſit Reipublicæ tam beneficialis, quam Agricultura.
Negat Reſpondens GEORGIUS LEONARD.

IV. An Status civilis oriatur ex Pactis.
Affirmat Reſpondens CAROLUS CHAUNCY.

V. An omnis moralis agens, moralem Legem obſervare obligetur.
Affirmat Reſpondens TIMOTHEUS PAINE.

VI. An Conſcientia conſtituat Identitatem perſonalem.
Affirmat Reſpondens ARTEMAS WARD.

VII. An Confiſcatio Bonorum Parentis ob Crimen læſæ Majeſtratis, Liberos innocentis Damnum injuſtè afficiat.
Affirmat Reſpondens JOSEPHUS ADAMS.

VIII. An origo Mali ſolvi poſſit ſalvis Dei Attributis.
Affirmat Reſpondens JAHAKOBUS CUSHING.

IX. An Idea adæquata juſtitiæ in Deo, a nobis formari poſſit.
Negat Reſpondens GULIELMUS COOKE.

X. An in Amicitiâ inæquali, ſit plus tribuendum et retribuendum majori, et minus minori.
Affirmat Reſpondens JONATHAN SEWALL.

XI. An detur Motus immediatè a Ventriculo ad Veſicam.
Negat Reſpondens RICHARDUS PERKINS.

XII. An Præſcientia divina tollat Libertatem agendi.
Negat Reſpondens GULIELMUS BALDWIN.

XIII. An Bellum aliquod ſit Juſtum jure Naturæ.
Affirmat Reſpondens PEREZ MARSH.

XIV. An Fides data in imperio civili Magiſtratum ſummum obliget.
Affirmat Reſpondens THOMAS SANDERS.

XV. An Vocatio ad Miniſterium in Eccleſiis Sacrum his Temporibus, ſit immediata.
Negat Reſpondens SAMUEL ANGIER.

XVI. An Timor in Amore neceſſariè includatur.
Affirmat Reſpondens SAMUEL WOODWARD.

XVII. An Decreta divina ſint omnino abſoluta.
Affirmat Reſpondens JOSEPHUS BEAN.

XVIII. An Poſitura humani Corporis erecta, requirat, Pericardium et ſeptum tranverſum coaleſcere.
Affirmat Reſpondens JOHANNES RAND.

XIX. An Leges Morales ex relatione entium Neceſſariò naſcantur.
Affirmat Reſpondens THOMAS HIBBERT.

XX. An Fructum prohibitum, Mortis *Adami* fuiſſe Cauſam Phyſicam, probabile ſit.
Affirmat Reſpondens JACOBUS HOBBS.

XXI. An Deus ex Seipſo Cauſaliter, *i. e.* ut a Cauſa exiſtat.
Negat Reſpondens GEORGIUS LESSLIE.

His Succedit *ORATIO* Valedictoria.

From an original (9⅜ × 15⅜) in Harvard College Library

THE QUESTIONS TO BE DEBATED BY THE CANDIDATES FOR THE DEGREE OF A.M., HARVARD COLLEGE, 1751

The house had a rear lean-to which had been used as a shoemaker's shop, and in this, on April 21, Ward opened a small general store. His stock ranged from dry-goods to rum.

Rum, be it remembered, was then an article of thoroughly good standing in New England, and a part of every man's diet, whether preacher or layman; as essential at church-raisings and ordinations as on strictly secular occasions. "Temperance societies" did not come into being for another half century, and total abstinence and prohibition were still longer delayed.

Most of his accounts were with men of Shrewsbury; a few were with residents of neighboring towns.

Some of his customers paid in cash. Others by merchandise—homespun cloth, "cyder," fish, etc.; or in labor—"making a saw, staples, etc.," "making a pair of [leather] breeches," "dressing one deer skin," carting, etc.

His marriage quickly succeeded the opening of his store. It was solemnized on July 31 at the Trowbridge home in Groton.

The following spring (March 4, 1751) the Shrewsbury farmers made him tax assessor—the first of his many civic appointments, and an office to which he was reëlected a score of times.

Three months later (June 22), though only twenty-three years old, he entered upon his long service as justice of the peace—an official of dignity and importance in that generation. It was undoubtedly with much pride that he received his commission issued "By order of the Lieutenant-Governor with the Advice and Consent of the Council": an imposing document with its round red seal, its conventional "greeting" by "George the Second, By the Grace of God, of Great

Bowker plot on the north, from Moses Hastings. The house stood a little to the west of the original structure of the present Sumner House, and nearer the road.

Three years later (February 15, 1753), Colonel Ward transferred the property as a gift to Artemas Ward ("in consideration of the love, good will and affection which I have and do bear towards my well beloved son Artemas Ward").

Britain, France, and Ireland, KING, Defender of the Faith, etc.," and its signature by Spencer Phips, Lieutenant-Governor and Commander-in-chief of the Province of the Massachusetts Bay.

The next year (1752) the town clerk's duties were added to his responsibilities, and he was also voted into the full dignity of a selectman: his first of twenty terms as such.

These township offices developed and shaped Ward's character and career.

Of special influence was the experience gained as one of the selectmen,—the executive officers of the township,—for he thus encountered the many-sided problems of human government.

Improving this experience was that as justice of the peace: both locally and in General Sessions at Worcester. The sitting-room of the Yellow House was his home court, and in it he married many couples, tried a large class of minor offenders, and balanced the scales of justice between disputant neighbors.

By province laws a justice of the peace had wide discretion in many cases—up to the point of sentencing a culprit to be whipped or to be put in the stocks. Drunkards, profaners of the Sabbath, and peace breakers were among those who could thus be punished.

A "profaner of the Sabbath" included any rash or self-indulgent person who essayed to travel on Sunday except on a very real and easily demonstrable emergency. And this law was strictly enforced in Shrewsbury—as, generally, in the other country districts of Massachusetts. Nor did Ward ever relax his early sabbatical vigilance: we find him, a generation later, a man of sixty-one years, a general and a chief justice, standing in the Shrewsbury highway to halt infractors of the Sunday law.

That these functions as selectman, justice of the peace, etc., were performed upon a small stage, gave them additional educative value, for the audience sat very close to the actors and was prompt to note and quick to protest any false step or sentiment.

Local opinion was very strong. It was indeed more than that—it was almost omnipotent in local affairs, for the town-meeting appointed all town officials and had the making or approval of all local laws and orders, subject only to the authority of the General Court;[3] and in town-meeting every inhabitant had an equal voice and spoke his mind—proposing, arguing, and disputing as his interests and sentiments moved him.

Ward's repeated reëlection as selectman and the continuous acquiescence of the townspeople in his tenure as justice of the peace, testify both to his willingness to assume responsibility and to his intelligent grasp of human relations: to a knowledge of, and respect for, local needs, sentiments, and traditions; and to a reputation for even-handed justice.

The cumulative responsibilities undertaken also testify to the industry which distinguished him. The combination of duties, clerical and otherwise, as selectman, town clerk, and assessor, added to those of justice of the peace, with the incidental drawing up of documents, letters, etc., which accrued from that office—all imposed upon the conduct of his store—must have made him the busiest young man in Shrewsbury!

On May 7, 1754, his father died, closing a much respected and enterprising life at the age of sixty-nine. His will, after carefully providing for his widow, divided his estate among his four surviving children and his two grandchildren by his eldest son Nahum, who had died in 1738.

Artemas and his brother Elisha were named as executors and residuary legatees.

On January 28 of the following year (1755), Ward was commissioned major of the Third Regiment of Militia in

[3] "General Court" was the customary abbreviation of "Great and General Court"—the title of the Massachusetts legislature under both the first and second charters. With the adoption of the state constitution, the abbreviation became the title.

the counties of Middlesex and Worcester, and captain of the First Company in the town of Shrewsbury.

Two years later (May 16, 1757) he was elected for the first of many terms as the township's representative in the General Court, and nine days thereafter he was in the capital for the short spring session.

The Boston to which he came as a provincial legislator, had led the continent for more than a century. It was only a little town of about 16,000 inhabitants, but it hummed with trade, and shipping, and shipbuilding. Its social life, too, was varied and attractive, and it treasured no small amount of luxury in the homes of its many well-to-do citizens. It was capable of a substantial brilliancy in display and entertainment, and on gala dates, such as the anniversary of the King's birthday, and Accession and Coronation days, it miniatured London with excellent effect.

It was at this time even more than ordinarily full of life and bustle, its normal industry enhanced by the activities of war. The Seven Years' conflict was flaming across the civilized world and, crossing the Atlantic, had locked France and England in the final struggle for supremacy in North America.

The Representatives' Chamber in which Ward took his seat under the carved wooden codfish, was on the second floor of the Old State House—the same building which stands today at the head of State Street, though then known as the Court House, or, locally, as the Town House.

Ward's assignments during his initial term were confined to committees to consider soldiers' petitions.

In the following August came his first call to arms in the excitement which swept Massachusetts on news of the fall of Fort William Henry to the French and their Indian allies—the story made lurid by the Indian atrocities which stained the French victory.

There was widespread fear that Montcalm would follow up his success: first with an assault on Fort Edward and then a general eastward invasion. Thousands of militiamen grasped their firelocks and marched west and north toward the fort to meet the enemy. Among them were Major Ward and his companies.

Montcalm, however, displayed no intent to attack, and General Webb, commander at Fort Edward, dispatched orders halting all militiamen on their way toward it. So Ward marched his men back to their homes after a very brief absence. And Montcalm, satisfied with his capture of all the supplies at Fort William Henry and his total destruction of the post, retired to Montreal, releasing his Canadians for the harvest.

Ward had thus missed the summer meeting of the legislature, but he was promptly on hand for the opening of its third session on November 23, and during the two months following he was again on committees to consider soldiers' petitions, and on others respecting army supply claims and subsistence payments, and town and guardianship detail.

He returned to Shrewsbury on January 26, 1758, and shortly after was enlisting men for a regiment to be commanded by Colonel William Williams in a new and formidable expedition against the French forces and positions at Ticonderoga and Crown Point—designated by Pitt as part of his threefold plan for the destruction of French power in North America. The Ticonderoga-Crown Point army was to be headed by Abercromby, the King's commander-in-chief on the continent.

Ward was commissioned as a major in Williams' regiment.

He was in Boston again on March 3 for the opening of the last session of the 1757–1758 legislature.

On the fourteenth he was named on a committee to examine a militia act passed January 25, and "Report whether it may not be expedient to suspend the Operation of some Parts thereof for some Time, and to prepare the Draught of a Vote accordingly." The Abercromby campaign would draw so many men away from farms and other callings that public opinion was opposed to the further interruption of essential labor by the general assembling of militia companies on "training-days" as required by the act.

On March 20 the committee reported a bill which the governor refused to sign. After much effort, a substitute bill came out as Chapter 26, Acts of 1757–1758.

Three days later, Ward was back in Shrewsbury to continue his enlistments.

The General Court had, on March 17, fixed the rate of pay for privates at £1 16*s*. a month. In addition it resolved that "each able bodied effective Man who shall voluntarily inlist . . . shall be intitled to Thirty Shillings and upon his passing Muster shall receive a good Blanket and Fifty Shillings more for furnishing himself with Cloaths."

The Council had, next, on March 25 and 27, "advised and consented" that warrants be made out for the payment of bounties, but the men's receipts show that in his anxiety to fill his companies Ward advanced some of his recruits part of their bounty money without waiting for the warrants.

Notice of the Council's action necessitated a return to Boston to draw the first £300 assigned to him.

With town, legislative, and military duties thus crowding his hours, Ward had little time to devote to the less congenial vocation of storekeeping, and it is not surprising that his profitable merchandise business rapidly fell away during 1757 and disappeared in May, 1758. Nor did he ever attempt to revive it.

This new "general invasion of Canada" had been planned on a large scale, but the preliminary arrangements were faulty. Ward was one of nine officers who in April addressed Governor Pownall stating that they esteemed it "absolutely necessary" to receive a proper equipment of "camp furniture"—particularly kettles and haversacks; to increase the pay offered to surgeons so that men of sufficient ability could be obtained; to have an armorer with at least one assistant for each regiment, as "Upon the Strictest Inquiry we find the Provincial Troops may not depend upon the King's Armorers for the repair of their Arms"; to obtain an increase in the pay offered to chaplains "in order to engage gentlemen of the best character"; to have a courier to carry dispatches. It was also desired that particular care be exercised "that ineffective persons may not be suffered to go in the army."

April saw Ward for a few days in Boston in his seat as a Representative, but by the end of the month he was back in Shrewsbury to make the final arrangements for his companies.[4]

On May 1 Colonel Williams dispatched orders[5] to "The Honble John Wheelwright," Boston, for supplies for his regiment. It included one to deliver

"60 Arms 228 Blankets 228 Haversacks 228 Flasks 42 kettles 42 axes	To Majr Artemas Ward's Man that comes with a Team. Shruesberry."

On May 6 Governor Pownall ordered Colonel Williams to collect his men without delay and to get everything in readiness for marching, giving regulations concerning the cartage of supplies and the subsistence of the men en route, etc.

Ward was obliged to make three additional journeys to Boston to draw the balance of the £770 12*s.* bounty money for his men and £440 of "billiting" money—the latter an allowance of sixpence a day for each provincial soldier for subsistence until his arrival at Northampton, where he would be placed on the commissary of the "regulars."

Ward's very moderate expense account for seven round

[4] On April 28 it was ordered in the House "that Capt. Barrett be of the committee appointed the 15th of December last on the petition of Jonathan Stone, and others, in the Room of Major Ward, who is engaged in the intended Expedition against Canada."

[5] *Williams Papers*, 172, Berkshire Athenaeum, Pittsfield, Mass.

trips to Boston on this business (including three trips for the vacating of the bonds given) was only £8.

Then quickly followed orders to march his four companies to Worcester and thence to Northampton to join the balance of the regiment.

The military machinery had been cumbrous in getting started and the army equipment was still deficient,[6] but the expedition was at last officially under way.

Abercromby had under him the largest army of white men ever to that date gathered in a single command on American soil: a total of more than 15,000—9024 provincials and 6367 regulars. Among its officers were several who were to be closely associated with Ward in later years: Charles Lee, four years his junior, captain of a company of His Majesty's Grenadiers of the 44th Regiment; and Brigadier-General Timothy Ruggles, Lieutenant-Colonel John Whitcomb, Major Israel Putnam, and Captain John Stark of the provincial forces.

Hope and confidence ran high. Success seemed certain. Newspapers contained rosy reports of what was going to happen at "Ti."

Those who knew him, held Abercromby in slight respect, but that mattered little, for next in command was Lord George Howe, beloved and respected by both regulars and provincials—a man of high military ability and great personal charm, blessed with a true understanding of both the value and the peculiarities of the colonial troops; a man whose adaptability was such that he not only eagerly absorbed what provincial leaders could teach him, but, in return, after thus learning from them, could devise and impart methods in forest and back-country travel which improved on his instructors. There is no danger of over-statement in paying tribute to

[6] There was a "great deficiency in the number of Arms belonging to the Province." It was hoped to complete the equipment of the regiments out of arms "ordered over by the Crown." The latter had, however, not arrived up to May 19 though they were "every day expected from Great Britain."—Governor Pownall to Colonel Williams, May 19, 1758, *Williams Papers,* 181, Berkshire Athenaeum, Pittsfield, Mass.

Lord Howe. Contemporary evidence is irresistible. Wolfe called him "the noblest Englishman that has appeared in my time, and the best soldier in the British army." Pitt spoke of him as "a character of ancient times; a complete model of military virtue." And in Westminster Abbey stands the monument which Massachusetts Bay erected to his memory.

Major Ward set out with his companies on the morning of May 30 and had made the twenty miles to Brookfield before sunset.

His transcript of his diary of the expedition has been preserved.[7] It throws no new light on the campaign, but it contains much interesting detail.

It records June 17 and 18, after the arrival at Fort Edward, the building of a breastwork by his men "on ye west end of ye encampment."

On the day following, the visit of Abercromby and his aides-de-camp is noted, and that the general "was pleased with Colo. Williams encampment."

We find a similar entry on June 22: "Ruggles & Williams's Regiment mustered by Brigdr. Genl. Gage who did Colo. Williams ye Honor to say was his Regt. in uniform it wo'd be one of the finest he ever saw."[8]

June 28, Williams' regiment reached the southern extremity of Lake George and encamped there.

July 2, boats were assigned to the provincial troops to be loaded by them with "flour, pork, etc.," for the voyage down Lake George toward Ticonderoga.

July 3, succeeding a parade of all the regiments for a general review, Ward was promoted to the rank of lieutenant-colonel.

The next day all "ye heavy baggage" was put on board, and the following morning the whole army embarked.

[7] Owned (1921) by Florence Ward, Shrewsbury, Mass.

[8] Parkman, *Montcalm and Wolfe,* II, 93, says that the provincials were "uniformed in blue," but Ward's diary is evidence that uniforming did not reach to all the Massachusetts regiments.

"The arrangements were perfect. Each corps marched without confusion to its appointed station on the beach, and the sun was scarcely above the ridge of French Mountain when all were afloat. A spectator watching them from the shore says that when the fleet was three miles on its way, the surface of the lake at that distance was completely hidden from sight. There were nine hundred bateaux, a hundred and thirty-five whaleboats, and a large number of heavy flatboats carrying the artillery. The whole advanced in three divisions, the regulars in the center, and the provincials on the flanks. Each corps had its flags and its music. The day was fair and men and officers were in the highest spirits."[9]

They rowed northward all that day; and then, as "the Genl gave out orders we sho'd push on,"[10] all the night following also.

The "second narrows" was reached at daybreak. A few hours later the entire army had debarked at the north end of the lake and commenced the march through the forest to lay siege to Ticonderoga. Montcalm still held there, though debating hourly whether to make a stand—and if so, on what line; or whether to abandon the fort in the face of the formidable army coming to its attack.

The afternoon brought a calamitous victory to the English—the death of Howe[11] in a blind skirmish with a French advance party in the dense thicket.

The Frenchmen were routed—with many killed and taken prisoners, but the English army was thrown completely out

[9] Parkman, *Montcalm and Wolfe,* II, 92.

[10] Colonel Partridge to his wife, July 12, 1758, *Israel Williams Papers,* II, 77, Massachusetts Historical Society.

[11] The news of the death of Lord Howe was everywhere received as a calamity and aroused much apprehension. "As to the Progress and Effect of these Successes, we must suspend our Accounts 'til further News—the losing Lord Howe is paying too dear for the advantages we have yet gain'd for nothing can compensate for so dear a Sacrifice, but the Total Reduction of Canada."—*Boston Gazette,* July 17, 1758.

On his loss, both provincial and regular officers blamed the disasters which followed. With him, declared Thomas Mante, "the soul of General Abercromby's army seemed to expire. From the unhappy moment the general was deprived of his advice, neither order nor discipline was observed, and a strange kind of infatuation usurped the place of resolution."—Parkman, *Montcalm and Wolfe,* II, 97.

of gear. "All in confusion," wrote Ward. Howe was dead, and Abercromby lost touch with his command. He collected "such parts of it" as were within his reach "and posted them under the trees, where they remained all night under arms."[12] The others, Williams' regiment among them, made their way out of the forest as best they could and "returned to ye place we landed at with 160 prisoners and incamped."[13]

The next morning (July 7), still ignorant of the whereabouts of a large part of his force, Abercromby also returned to the landing place, there to find it awaiting him.[14]

His army reunited, the English commander-in-chief took up his plans anew. First to set out was Lieutenant-Colonel Bradstreet with a detachment of redcoats and provincials—Williams' regiment among them. They "marched and took possession of ye mills"—the sawmill at the Falls, an advanced French post which Montcalm had held in strong force until the preceding day. Thence, the Williams, Preble, and Doty regiments, and Partridge's battalion, went forward to

[12] Abercromby's Report to William Pitt, Secretary of State, July 12, 1758, Public Record Office, London, C. O. 5, Volume 50, page 353 (page 259 in British Transcripts in Library of Congress).

[13] *Ward's Diary.*

[14] Parkman, *Montcalm and Wolfe*, II, 98, says "the effect of the loss [of Howe] was seen at once. The army was needlessly kept under arms all night in the forest, and in the morning was ordered back to the landing place whence it came." The same statements appear in the accounts by Bancroft and others. The impression thus conveyed is inaccurate. The conditions were considerably worse. Instead of merely an army "needlessly kept under arms all night," it was, as noted above, a disjointed army largely out of touch with its commander-in-chief. A number of regiments were "missing" and Abercromby's aides did not know where to look for them.

Contemporary accounts tell the story. Ward's diary entry I have quoted above. See also: the diary of Lemuel Lyon, of Fitch's Connecticut regiment (*The Military Journals of Two Private Soldiers*, 22), July 6—"at Sondown . . . our men came back again to the Landing place and Lodged their"; Colonel Partridge's letter, July 12 (*Israel Williams Papers*, II, 77, Massachusetts Historical Society)—"The Regt. got so dispersed we were obliged to retire to open ground to Form anew where we camped"; and the continuation of Abercromby's report—"The 7th, in the Morning, having yet no Intelligence of the Troops that were missing, (being several Regiments,) not knowing which Way they had gone; Our Intelligence uncertain, Our Guides ignorant, & the Troops with me greatly fatigued, by having been one whole Night on the Water, the following Day constantly on Foot, and the next Night under Arms, added to their being in Want of Provision, having dropped what they had brought with them, in Order to lighten themselves, it was thought most Adviseable to return to the Landing Place, which we accordingly did, and upon Our Arrival there, about 8 that Morning, found the Remainder of the Army."

"within ¾ mile of ye french" and there built a breastwork and encamped.

Bradstreet also "rebuilt the bridges destroyed by the retiring enemy, and sent word to his commander that the way was open; on which Abercromby again put his army in motion [and] reached the Falls late in the afternoon."[15]

Montcalm resolves to hold Ticonderoga despite the dangers of the position and his lesser numbers, and to make his stand upon the ridge immediately to the west of his stronghold. The decision reached, his Frenchmen ply their axes with furious energy, felling trees by scores, by hundreds, by thousands.

The fort stood at the point of a tongue of land—a rocky plateau, with low ground on both sides—washed on the east by the head of Lake Champlain and on the west by the outlet of Lake George. Its new defenses so hurriedly being prepared stretch across the tongue from water to water. The ridge chosen for the main defense crowns the plateau at a distance of about half a mile from the fort, and upon it swiftly rises a mighty log breastwork zigzagging along its entire length. In front of this is set a barrier of heavy boughs interwoven with sharp points bristling everywhere. Again in front, on the descending slope—as also on the low ground to the sides—lie the trees as they fall, crowding each other in a thicket of underbrush: acres of trunks presenting a myriad obstructions: a vast abattis—a position of a thousand man-traps, and every trap a target for the Frenchmen posted behind the zigzag breastwork.

On the next day (July 8) Abercromby, misled by his own incompetence and an engineer's faulty report, ordered the taking of the position at the point of the bayonet. Any one of several other methods would have spelled the certain defeat or capitulation of the French—with, probably, slight English losses. But Abercromby and his officers, possessed

[15] Parkman, *Montcalm and Wolfe,* II, 98.

by the devils of unreasoned recklessness and gross ill-judgment, must hurl their men at the French breastwork in a frontal assault. Hurry, hurry—reinforcements are coming to Montcalm! No time to bring up the cannon! Charge with the bayonet!

In the van, driving in the French outposts as the army moves forward through the forest, are Rogers' rangers, "Bradstreet's armed boatmen," and a detachment of regulars (Gage's Light Infantry).

Next come several thousand provincials, halting just within the concealment of the trees and underbrush[16] and taking up positions at intervals, extending thus across the tongue from shore to shore—Williams' regiment to the right of the center.

Then—the main body of the English regulars. Forming in "columns of attack" they pass between the provincial regiments, march briskly out of the obscurity of the forest, and push forward to the attack.

"Across the rough ground, with its maze of fallen trees whose leaves hung withering in the July sun," the Englishmen "could see the top of the breastwork, but not the men behind it; when, in an instant, all the line was obscured by a gush of smoke, a crash of exploding firearms tore the air, and grapeshot and musket-balls swept the whole space like a tempest; 'a damnable fire,' says an officer who heard them screaming about his ears. The English had been ordered to carry the works with the bayonet; but their ranks were broken by the obstructions through which they struggled in vain to force their way, and they soon began to fire in turn. The storm raged in full fury for an hour. The assailants pushed close to the breastwork; but there they were stopped by the bristling mass of sharpened branches, which they could not pass under the murderous cross-fires that swept them from front and

[16] Colonel Partridge to his wife, July 12, 1758, *Israel Williams Papers,* II, 77, Massachusetts Historical Society.

flank. At length they fell back, exclaiming that the works were impregnable."[17]

Abercromby sent orders to attack again—and again they set themselves to the task.

"The scene was frightful: masses of infuriated men who could not go forward and would not go back; straining for an enemy they could not reach, and firing on an enemy they could not see; caught in the entanglement of fallen trees; tripped by briers, stumbling over logs, tearing through boughs; shouting, yelling, cursing, and pelted all the while with bullets that killed them by scores, stretched them on the ground, or hung them on jagged branches in strange attitudes of death."[18]

The provincial troops poured from their concealment in the forest and crowded forward to the aid of the redcoats—but without avail, for the flank fires of musketry and grape beat down every approach.

Several times the English attacked with the most desperate courage, but their officers had set them an impossible task. The last assault was made at about six o'clock: it was as fruitless as those which had preceded it.

"From this time till half-past seven a lingering fight was kept up by the rangers and other provincials, firing from the edge of the woods and from behind the stumps, bushes, and fallen trees in front of the lines. Its only objects were to cover their comrades, who were collecting and bringing off the wounded, and to protect the retreat of the regulars, who fell back in disorder to the Falls. As twilight came on the last combatant withdrew, and none were left but the dead. Abercromby had lost in killed, wounded, and missing nineteen hundred and forty-four officers and men."[19]

The regulars had suffered the most severely—their dead and wounded reached a full fourth of their entire strength;

[17] Parkman, *Montcalm and Wolfe,* II, 105–106.

[18] *Ibid.,* 106.

[19] *Ibid.,* 110.

but the provincial casualties were also considerable, nearly equaling the total of the French losses.

Captain Charles Lee was one of the many English officers wounded—a musket-ball passing through his body and breaking two of his ribs.

A start had been made to build breastworks to check the enemy if he should follow up his victory, but Ward's diary tells us that the work was soon abandoned and that the army "shamefully retreated."

Williams' regiment fell back only a short distance, however, halting and encamping, together with Partridge's battalion, at their "old Breastwork" between the French lines and the mill.

The English were still strong in numbers and well able to hold their own even if Montcalm should receive his expected reinforcements, but Abercromby had been completely unnerved by the losses he had sustained. His rashness "before the fight, was matched by his poltroonery after it."[20] At about midnight Colonel Williams and Colonel Partridge accidentally discovered "to our great surprise" that the army was in full flight southward to its boats, and they perforce again set out to follow it.[21]

The troops "arrived at ye battoos" in the morning and went on board—then south the length of Lake George, returning humbled, disgusted, and defeated to the encampment which they had left a few days earlier full of confidence and national pride.

The New England provincials thenceforth referred to Abercromby as "Mrs. Nabbycrombie" ("Nabby" being the familiar of Abigail). And Charles Lee's sharp tongue speaks of him as "our Booby in Chief."

For another three months the southern extremity of Lake George served as the main basis of the army. A camp of ill-

[20] Parkman, *Montcalm and Wolfe,* II, 114.

[21] Colonel Partridge to his wife, July 12, 1758, *Israel Williams Papers,* II, 77, Massachusetts Historical Society.

fortune, its depleted ranks stricken by fever and dysentery. Sanitary conditions were bad, the food often unwholesome, and hospital supplies frequently lacking.[22] On September 24 Ward recorded, "This day according to ye returns given in, there are but 1657 R. F. [rank and file] of the Provincials fit for duty."

There were, however, occasional bright spots in those dreary months. The camp drew great satisfaction from the victory of Rogers' detachment in a hot skirmish with Marin. Ward wrote, "ye truth is they gave ye Enemy a good drubing this time!"

Again, on August 20, glorious news came to headquarters by a letter from Lieutenant-Governor Hutchinson of "ye surrender of Cape Breton that it surrendered ye 26th of July last"; and, later, word of the capture and destruction of Fort Frontenac by Bradstreet and 3000 men, nearly all of them provincials of the Ticonderoga army.

Yet more weeks passed, then "Amherst, with five regiments, from Louisbourg, came . . . to join Abercromby at Lake George, and the two commanders discussed the question of again attacking Ticonderoga. Both thought the season too late. A fortnight after, a deserter brought news that Montcalm was breaking up his camp."[23]

Abercromby followed his example. The regulars were withdrawn and the specially raised provincial regiments were marched homeward and disbanded: Williams' regiment, together with Preble's and Nichols', setting out on October 24.

The campaign had ended, and during the following winter "only a few scouting parties kept alive the embers of war on the waters and mountains of Lake George."

On his return, Ward made a brief stay in Shrewsbury and

[22] "Our sick, destitute of everything proper for them; an empty medicine-chest; nothing but their dirty blankets for bed and bedding in malignant and slow fevers; Dr. Ashley dead, Dr. Wright gone home low eno', Bille worn off of his legs. Such is our case. . . . I have near 100 sick."—Colonel Williams, Sept. 4, 1758, *Israel Williams Papers,* II, 84, Massachusetts Historical Society.

[23] Parkman, *Montcalm and Wolfe,* II, 129–130.

then proceeded to Boston for the discharge of his bounty and billeting-money bonds.

This concluded a campaign of such dangers and difficulties as test not only a man's physical courage, but also his moral fortitude in the face of disease and disorder, and his patience and constancy when suffering from delays bred both by ill circumstances and by the incompetence of military and civilian superiors.

Quick recognition of the excellence of Ward's record during that trying year is seen in another upward step in military title. In the field he had earned promotion from major to lieutenant-colonel. Within two months of his return he was commissioned as colonel—his command being the Third Middlesex and Worcester County Regiment, in which he had formerly served as captain and major.

The Ticonderoga expedition had proved little short of an utter failure, but England's honor had been retrieved by Amherst and Wolfe at Louisburg; and 1759—the year in which both Montcalm and Wolfe gave their lives for their countries—tendered rich promise that thereafter England was to be overlord in North America.

These successes must be permanently secured. And 1760 again saw preparation for the "complete reduction of Canada."

The Ticonderoga campaign had seriously impaired Ward's health, and during 1759 he had made no effort to return to service in the field; but he was ready for the call in 1760, was commissioned colonel of a provincial expeditionary regiment, and was active in enlisting men to fill its ranks.

His constitution had, however, been more seriously undermined than he had supposed, and he was compelled to relinquish the expeditionary command and to content himself with that of his standing militia regiment and the inspection of expeditionary enlistments in the post of Commissary of Musters. He indeed never regained robust health, and calculus, his arch-enemy henceforth, plagued him intermittently all his life.

In civil affairs he steadily gained stature both in county and township. In the latter he had become the accepted leader of the community.

To his township offices were added those of town moderator (in 1761, and somewhat later for a series of terms); church moderator, in 1760, 1761, and 1762, following the death of the Reverend Job Cushing, his old tutor, and until arrangements were completed for the settlement of the Reverend Joseph Sumner; and treasurer—commencing with 1760, and thereafter every year except one until the Revolutionary War.

As Representative he was reëlected without intermission, save only the year of the Ticonderoga campaign and 1762 (when no Representative was sent from Shrewsbury), until he entered the Council.

And he was on January 21, 1762, appointed a judge of the Worcester County Court of Common Pleas;[24] and commissioned as a justice of the peace "of the quorum."

In the House, Ward was known to his colleagues as an indefatigable worker, and we find him, both at this period and in succeeding years, shouldering a great deal of committee work: considering all manner of applications and petitions; preparing currency and tax bills, etc. He also served by House authority as trustee for the Hassanamisco Indians.

It was in 1763 (January 12), the year following his appointment as judge of the Court of Common Pleas, that Colonel Ward purchased from his brother Elisha the house opposite the old Nahum Ward home which their father had erected early in the history of Shrewsbury. The sale included seventy acres of land fronting on the Great Country Road.[25]

Into this house, a frame structure of seven rooms (the

[24] The chief justice was Brigadier-General Timothy Ruggles.

[25] Ward had, on December 28, 1762, sold his home, the Yellow House and farm (page 10, note), to the Reverend Joseph Sumner, the new minister. Mr. Sumner moved in on June 8, 1763.

"Old Part" of the present Artemas Ward House), he soon after moved his family (already a typical old-time Massachusetts family of six children), and under its roof he held court and dispensed law and order for more than a score of years.

CHAPTER III

February, 1763–May, 1774: Age 35–46

Massachusetts after 1763. The Stamp Act dispute arouses Colonel Ward. Governor Bernard cancels his commission. On many committees of political protest. Elected to the Council in a contest with Lieutenant-Governor Hutchinson. Rejected by Governor Bernard. One of the "Glorious Ninety-Two." Again elected to the Council and again vetoed. A third time elected—and at last grudgingly admitted to the Board. General Charles Lee arrives in New York. The "Tea Party" of 1773 and the Boston Port Act.

WITH the signing of the Treaty of Paris, on February 10, 1763, we enter a new era. English arms have driven the French flag from the North American continent. They have triumphed also in Asia. England has won the supremacy of the seas and has become the greatest of colonial powers.

The English colonies in North America have increased from the scant half million whites of Artemas Ward's birthdate, thirty-five years before, to a total of one and a half million. And many thoughtful minds contemplatively regard the vast undeveloped Indian-peopled regions which the fortune of war has passed from French to English dominion.

The crushing of French sovereignty quickened the hundred converging causes which formed the river that within a few short years swept all before it in its course to the wide seas of American independence.

The outcome might have been long delayed if it had been possible to make the men directing England's policy comprehend that her North American colonies held in full the

English tradition that the right of self-taxation is the fundamental of liberty.

In 1765 came the historic Stamp Act—both the levying and the expenditure to be under the control of the English Parliament. Every student is familiar with the storm that it raised during its short and impotent life.

The whole subject of overseas authority was suddenly and violently illuminated. Here was a clear, clean issue, uncomplicated by the generations of mercantile compromises and evasions which befogged the operation of the Navigation and Trade acts. Here was an act, in no way related to the regulation of the commerce of the empire, designed to collect a tax specifically for revenue. The revenue was to be employed to assist in defraying "the necessary expenses of defending, protecting, and securing" the colonies; but this provision did not soften the American attitude toward the two questions: Had Parliament the right to levy the tax? Shall it be paid? The answer to both questions was an emphatic negative.

In Massachusetts, the Stamp Act aroused thousands who had taken only a fitful interest in the Sugar and Molasses disputes, and had not been enduringly stirred even by the "Writs of Assistance." It blew to a white heat the flame relit in the brilliant erratic mind of James Otis,[1] at this date still bearing the title of the "great incendiary" of the patriot party. It initiated the political activity of several men who figured prominently in the struggle for independence.

Artemas Ward was among those inspired. He had been little affected by the disturbances bred by the Navigation and Trade acts, and had taken no part in either provincial or local quarrels with holders or supporters of the prerogative—but the Stamp Act struck fire in him; his activity in patriot circles commences with its date.

[1] My reference, except where otherwise noted, is always to James Otis, the son, of Boston, immortalized by his speech against Writs of Assistance; not to James Otis, the father, of Barnstable.

This new strong sentiment rapidly widened the breach separating the two parties which in their later development are best recognized by modern students under the titles of "Loyalist" and "Patriot."

In Boston, the loyalists formed a superstructure of wealth and large social importance, centering chiefly around the Anglican church. Within their lines were the governor and his friends and appointees, the higher justices and numerous lawyers, and a fair proportion of the merchants of the town, together with a coterie whose concerns were not materially affected by either party but who gravitated to the loyalist side by the weight of inherited reverence for English institutions—or at the less admirable behest of social ambitions and aspirations.

Less socially brilliant, but very formidable, was the patriot party. It included many merchants and professional men, most of the clergy excepting those of the Anglican church, and almost the entire body of mechanics. The strongest figure in its councils was Samuel Adams—"master of the town-meeting" and ever ready of tongue and pen.

The Boston of Samuel Adams and his clan constituted the head and mouth of the radical patriots, but their weight and strength lay in the country townships. It was fear of the manhood of the country townships which held the loyalist officials and partisans in check during the years of wrangling which preceded the outbreak of the Revolution. Without the menace of the rallying of thousands of armed farmers, the Boston patriot leaders would have enjoyed short shrift. This menace outweighed even the guns of the English navy and the bayonets of the regulars.

Unanimity was, nevertheless, rare even in the country districts. Nearly every township held its exceptions.

The General Court opened its fall session on September 25—just thirty days after the sacking of the mansion of Lieutenant-Governor Hutchinson by a Stamp Act mob. During its very brief duration, Samuel Adams entered it as a newly enrolled Representative—his first direct participation in the government of the province.

Governor Bernard addressed the delegates on the riots and the necessity of submission to the provisions of the Stamp Act. He painted in strong sentences the dangers of refusal to abide by them—the loss of trade by the cessation of navigation, and a general state of outlawry; and argued for the compensation of those who had suffered in the riots.

Colonel Ward's stand against imperial taxation had been quickly recognized, and on the following day he was added to the committee which was preparing an answer to the governor's message. This was Ward's first appointment on a committee of political protest.

During the same afternoon came an appointment on another committee to deliver the Representatives' reply to the governor's notification that a stamp ship had entered the harbor and his request for assistance in the care and preservation of the Stamped Papers that it brought.

The Representatives' reply expressed their entire unwillingness to have anything whatever to do with the Stamped Papers.

Bernard's retaliation was an excuse-coated order adjourning the General Court to October.

Shortly after the adjournment came the Stamp Act congress in New York. Its labors resulted in addresses to the King and the two houses of Parliament. Timothy Ruggles, chief justice of the Court of Common Pleas of Worcester County (on whose bench Ward had now sat for three years), served as president of the congress—but the stand he took was strongly prerogative and he refused to sign the addresses adopted.

The General Court met again on October 23, and on the following day a House committee which included Samuel Adams and Colonel Ward presented the reply to Bernard which had been held up by the sudden adjournment of the preceding month. The reply respectfully acknowledged the authority of the English Parliament, though emphasizing its limitations, but its tone toward the governor was of sarcasm and dislike. With this committee appointment began Ward's close political association with Samuel Adams—a bond which held for a quarter of a century.

Five days later the House drew up resolves of the "just rights" of the inhabitants of the province—disavowing taxation by Parliament, and declaring that "all acts made, by any Power whatever, other than the General Assembly of this province, imposing Taxes on the Inhabitants are Infringements of our inherent and unalienable Rights."

On November 7, Ward was placed on the committee to draft a letter on the Stamp Act and restrictions of American trade, to be sent to Massachusetts' English Agent.

The session terminated on the next day.

The winter following saw a flourishing crop of the non-importation resolutions so distasteful to English pocket-books, an unrelenting opposition to the use of the reviled stamps, and a great making of homespun to take the place of imported clothes.

The spring records the repeal of the Stamp Act amid rejoicing on both sides of the Atlantic. American patriot leaders looked askance, however, at the accompanying Declaratory Act, which emphatically asserted the "full power and authority" of the King and Parliament "to make laws and statutes . . . to bind the colonies and people of America . . . in all cases whatsoever."

And, further, in Boston, there was little peace within legislative walls, for Bernard made the first session of the new General Court lively by quarreling with the Representatives for failing to elect Hutchinson, the Olivers, and Trowbridge to the Council (which omission he had countered by negativing six of the councilors returned). He also made very emphatic his demand for the compensation of Hutchinson and others who had suffered property losses during the Stamp Act riots.

The Representatives retorted with objections to his temper, expressions, and methods.

Ward was a member of the committee appointed, June 27, to reply to Bernard's second message concerning compensation. Its answer, delivered on the following day, stated that the House felt that it had done all "that our Most Gracious Sovereign and his Parliament" could "reasonably expect from" it, but that it had appointed a committee to investigate during the summer recess and would act on its report during the next session. It concluded by saying: "Your Excellency is pleased to enforce the immediate compliance of the House with this requisition, by an argument drawn from a regard to the town of Boston, the reputation of whose inhabitants your Excellency says has already suffered much for having been tame spectators of the violences committed, and that this disgrace would be removed thereby. We see no reason why the reputation of that town should suffer in the opinion of any one, from all the evidence which has fallen under the observation of the House. Nor does it appear to us how a compliance would remove such disgrace, if that town had been so unhappy as to have fallen under it."

The same afternoon the House was adjourned without any untoward event.

The trend of Ward's political sentiments had not been overlooked by the prerogative party, and Bernard reached the conclusion that he was a dangerous man to hold a colonel's command. His removal quickly followed: his commission was canceled within two days of the closing of the spring session.

The delivery, on July 7, of the governor's order of removal formed a dramatic little scene which was long treasured in Shrewsbury. The most circumstantial account handed down to posterity is that of the Reverend Joseph Sumner,[2] for sixty-two years the township's much beloved and influential preacher.

[2] A. H. Ward, *History of the Town of Shrewsbury, Mass.*, 492.

Bernard's message was carried by a mounted officer in full uniform. He found Ward on the common among a number of the townspeople who had come together to tear down the old meeting-house. He delivered his dispatch and then, still seated on his horse, appeared to await a reply. Ward read the letter—a short one and to the point, as follows:

"Boston, June 30, 1766.

To ARTEMAS WARD, Esq., Sir:

I am ordered by the Governor to signify to you, that he has thought fit to supersede your commission of Col. in the Regt. of Militia lying in part in the County of Worcester, and partly in the County of Middlesex. And your said commission is superseded accordingly.

I am, sir, your most obt. and humble servt.,

JOHN COTTON, *Dep'y Sec'y.*"

As Ward finished reading, one of the onlookers asked if the message contained "important news." Whereupon Ward read the letter aloud, and then, turning to the messenger, said, "Give my compliments to the Governor, and say to him, I consider myself twice honored, but more in being superseded, than in having been commissioned, and that I thank him for this," holding up the letter, "since the motive that dictated it is evidence, that I am, what he is not, a friend to my country."

The story goes steadily forward during the fall and winter sessions. Ward (December 5) voted "Yea" (with Samuel Adams, Otis, Hancock, the Whitcombs, Foster, and other well-known patriots) on the bill which granted compensation to the Stamp Act Riot victims but joined with it a "general Pardon, Indemnity and Oblivion to the Offenders."

Bernard hesitated to accept this, but finally decided to make the best of it.

On January 29, 1767, Ward was with Samuel Adams,

Otis, Cushing, and Hawley on a committee to report a reply to Bernard's opening address of the preceding day; and two days later on a new committee to present the answer prepared—which referred somewhat sarcastically to the spirit of the address and objected to the uninvited presence of Hutchinson in the Council Chamber during the attendance of the General Court on the governor.

February 3, he was with Samuel Adams, Otis, Cushing, Hawley, Dexter, and Sheaffe on a committee to consider the governor's acknowledgment that, through the Council, money had been expended for the maintenance of an artillery company which had arrived in the fall.

The reply drawn up by the committee was a strong rebuke to the governor for having taken money from the treasury without the knowledge of the House.

Also on February 3, Ward was with Brigadier-General Preble and others on a committee to inquire into the state of the militia.

In June the English Parliament passed the Townshend "Act for granting certain Duties in the British Colonies and Plantations in America, etc." It levied on importations of glass, red lead, white lead, painters' colors, paper (and pasteboard, etc.), and tea; and legalized Writs of Assistance. The anticipated revenue was to be applied first to the payment of the colonial civil list.

The expressed intent of the Townshend Act to collect a revenue, set it, like the Stamp Act, outside the theory of the earlier Navigation and Trade acts, but as "external" taxation it was hoped that it would be swallowed. A few years earlier it might have gone down without much trouble, but patriot political analysis had progressed and now would not brook any taxes, external or internal, levied for revenue.

Historians note, with varying sentiments, the development and expansion of Massachusetts' views of her relations with England, and of her progressive objections to forms of taxation. But this evolution of claim and assertion, as she struggled to prevent colonial autonomy from being submerged by new extensions of imperial control, should not surprise the student. Both colonial and English leaders were sailing on seas imperfectly charted. England herself had not then formulated a clear theory of the constitution of the British Empire.

The personal side also made itself strongly felt. Massachusetts leaders held themselves fully the equals of English statesmen, and had no inclination to bend the knee to them.

The England of George III was feared and respected, but with few exceptions its politics and politicians were, by modern standards, both incompetent and venal. Parliamentary representation, church livings, army and navy commissions, and government appointments were publicly bought, sold, and bartered: were publicly advertised for sale. All branches of the government were saturated with corruption.

General conditions were equally bad. Greater wealth than the nation had ever before known had followed the stretching of the empire and the tapping of India, but its possession jostled a great deal of bitter poverty; highwaymen were an expected episode on even the most frequented roads; gross immorality was rife; rioting was common.

It is not surprising that the leaders of thought in the cleaner, more orderly atmosphere of the colonies—especially the Massachusetts leaders—resisted firmly, and sometimes most acrimoniously, every attempt to bring, or which seemed to threaten to bring them under the thumbs of English officeholders.

By natural gifts and inclination, and by the experience of well-tried generations, the people of Massachusetts were fully qualified to govern themselves without any imperial aid, superintendence, or advice. Despite their place upon the calendar of the eighteenth century, instead of the nineteenth or twentieth, they were as competent and full-fledged as are the self-governing, or "responsible government," colonies of the British Empire of today.

In practice, though not in formal recognition, they had indeed traveled a long way toward the status of a self-governing colony, and men of the Samuel Adams type desperately fought every attempt to make them retrace their steps—even if only a short distance and for good imperial reasons.

In the following January (1768) the Massachusetts House met the Townshend revenue act with a petition to the King and addresses to members of the English ministry, remonstrating against taxation levied by Parliament, and it succeeded this on February 11 with Samuel Adams' "Circular Letter" to the other colonies, informing them of its action and suggesting that "all possible care" be taken that the provinces "upon so delicate a point should harmonize with each other."

Next one comes to May 25, biographically important as the date of Ward's election to the Council in a contest with Lieutenant-Governor Hutchinson.

The Council at this period, it should be remembered, held a large measure of power, for it shared both in legislation and in executive authority, combining the duties now resting separately on the Senate and Council.

Eighteen councilors were to be chosen from within the old Massachusetts Bay Colony. Seventy-one votes were required for election. The first ballot disclosed only seventeen men who had received the requisite number. Hutchinson had been given sixty-eight—the highest number of those who failed of election. The prerogative party expected to seat him on the next ballot, but Samuel Adams spread the news, freshly arrived, that Hutchinson had received a grant from the crown—that he had become a government "Pensioner," and Otis hurried from member to member crying for votes for Colonel Ward. The result of their efforts was the immediate election of Ward to complete the Council roll.

Bernard promptly retaliated by vetoing Ward.

In his letter to ex-Governor Pownall,[3] one of several on the subject, Hutchinson describes Ward as "a very sulky fellow, who I thought I could bring over by giving him a commission in the provincial forces after you left the government, but I was mistaken."

Telling of Bernard's veto, he adds, "Ward was sacrificed to my *manes!*"

A month later (June 21) Bernard presented the instructions of Lord Hillsborough, England's Colonial Secretary, that he "require of the House of Representatives, in his Majesty's Name, to Rescind the Resolution which gave Birth to the Circular Letter from the Speaker [that of February 11 to the other colonies referred to on page 39] and to declare their Disapprobation of, and Dissent to that rash and hasty proceeding."

The House came to a vote on the subject June 30. By ninety-two to seventeen it refused to rescind, and was promptly dissolved.

The Representatives who thus defied England were extolled throughout the length and breadth of the colonies, and in and out of print, as the "Glorious Ninety-Two." Prominent among them was Artemas Ward. The seventeen members who voted to rescind were led by Timothy Ruggles.

Official voices were now reiterating demands for troops to hold the people in check. A little later, the report that troops were coming resulted in a Boston town-meeting which resolved against taxation except by their own Representatives, and against a standing army; voted that all inhabitants, not already provided, should furnish themselves with arms, "as provided by a good & wholesome law of the Province"—giving as excuse the possibility of another English-French war; and invited a general convention of town committees.

Ward was on September 20 unanimously chosen Shrewsbury's representative in the "Committee of Convention"—

[3] MS. copy, June 7, 1768, *Massachusetts Archives*, XXV, 262.

the title applied to the gathering of town delegates thus called to the capital.

The convention held its opening session on September 22, sixty-six towns and several districts being represented in the "upwards of seventy" delegates present. Later arrivals swelled their number until ninety-six towns and eight districts were represented.

The delegates' first step was to petition the governor to cause an assembly "to be immediately convened." Bernard refused to receive the petition, denounced the calling of "an assembly of the people by private persons" as a "notorious violation" of the King's authority—"for a meeting of the Deputies of the Towns is an Assembly of the Representatives of the People to all Intents and Purposes; and it is not the calling it a Committee of Convention that will alter the Nature of the Thing," and admonished the delegates "instantly" to break up the assembly, or he should be obliged to "assert the Prerogative of the Crown in a more public Manner." "The King," he concluded, "is determined to maintain his entire Sovereignty over this Province; and whoever shall persist in usurping any of the Rights of it, will repent of his Rashness."

The delegates ignored the demand that they disperse, and on the third day replied to him lengthily and argumentatively. But this communication also Bernard refused to receive.

The convention concluded its proceedings on September 26 with a public statement, "unanimously agreed upon," which is lavish in expressions of loyalty but which repeated the protest of the dissolved House of Representatives against taxation for revenue and against a standing army being maintained in the province.[4]

A squadron from Halifax arrived on the last day of the convention, bringing a detachment of regulars under the command of Lieutenant-Colonel Dalrymple. From their

[4] A full account of the proceedings is in the Boston newspapers of the time.

presence and those from Ireland, arriving soon after, sprang a new and very thorny crop of disputes—over their quarters and their supplies, the legality of their presence, etc.—a wordy warfare with many threats exchanged by "lobster backs" and "Sons of Liberty."

Officials and their supporters of the prerogative party rejoiced, for they felt that they had achieved the upper hand. The troops garrisoned the capital, ready to uphold them, despite all the patriot protests. But this temporary success served, nevertheless, chiefly to mark the consummation of another grave error of judgment. The use of soldiery to suggest coercion was another defiance of the traditional sentiments of the race.

On through the winter, enlivened in England (now that Boston was possessed by the regulars) with Parliamentary plans to seize the patriot leaders for trial in England. These plans, and variations of them, were duly reported in the colonies, and with the inflammatory result that might have been expected.

Next spring (1769) came the publication of some of the letters Bernard had written to England during the preceding year. He had handled American conditions in an uncommonly adverse spirit and had suggested various changes in the provincial government.

The letters excited a great deal of anger throughout the province—somewhat to the perturbation of Lieutenant-Governor Hutchinson, for he also had been writing in similar strain. Exposure was, however, in his case deferred for several years.

When the General Court convened on May 31, the House addressed the governor requesting the removal of the fleet and soldiers. He retorted that he had no authority over either.

On the same day Ward was again elected to the Council, only to be vetoed on the morrow.

The House, after much consideration and several reports (Ward was added to the second committee of consideration), drew up a strong paper disputing Bernard's plea of impotence, and expressing the alarm of the province, if he were correct, at the presence of an army "uncontrollable by any civil authority in the province." Further, it objected to the idea that the regulars were needed, declaring that disturbances in Massachusetts had been "greatly misrepresented"; that they were not nearly so bad as many in Great Britain "at the very gates of the palace and even in the Royal Presence."

Bernard replied that he could not remove the troops, but could the General Court—and did so, to Cambridge.

On June 22 Ward was on the committee appointed to present to the Council the House approval of the "zeal and attention" the preceding Council had displayed in writing to Colonial Secretary Hillsborough to refute the statements in the Bernard (and Gage) letters. The Council's letter of April 15 had complained of the governor's representations, denying their accuracy; and charged him with planning "the Destruction of our Constitution." It had closed with the declaration that by the mutual lack of confidence his usefulness as governor had been destroyed.

June 27, Ward took part in a vote unanimously approving a petition requesting Bernard's removal.

On July 8 and 12 he was with Samuel Adams, Hancock, Otis the father and Otis the son, Hawley, and Colonel Williams, on committees to answer the governor's messages of July 6 and 12.

Their reply, unanimously approved by the House, was presented to Bernard on July 15. It refused to appropriate money to defray the expense of quartering the troops, and strongly protested against the governor and Council having authorized disbursements on that account. It concluded by asserting that "as we cannot, consistently with our honor, or interest, and much less with the duty we owe our constituents, so we shall never make provision for the purposes in your several messages above mentioned."

Meantime, the renewal of the taxation controversy had again aroused the South, and also, in this year of 1769, brought George Washington into the arena as the introducer of the articles of association which gave birth to the Virginia non-importation agreement.

The numerous violations of non-importation agreements only added to the heat of the conflict. The life of a merchant of the period held a greater possibility of exciting incident than is usually attendant on such a career. The ordinary equation of business uncertainty was liable to be varied at any moment by a customs agent with an omnipotent searching Writ of Assistance or by an equally aggressive patriot committee set in full cry by a report, false or otherwise, of "prohibited" importations.

In Boston the community was continually disturbed by many-sided quarrels engaging naval revenue officers,[5] soldiers, citizens, and seamen; the disputes occasionally swelling into violence, as in the assault on Otis and the shooting of the boy Snider, and culminating in the "Boston Massacre" on March 5, 1770.

Acute indeed was the crisis following the "Massacre." Crowds of men, of Boston and all the neighboring towns, armed and protesting, filling the streets; other scores and hundreds continuously coming in from the country districts; the local militia posted everywhere to avert any further clash with the soldiers—Samuel Adams and John Adams and Dr. Joseph Warren, as other prominent citizens, muskets in hand, taking their turns in policing the town both night and day.

[5] The average layman reading that excise duties were collected by officers of the English navy, pictures the collectors as men of the style of those who now command His Majesty's ships—men of the same type as those in our own navy of today—but "The British naval lieutenant of 1765 was a very rough person. He had often been 'made' by a post-captain who in an emergency did a little press-gang work among merchantmen, and filled up the minor posts on the King's decks from the impressed mates and captains of the mercantile marine. Edward Thompson, in his letters, says that in his time 'a chaw of tobacco, a rattan and a rope of oaths' constituted the simple qualifications for a lieutenancy in the King's fleet. Lieutenants according to this sample did very little to promote good feeling between Colonial traders and the British Navy."—Belcher's *First American Civil War,* I, 34–35.

The wrath of the people rose steadily higher, and a pitched battle with the soldiers was averted only by the governor and the English commander submitting to Samuel Adams' demand that the troops be removed from the town.

The following month saw the repeal of the taxation provisions of the Townshend revenue act—excepting the duty on tea. Parliament might as well have let the act stand entire, for the exception was eventually to defeat the purpose of the repeal.

The new General Court convened on May 30. It for the third time elected Ward to the Council, giving him 115 out of a total of 125 votes. Hutchinson, now acting-governor, had marked him and also Thomas Sanders for slaughter again, but took the advice of his associates and concluded to accept them; partly in gratitude for the election of several "very moderate men," and partly for fear that a new refusal would "increase the bad spirit in the House and through the province."[6]

Thus we find Colonel Ward at last a Councilor of Massachusetts. He takes his seat at the Board with twenty-four other councilors, all of them rather gorgeous in appearance because of their large white wigs and their scarlet-cloth coats —"some of them with gold-laced hats . . . on the table before them, or under the table beneath them." Hutchinson is at the head of the table.

Prominent on the walls are "glorious portraits of King Charles II and King James II, to which might be added and should be added, little miserable likenesses of Governor Winthrop, Governor Bradstreet, Governor Endicott, and Governor Belcher, hung up in obscure corners."[7]

Ward's class at Harvard is well represented, for he is joined at the Board by two of his classmates, both there also for the first time: Thomas Sanders of Gloucester—he who was all but vetoed together with Ward, and who had been

[6] MS. copy, June 8, 1770, *Massachusetts Archives,* XXVI, 500.

[7] *Works of John Adams,* X, 250, 249–250.

previously several times vetoed; and George Leonard, from Norton, one of the twenty-three members who had been willingly accepted.

From this date until the time of the hated "mandamus councilors," Ward was each year reëlected to the Board. He was, however, never persona grata to the governor's party because of his known antagonism to any encroachments on American rights.

In the background, meantime, hung the strong sentiment that the Stamp Act had raised. The patriot element fluctuated in fervor, and non-importation resolutions broke down, but one did not have to go very deep to touch strong resistance.

No new revenue laws were attempted, but other changes in control were essayed. All of them were perhaps justifiable from the English standpoint, but they looked dangerous to those Massachusetts leaders who had sniffed suspiciously at the Declaratory Act and the exception to the Townshend Act repeal, and they kept the alarm-bells ringing.

A brief spell of comparative political peace and then in the fall of 1772 Hutchinson (governor since March of the preceding year) is startled by a new upheaval. It had been set mounting by the report that the judges of the Superior Court were to be carried on the King's payroll in place of their payment by the provincial House of Representatives—thus depriving the popular branch of the provincial government of its only means of exercising any control over the judiciary; and it brought into life the famous Committees of Correspondence.

Hutchinson convened the General Court on January 6, 1773, and in a lengthy speech set forth his views on the relative positions of the American colonies and the English Parliament, and deplored the recent town-meetings throughout the province in which the "supreme authority of Parliament" had been denied.

A long argument followed in which both House and Council took part.

Ward was on the Council committee appointed to reply to Hutchinson. Its answer, presented January 25, declared that the unrest in the province rose from attempts of Parliament to subject the inhabitants to taxes without their consent; and it cited Magna Charta and other authorities in support of its declaration that Parliament could not constitutionally levy taxes "in any form," direct or indirect, on the people of Massachusetts.

Ward was also on the committee which prepared the Council's answer to Hutchinson's reply.

The Council's answer recapitulated its statements of January 25, again referring to "Magna Charta, and other authorities" to prove that the province was not constitutionally subject to parliamentary taxation: "The argument, abridged, stands thus," it said, "that, from those authorities, it appears an essential part of the English constitution, that no tallage, or aid, or tax, shall be laid or levied, without the good will and assent of the freemen of the commonality of the realm. That, from common law, and the province charter, the inhabitants of this province are clearly entitled to all the rights of free and natural subjects, within the realm. That, among those rights, must be included the essential one just mentioned, concerning aids and taxes; and therefore, that no aids or taxes can be levied on us, constitutionally, without our own consent, signified by our Representatives. From whence, the conclusion is clear, that therefore, the inhabitants of this province are not constitutionally subject to Parliamentary taxation."

On March 5 Ward was on the Council committee which presented a message to Hutchinson protesting against the King's order, duly arrived, which made the judges of the Superior Court financially dependent on the crown. The Council declared that "as the Happiness of a Community so much depends on an impartial Administration of Justice" it could not "but be deeply affected by the thought, that by this Innovation in Government, a Foundation may be laid for rendering the Rights, Liberties and Properties of this People, in Many Respects, precarious and insecure."

Next to hand—of slight historical but large temporary importance—is the publication of the letters written to Thomas Whately of London, ex-member of Parliament, by Governor Hutchinson (when Lieutenant-Governor), Lieutenant-Governor Andrew Oliver (when Secretary), and others, which had been sent back across the ocean by Benjamin Franklin. Much curiosity and apprehension had been aroused by various rumors disseminated concerning the letters, and when they finally appeared in print they were eagerly read by the entire province and denounced from a long list of pulpits.[8]

It happened that the letters were comparatively innocuous, but the Massachusetts ear was not so tuned as to enjoy the suggestions they contained that there "must be an abridgement of English liberties" and that something more than "declaratory acts or resolves" was needed to secure the dependence of the colony. If Franklin had obtained some of Hutchinson's other letters—those to Hillsborough and Bernard, for example—there would have been still greater heat in the province.

Time has mellowed the criticisms of Hutchinson and we of today can generally visualize his viewpoint and appreciate both his abilities and the difficulties of his position. But the views he expressed and the advice he gave to English authorities were bitterly resented by his patriot contemporaries.

The new legislative year opened May 26. Ward did not reach Boston until June 15, but he was on the morrow ap-

[8] The use of these letters is harshly condemned by loyalist writers and is deplored by many others, but there is no need to dodge or gloss over the issue. The alleged exaggeration of the import or design of the letters is a subject that may be debated, or criticized, or deplored (according to the individual viewpoint), but the procuring of them by Franklin and their forwarding to Boston does not call for apology. In those days no one held letters on political subjects as sacred, no matter by whom written or to whom addressed. Everyone in public life in England, from the King down, read and used other people's letters at every opportunity, both during their transit through the mails and after their delivery.

pointed on the Council committee which notified Hutchinson that the House possessed several of his letters and requested him to inform them if he had written any "of the same Tenor with the copies herewith exhibited."

Hutchinson asked to see the originals, and, after inspecting them, did not deny their authenticity.

A few days later (June 25) the Board passed twelve resolves condemning the Hutchinson and Oliver letters and a thirteenth requesting the removal of both the governor and lieutenant-governor.

But such appeals were doomed to failure, for they could not stem the tide that in English official circles had set against patriot viewpoints, ambitions, and representations. English officialdom was confirmed in its stand and fed in its prejudices by the reports and opinions of sincere loyalists such as Hutchinson; by the insincere testimony of place-hunters; and by the venom of mischief-makers.

At this session Colonel Ward had the pleasure of sitting in the Council with John Winthrop, his Harvard instructor in higher mathematics and natural philosophy. In the quarter-century that had elapsed since the day of Ward's graduation, Winthrop had achieved wide recognition as a scientist: Edinburgh had conferred an honorary LL.D. on him and the Royal Society of London had made him a Fellow.

General Charles Lee arrived from England in the fall—the same Lee who as a captain of the Royal Grenadiers had fought at Ticonderoga. This is his first visit to America since the close of the French war; but for fame and disgrace, for adulation and censure, it is to be his home henceforth. He is to play a heavy part in the Revolutionary drama.

During the ten years which have passed since the signing of the Treaty of Paris, Lee has grown notably in experience and personality. He has won distinction in Portugal, and has held the rank of major-general in the Polish army.

English government and army circles know him well—but deny him favor, for his sharp tongue and ready pen have made him many enemies.

A peculiar, brilliant man—driven by an abnormal excitability and restlessness which have swept him hither and thither, to and fro. Now forty-two years of age; of proved courage both in the field and the duello; well versed in military subjects, judged by the standards of the time; and possessed of a comfortable private fortune. A tall, thin man with a huge nose; slovenly in his dress; of erratic disposition and violent temper; intermittently ingratiating, caustic, and arrogant.

Lee landed in New York on November 10. For a while the gout kept him inactive, but as soon as his malady had been alleviated he commenced the talking, writing, and visiting which so strongly fixed the attention of the colonies upon him. His aggressive espousal of the patriot cause inspired and inspirited all who came in contact with him; and his enthusiasm brought out and developed all that was best and most attractive in his complex character.[9]

Next one views Boston's defiance of the English attempt to make efficient use of the tea duty—that relic of the Townshend revenue act which had been smouldering now for several years, remaining on the statute books as a levy on all tea brought into the colonies, but actually reaching less than ten per cent. of the large quantity imported. The new plan was to employ the act for the assistance and profit of the English East India Company, the empire's greatest monopoly, and, incidentally, by the same stroke to make tea smuggling unprofitable and customs collections a source of appreciable revenue.

[9] Many modern writers dismiss or disparage Charles Lee's military ability and reputation as largely spurious, but to do so is to affront the judgment and experience of his most famous and most competent contemporaries. After months of close association at the siege of Boston, Washington was still a party to the universal American admiration of Lee's abilities (Washington's letter to Lee, March 14, 1776, *Lee Papers*, I, 358; to John A. Washington, March 31, 1776, Ford's *Writings of George Washington*, III, 508).

An interesting story is entwined in this English spinning of the fuse of the American Revolution.

Its first and chief point is found in the exigencies of the great corporation licensed to exploit the millions of India but dangerously close to a bankruptcy that might involve imperial credit, for its finances were interwoven with those of the English government and its tentacles stretched through high English circles. Second, is an overstock of tea and other goods bulging its warehouses. Third, is the possibility of unloading the tea on the American market by offering it at a low price direct to retailers through special agents—the English government aiding by the removal of the English customs, leaving only the American import duty. Fourth, is the political error of leaving the American duty payable in the colonies instead of making it payable in England.

To Massachusetts the project came to ride upon the storm raised by the judges' salaries and the Hutchinson-Oliver letters. It revitalized the taxation controversy and excited the anger of the large patriot following which had declared against taxation for revenue. It alienated tory merchants—and backsliding whig merchants—who had laid in Dutch and other teas, smuggled or otherwise, and who saw their stocks about to drop in value. And it spread wide apprehension among merchants of all political persuasions lest their future trade—not only in tea, but also perhaps in other commodities—be engulfed by monopoly control.

"The King meant to try the question with America"—and he got his answer quickly!

The story of the tea-dumping has been told too often to need recapitulation here, but let it not be forgotten that the moral effect on the King's representatives in Massachusetts was greatly enhanced by their knowledge that, in essentials, the big and sometimes noisy following of Samuel Adams was supported by the patriot members of the Council.

On the day (Saturday, November 27) preceding the arrival of the *Dartmouth,* the first of the three tea-ships to enter the harbor, the Council replied to the application of the governor and the tea agents with a refusal to aid the landing or safeguarding of the tea, giving as its reason that to do so would be to assent to the collection of the duty and thus to the principle of taxation by Parliament.

Hutchinson deemed the reply so radical that he warned the Council "of the consequences of it; that it would be highly resented in England, and would be urged there, to shew the necessity of a change in their constitution."[10]

On the following Monday, while the *Dartmouth* lay at anchorage and townspeople and visitors filled the Old South Meeting House to hang on the words of Samuel Adams, and Joseph Warren, and Hancock, and other speakers, Hutchinson was renewing his futile debate with the Council in the Court House.

The patriot members adhered to their report—"all advice to secure the tea, upon its being landed, being expressly refused, because such advice would be a measure for procuring payment of the duty."

Thus firmly upholding the hands of the Samuel Adams party were Ward (present at both the meetings mentioned), James Bowdoin, John Winthrop, George Leonard, James Pitts, and Samuel Dexter.

Seventeen days later (December 16), in the semi-darkness of the candle-lit meeting-house, Samuel Adams gave the signal: and his historic troop of "Mohawks" descended upon the tea-ships and emptied their proscribed cargoes into the harbor.

A pregnant intermission now, while Hutchinson's dispatches are tossed about on the wintry Atlantic as old-fashioned sailing-vessels tack across the ocean. There was little to be done by either party until the English government disclosed its intent on the receipt of the news.

On February 1, 1774, Ward was on the committee ap-

[10] Hutchinson, *History of Massachusetts Bay,* III, 428–429.

pointed to present the Council's answer to the governor's message of January 26.

Hutchinson in his closing paragraph had conveyed "His Majesty's disapprobation of the appointment of Committees of Correspondence." The Council's answer declared that, "so far as this matter relates to the Board," the King's disapproval could apply only to committees appointed to advise the colony agent in England, but it warmly defended the right to appoint, and the necessity for, such committees.

The last days of the session were distinguished by the final chapter of the trouble over the judges' salaries: the House impeachment of Chief Justice Peter Oliver of the Superior Court for accepting his salary from the crown.

The Council on March 7 appointed a committee (Ward a member) to wait on the governor with an address, dissenting from his opinion, expressed to the House, that the process by impeachment and the governor and Council proceeding and determining upon it were unconstitutional; declaring the readiness of the Board "to hear and determine on the impeachment abovementioned, or to hear and determine on the charge and complaint since exhibited by the House of Representatives on the same subject"; and requesting that he "with the Council" would appoint a time for the hearing.

Realizing that he could not control the Council, Hutchinson stopped the proceedings by dissolving the House. Technically, he had the last word—but Peter Oliver never again presided in court and the committees of correspondence carried on the work of the assembly.

Word of the "Boston Tea Party" reached England before the end of January. Lord North struck back with his bill to close the Port of Boston. The measure traveled rapidly through Parliament. It was not presented until March 18 but three readings and passage in both Commons and Lords, debates in both Houses, and the affixing of the King's signature were all crowded into fourteen days.

The act prohibited the shipping or unshipping of any goods at any point within the harbor, excepting only His Majesty's stores, and consignments of food and fuel for the inhabitants of Boston—and these consignments were to be rigidly inspected, and closely limited to "necessary use and sustenance."

CHAPTER IV

May 10, 1774–April 19, 1775: Age 46–47

The closing of the Port of Boston. The Regulating Act, and that for the "Impartial Administration of Justice." Ward a delegate to the Worcester County Convention. The closing of the courts. Ward's old regiment elects him Colonel. A delegate to the First and Second Provincial Congresses. Appointed second general officer of the province. The battle of April 19, 1775, and the land blockade of Boston.

ON May 10 two merchantmen brought copies of the Port Act to Boston.

Three days later His Majesty's ship *Lively* beat its way into the harbor and from it landed General "Tom" Gage—for a number of years commander-in-chief of the King's forces in North America, and now also commissioned to succeed Hutchinson as governor of Massachusetts. He had come with instructions to close the harbor of Boston; to transfer the port of entry to Marblehead; to remove the capital to Salem; and to punish the leaders of the opposition to British legislation. He was to be followed by a new influx of redcoats to uphold royal authority.

Next morning Paul Revere set out on a big gray horse, riding fast, bound for New York and Philadelphia with Massachusetts' appeal for the support of her sister colonies, and her prayers for joint retaliation by stamping out all trade with Great Britain. Every country town through which he passed, received the word and radiated it for miles around. Other riders, traveling many routes, spread the news still wider; and a hundredfold echoed it and its appeal.

The General Court convened on May 25. Gage's initial

speech, delivered on the following day, made no reference to the new conditions except to notify the assembly that by royal order it was after June 1 to meet in Salem.

The Representatives accelerated their proceedings, planning to conclude them before that date and thus avoid, temporarily at all events, the change in the seat of government, but Gage upset their calculations by suddenly adjourning them to meet at Salem on June 7.

On Wednesday, June 1, the closing act went into effect. The King's ships took possession of the harbor and nothing thenceforth could stir upon the face of the water without their permission.

A pall of enforced idleness settled upon the town. So large a part of its trade and livelihood had been of and by the sea—both coastwise and ocean-going: ships and shipping, imports and exports, and many subsidiary interests and activities along the docks and in warehouses and shops—that the closing of the port threw hundreds out of employment and brought scores of business houses to an abrupt halt. It would have spelled destitution to many but for donations, in money and kind, by sympathizers throughout the country, brought in by the Roxbury road over Boston Neck—the isthmus connecting Boston with the mainland. That one road had become the capital's only free line of communication with the continent.

On June 9, the third day of the General Court session at Salem, the House and Council delivered their replies to Gage's address of May 26. The House answer consisted largely of objections to moving the seat of government, and was received without protest. But the Council's reply, prepared by Ward,[1] stirred the governor to great ire.

The Council's reply recognized that the position that Gage was assuming had been rendered more difficult by "the pecu-

[1] The draft, in Ward's hand, is among the *Artemas Ward MSS.* (owned by Artemas Ward, New York). The completed reply retained all of the ideas and much of the language.

liar circumstances of the times," but it hoped that his administration, in "principles and general conduct," might be a "happy contrast" to that of his "two immediate predecessors," for there was "the greatest reason to apprehend, that from their machinations, both in concert and apart," were "derived the origin and progress of the disunion between Great Britain and the colonies, and the present distressed state of the province." It stated that the people of Massachusetts claimed "no more than the rights of Englishmen"—but that they claimed those rights "without diminution or abridgement." Plainly and firmly it continued with the declaration that those rights, as it would be their indispensable duty, so it should be their constant endeavor, to maintain, to the utmost of their power—"in perfect consistence, however, with the truest loyalty to the Crown; the just prerogatives of which, your Excellency will find this Board ever zealous to support."

The committee which presented the reply reported that when the chairman had read so far as that part which expressed a wish that his administration might be "a happy contrast" to that of his two immediate predecessors, the governor told the chairman to stop, declaring that he could not receive an address which reflected so severely on his predecessors.

He followed this, June 14, by a formal communication denouncing the address "as an insult upon his Majesty, and the Lords of the Privy Council" and an affront to himself.

Three days later, on June 17, exactly a year before the battle of Bunker Hill, the House appointed delegates to a meeting of "Committees or Delegates" from all the colonies—a "Continental Congress"—to be held in Philadelphia: Samuel Adams, key in pocket, guarding the vote, and warding off the governor's attempt to dissolve the House, by keeping the tories locked in and the governor's messenger locked out.

Meanwhile, back in Colonel Ward's home county, the justices of the Court of Common Pleas, with Ward the only exception, were hastening to place themselves on the tory side—Judge Timothy Ruggles leading them. As also were the justices of the peace attending the Court of General Sessions. Together, they prepared a letter to Gage which arraigned the "inflammatory pieces" of the Boston and Worcester committees as creating "discord and confusion," and promised to do everything in their power "to discountenance such proceedings, and to support the execution of the laws, and render your Excellency's administration successful and prosperous."

For this production, delivered by Sheriff Chandler on June 21, the early fall was to bring much retributive humiliation.

Among the justices of the peace who signed it was Timothy Paine, who as a youth had sat next Ward at Harvard.

In the country districts, every tavern served as a political club and all were abuzz with discussion. John Adams, in a reminiscent letter, records one of these familiar debates.

"I stopped one night at a tavern in Shrewsbury, about forty miles from Boston, and as I was cold and wet, I sat down at a good fire in the bar-room to dry my great coat and saddle-bags till a fire could be made in my chamber. There presently came in, one after another, half a dozen, or half a score, substantial yeomen of the neighborhood, who, sitting down to the fire after lighting their pipes, began a lively conversation upon politics. As I believed I was unknown to all of them, I sat in total silence to hear them. One said, 'The people of Boston are distracted.' Another answered, 'No wonder the people of Boston are distracted, Oppression will make wise men mad.' A third said, 'What would you say if a fellow should come to your house and tell you he was come to take a list of your cattle, that Parliament might tax you for them at so much a head? And how should you feel if he was to go and break open your barn, to take down your oxen, horses and sheep?' 'What should I say?' replied the first; 'I would knock him in the head.' 'Well,' said a fourth, 'if parliament can take away Mr. Hancock's wharf and Mr. Rowe's wharf, they can take away your barn and my house.' After much more reasoning in this style, a fifth, who had as yet been silent, broke out: 'Well, it is high time for us to rebel; we must rebel sometime or other, and we had better rebel now than at any time to come. If we put it off for ten or twenty years, and let them go on as they have begun, they will get a strong party among us, and plague us a great deal more than they can now.' "[2]

The Shrewsbury farmers, envisaging the growth of the tory party, displayed remarkably clear insight. It was but a very little while later that Gage was rejoicing at tory developments. He wrote, July 5, to Lord Dartmouth, Secretary of State for the American Department: "There is now an open opposition to the faction, carried on with a warmth and spirit unknown before, which it is highly proper and necessary to cherish, and support by every means; and I hope it will not be long before it produces very salutary effects."[3]

Swiftly after the closing of the port came the news of the passing by the English Parliament of "An Act for the Better Regulating the Government of the Province of the Massachusetts Bay" and "An Act for the Impartial Administration of Justice."

The first law struck at the very heart of the political system of the province. It prohibited the calling or holding of town-meetings, save by the express permission of the governor, excepting only annual gatherings confined to the election of town officers and Representatives. It snatched the choice of councilors from the province and vested their naming in the King. It placed the appointment of judges, sheriffs, and other civil officers in the hands of the governor —who was answerable only to the King. It took away the

[2] *Works of John Adams,* IX, 597.

[3] *American Archives,* 4th, I, 515.

right to elect jurors and gave their selection to the sheriffs who had thus been made amenable to the governor's fiat.

The second law took from the province its right to try for capital offenses either government officials or those acting under their orders, and provided that they might be sent to any of the other colonies or to England for trial.

The official copies of the acts were not received until August 6 but their general tenor was known and debated early in June, and the threat of coercion was reiterated by each ship which unloaded reinforcements of British regulars. Boston wrote in indignation to the other provinces as well as to the country towns of Massachusetts, and both provinces and country towns echoed her anger in the heightened tone of their letters and resolutions.

Many and great were now the grievances. The province could be taxed by men, three thousand miles away, who had never set foot upon its soil and knew nothing of, or knew badly, its circumstances, needs, and traditions; its customary life as it pulsed in every township, great and small, was to be halted and cribbed by the town-meeting edict; its properties and liberties were to be thenceforth in the hands of judges and juries over whom it had no longer even the shadow of either selection or control; it was to be held impotent to punish official violence; and it must submit, whether or no, to an English army ever in its midst.

With the official copies of the new acts had come a list of "mandamus councilors" (Timothy Ruggles and Timothy Paine among them)—a Council appointed in London, instead of, as heretofore, one elected by the Massachusetts House of Representatives.

The councilors who accepted their appointments speedily became objects of local patriot attention, but it was everywhere realized that, unless untoward events should earlier precipitate trouble, the first important test of strength would come when the courts opened their sessions under the new laws.

On August 9 there gathered in Worcester its first county convention of committees of correspondence and delegates.[4] The fifty-two men who came together in "the house of Mary Sternes [Stearns] inholder"[5] represented twenty-two townships. Some towns were represented by single delegates; others by two or more. One town mustered eight, including three captains, a doctor, and a deacon. From Shrewsbury came Colonel Ward, accompanied by Phinehas Heywood, who had succeeded as Representative on Ward's election to the Council.

The student finds much interest in the proceedings of these county conventions, for by means of simple "resolutions" they abolished all authorized government and judicature in Massachusetts. The general enforcement of their resolutions demonstrates the strength of the public patriot opinion of the province.

The prohibited town-meetings ruled the townships, and the county conventions directed them to concerted effort. It was the interlocking framework of the two which gave the Provincial Congress its vigorous life.

Not one of Ward's associates of the Worcester County Court of Common Pleas was present at the convention. Timothy Ruggles had broken with his fellow-townsmen and made his way to the capital. The other judges—Thomas Steel and Joseph Wilder—had signed the tory letter to Gage and were also conspicuous by their absence. The lawyers of the county had likewise declared for the crown, following the lead of Jonathan Sewall (another of Ward's college classmates), now become attorney-general of the province.

The convention adopted a letter to the Massachusetts delegates to the Continental Congress, issued a call to the

[4] The journal of the Worcester County convention is in Lincoln's *Journals of each Provincial Congress*, 627–652.

[5] This was the King's Arms Tavern, but patriot records balked at thus describing it. The offending sign and title were taken down in July, 1776. A vaudeville house now stretches across the site of the tavern, and the Lincoln House Block (Main Street, Maple to Elm) covers its front yard.

towns not represented, and drew up a set of resolutions declaring that the people of Massachusetts owed no obedience to the English Parliament, that they recognized no right but their own to legislate for them, that the charter of the province was the basis of their allegiance to the King of England, and that any attempt to vacate the charter would have a "tendency to dissolve the union between Great Britain and the province." It also "greatly" approved the non-consumption agreement as likely to convince their "Brethren in Britain, that more is to be gained in the way of justice, from friendship and affection, than by extortion and arbitrary power."

Sixteen days later, on a call inspired by the town of Worcester, a considerable body of delegates gathered in the capital. They had come from the counties of Worcester, Middlesex, and Essex, to confer with each other and with the Boston committee of correspondence. They declared that "no power on earth hath a right without the consent of this province to alter the minutest tittle of its charter"; moved for a Provincial Congress; urged the obstruction of the courts until such a congress convened, and the boycott of their officers and adherents; and advised the practice of the military art.

Partisan feeling mounted high. The Quebec Act heightened the tension. "Liberty Poles" were erected, and many of the wealthier classes of the country townships fled into Boston. The English ministry were roundly denounced with picturesque epithets. Copies of the Port Act were publicly burned.[6]

The presence of the garrison calmed the fears of the tories

[6] Burning obnoxious literature was a favorite pastime on both sides of the Atlantic, and was indulged in by both government and objectors. Attempts to thus uphold ministerial dignity sometimes resulted in ludicrously undignified disturbances. A good example is found in the execution of the House of Commons order of February 27, 1775, that the "Common Hangman" burn a copy of an offending issue of the vituperative little London *Crisis* in the New Palace Yard, Westminster, and another copy in front of the Royal Exchange; and that "the sheriffs of London and Middlesex do attend at the same time and places respectively."

At Westminster the copy was successfully burned, but immediately thereafter "a man threw into the fire the Address of both Houses of Parliament to his Majesty, declaring

in Boston—alike those who claimed it as their home and those who had come in from the country—but otherwise life was not entirely pleasant even there for crown adherents. They suffered from the scorn of their patriot neighbors, and, jointly with them, had to bear the many ills which marched step by step with the soldiery of those days. Sickness was rife and dissolute female camp-followers were numerous.

The second Worcester County convention—a two-day session, commencing August 30—brought together one hundred and thirty members of committees of correspondence and "a number of deputies and gentlemen from several towns."

Their first vote after the chaplain had opened the meeting with prayer, was, "by reason of the straitness of the place, and the many attending," to adjourn from Mary Stearns' house to the court-house.

There, on the following day, they issued a call to the men of the county to be at Worcester on September 6 to prevent the sitting of the Court of Common Pleas and the General Sessions of the Peace under the new laws; recommended the towns and districts of the county to elect delegates to a "general provincial convention" at Concord on October 11; and published the means to be taken to spread the alarm in the event of "an invasion, or danger of an invasion" of any town in the county.

Men were already thinking in terms of war. Before the meeting of the Continental Congress, before the meeting of the Provincial Congress, the men of Worcester County were thus counseled to be ready to repel an *invasion* by the enemy.

The convention had barely dispersed when the province

the Bostonians in actual rebellion; likewise the Address of the Bishops and Clergy assembled in Convocation. The Sheriffs were much hissed for attending, and the populace diverted themselves with throwing the fire at each other."

The burning of the second copy was a still more exciting and riotous event. "As soon as the fire was lighted before the Exchange, it was put out, and dead dogs and cats were thrown at the Officers; a fire was then made in Cornhill, and the pelting continued. Sheriff Hart was wounded in the wrist, and Sheriff Plomer in the breast, with a brickbat; Mr. Gates, the City Marshal, was dismounted, and with much difficulty saved his life. Three of the ringleaders were taken into custody but were soon after rescued by the mob."—*Kentish Gazette,* March 8, 1775.

was aroused by the "Powder Alarm." Bred by the excitement raised by Gage's seizure of powder and field-pieces in Charlestown and Cambridge, a report ran wild that the redcoats had fired on the people and that the English army and English ships were cannonading Boston. A great rush of men started toward the capital and several thousand arrived in Cambridge and other near-by towns before the denial of the report could reach them.

When they had been fully convinced that they were not needed, the men tramped back to their homes. For those of Worcester County, the return was accepted as only a brief respite! A day or two with their families—then afoot again to march to the county-town to prevent the opening of the courts.

Gage had taken no steps to protect the courts in the western counties, but the province had been warned that he intended to act decisively to prevent or overcome any obstruction at Worcester; and that the courts scheduled to open there on September 6 would do so under the protection of English bayonets.

The morning of September 6 saw Worcester occupied by a patriot army of 6000 men. They filled the main streets, the common, and the immediate vicinity to overflowing. They were expecting trouble and they were ready for it.

Judges Thomas Steel and Joseph Wilder[7] had come in with the intention of sitting at the court's opening, despite the anger which they had aroused as signers of the justices' tory letter to Gage. But Judge Timothy Ruggles, fearing for his life, had told the governor that it would not be safe for him to attend.

The county convention regathered in Timothy Bigelow's house, adjourning later to the "green beyond Mr. Salis-

[7] Numerous authorities state that Judge Wilder died in *1773*, the year preceding the Worcester County convention. Some of them give his death date as April 20, 1773. These statements are incorrect. It was Wilder's first wife, Deborah Joscelyn, who died on April 20, 1773. Wilder survived her, and the year following the Worcester County convention, he took to himself a second wife, the widow Rebecca (Richardson) Locke.

bury's." Its initial resolution was that *"the court should not sit on any terms."* It next requested the people to come together on the common and choose one man from each company "as a committee to wait on the judges to inform them of a resolution to stop the court's sitting, if the people concur therein."

There followed a considerable delay, selecting the company representatives and then hunting up the justices to inform them officially—of what they had already learned beyond any manner of doubt!—that they would not be permitted to hold court.

The justices were also told that they, together with the court officers, must show their submission to the will of the people by walking through the militia ranks to the court-house, there to affix their signatures to a promise to stay all judicial proceedings.

Next for attention were the local subscribers to a tory protest of June 20. Most of them had signed a recantation and begged to be taken back into the good will of the community, but this was not considered sufficient—the convention instructed them that they must follow after the judges and publicly read their disavowals.

Then, "notice" was taken of the justices who had signed the tory letter to Gage.

The actors having been coached, the assembled militiamen massed in deep ranks on both sides of Main Street, extending from the Old South Church to the court-house.

A great sight for patriot eyes—but it bred misgivings among the timid of the townspeople, whether patriot or tory. What would come of this show of force, this military array, this massing of the county militiamen against the edict of the King and in defiance of the English governor and commander-in-chief? Many apprehensive thoughts turned toward the Boston road, along which the redcoats might even then be approaching. Any moment might hear the galloping of horses bearing the alarm.

Then came the play—designed by its producers to impress upon all men the resolution of the people of Worcester County to maintain their supremacy; that higher than the law's officials were the people themselves, who would brook no laws other than of their own making.

The word was given and the procession started. First through the "ranges" of the people came the judges of the Court of Common Pleas—two of the three (it would have been three of four if Ruggles had ventured from Boston) to be pointed at as men who had taken sides with the English Parliament and against their own people. Artemas Ward was the one exception.

After the judges, the officers of the court.

Next followed the justices of the peace—many of these also to be pointed at as having signed the tory letter. A humiliating experience for men who had hitherto held themselves proudly among their fellows!

Last came the townsmen who had subscribed to the local tory protest.

Every minute or two the procession stopped while the "leaders," or chief men, among the local protesters humbly read their recantations.

Arrived at the court-house, the "protesters" were dismissed, but the justices and their attendants continued into the building and signed the following declaration:

"Gentlemen: You having desired, and even insisted upon it, that all judicial proceedings be stayed by the justices of the courts appointed this day, by law, to be held at Worcester, within and for the County of Worcester, on account of the unconstitutional act of the British parliament, respecting the administration of justice in this province, which, if effected, will reduce the inhabitants thereof to mere arbitrary power, we do assure you, that we will stay all such judicial proceedings of said courts, and will not endeavor to put said act into execution."

It goes without saying that Ward's signature was affixed to the document, for he was an active member of the convention which required its acknowledgment. More to the point is it that Judges Steel and Wilder, ex-mandamus councilor Timothy Paine, and other justices of the peace who had signed the tory letter, were compelled thus to place themselves on record.[8]

The convention proceedings included also resolutions that all militia officers resign the commissions which they held in the name of the crown; that the towns elect new company officers; and that every town "immediately" equip itself with one or more field-pieces, "mounted and fitted for use," and sufficient ammunition to make them effective.

And thus the day journeyed on to its end. Its purpose had been achieved without a moment's disturbance, without a shot being fired. Gage had reconsidered his plan of sending troops, fearing to cast the die. The patriots of Worcester County had demonstrated their full control.

On the morrow, those of the justices present who had participated in the letter to Gage were confronted with a new separate paper of complete submission, which also they signed.

The convention next requested justices of the peace (with the exception of Timothy Ruggles, John Murray, and James Putnam), judges of the probate, sheriffs, and coroners appointed under the old province laws, to continue in office irrespective of any notices or proclamations removing them or interfering with them, and recommended to the people of the county "that they consider and treat them as being in their said offices, and support and defend them in the execution thereof."

After other sundry votes of less importance, it then adjourned to September 20.

[8] This narrative of the closing of the Worcester courts differs in details from every printed account that I have seen. It is, however, I believe, accurate in these differences. The most important source is the journal of the convention in Lincoln's *Journals of each Provincial Congress,* 635–639.

Gage's troubles increased even in Boston and he prepared to meet the future by fortifying Boston Neck. Thus he could at a moment's notice sever the capital from the province.

September 8, the blacksmiths of the county of Worcester, with Ross Wyman of Shrewsbury as president, resolved that they would not work for any tories, nor for anyone of any political persuasion who did not sign and live up to the non-consumption agreement, and asked all other "artificers" to take similar action.

On the ninth the Suffolk County convention unanimously adopted the famous "Suffolk Resolves" drawn up by Joseph Warren. Warren spoke as leader of the Boston patriots in the absence of Samuel Adams, who was then with John Adams, Robert Treat Paine, and Cushing in Philadelphia, representing Massachusetts in the First Continental Congress.

In Philadelphia, the Massachusetts men found "a certain degree of jealousy in the minds of some" from the central and southern colonies. These jealous ones even feared that the New Englanders aimed "at a total independency, not only of the mother country, but of the colonies, too"; and that being a "hardy and brave people," they might in time "overrun them all."[9] Nevertheless, to the consternation of the tory faction, the Congress adopted Warren's Suffolk Resolves, drew up a statement of "rights and grievances," and entered into a non-importation, non-consumption, and non-exportation agreement. And—equally important in its after-results—Colonel Washington of Virginia so impressed the other delegates that Patrick Henry was moved to pay him the unstinted compliment that in "solid information and sound judgment" he was "the greatest man" of them all.

Charles Lee was in Philadelphia while the Congress sat. He had completed a tour of the colonies and declared them

[9] Samuel Adams to Joseph Warren, September 25, 1774.—Cushing, *Writings of Samuel Adams,* III, 158.

full of resolution to support and succor Boston. He asserted that the very character of the provincials had changed and strengthened under the stress. He was ever talking, writing, and visiting; talking, writing, and visiting: red-hot for the patriot side. Higher and higher grew his ambition to crown his adventurous life by leading the colonies in rebellion against England.[10] And more and more, men's minds tended toward him, and patriot councils everywhere rejoiced that America was assured of his hand and sword if war should come.

The Worcester County convention sat again on September 20 and 21.

It voted "that the sheriff adjourn the Superior Court appointed by law to be held this day."

It also directed him to issue precepts for the choice of Representatives to the General Court called by Governor Gage for October 5 (writs for which had been issued on September 1), but it counseled the towns and districts to instruct the Representatives chosen to refuse to be sworn by any officers save those "appointed according to the constitution," or to act in concert with the mandamus councilors, or to attend in Boston "while the town is invested with troops and ships of war." And "should there be anything to prevent their acting with such a governor and council as is expressly set forth in the charter, that they immediately repair to the town of Concord, and there join in a provincial congress, with such other members as are or may be chosen for that purpose, to act and determine on such measures as they shall

[10] December 16, 1774, Lee wrote to Edmund Burke, in London, deprecating an English report that he had been "busy in dissuading the people of Boston from submitting" and that he had offered to put himself at their head. He added that he hoped people did not believe that he possessed "so much temerity and vanity" as to think himself "qualified for the most important charge that ever was committed to mortal man." But, apart from this most uncharacteristic modesty, the reason he advanced against the idea was *not* his foreign birth, which barred him in the minds of the New England leaders and many others; it was instead that he did not think the Americans would give the supreme command to anyone who had no property interest in the country.—*Lee Papers,* I, 148. Then shortly after—with great anxiety to complete the transaction—he set about purchasing an estate in Virginia and thus became himself an American property-owner.

judge to be proper to extricate this colony out of the present unhappy circumstances."

Following this, the convention emphasized its earlier appeal that every town provide itself with one or more field-pieces, mounted and fitted for use; resolved for the redivision of the county militia into seven regiments; again advised the election of new officers—the company officers to be chosen by the men, and the company officers thus appointed to elect their field-officers; and recommended that one third of the men between sixteen and sixty years of age be enlisted, "to be ready to act *at a minute's warning*"—the famous organization of "minute-men."

As county after county endorsed the cry for a Provincial Congress, the activities of the country townships increasingly alarmed Gage. On the day that the Worcester County convention met for the fourth time, he wrote to Lord Dartmouth: "The country people are exercising in arms, in this Province, Connecticut and Rhode Island, and getting magazines of arms and ammunition . . . and such artillery as they can procure, good and bad."[11]

Eight days later, because "of the extraordinary resolves which have been passed in many of the counties," Gage issued a proclamation countermanding his summons for a General Court on October 5. He feared, and probably with good reason, the outcome of a general gathering of Representatives.

October 3, a week earlier than the date suggested in the Worcester County convention, we find Ward's old regiment putting him at its head. The following report is from the *Massachusetts Spy,* October 20:

"On the third instant, the regiment formerly belonging to the Hon. Artemas Ward, Esq., of Shrewsbury, in the county of Worcester, and who for his integrity was dismissed in a former administration, from being Colonel of said regi-

[11] September 20, 1774, *American Archives,* 4th, I, 795.

ment, met, and taking into serious consideration the present oppressed and distressed condition of this province in general, and the poor garrisoned and blockaded town of Boston in particular, after proper solemnity, proceeded as follows, 1st.—They cheerfully, yet with a degree of indignation, flung up their commissions, which they sustained under the late Governor Hutchinson; then they proceeded very regularly to the choice of their field and commission officers, and unanimously made choice of the following gentlemen, viz.: the Hon. Artemas Ward, Colonel; Stephen Maynard, Esq., Lieut.-Colonel; Jonathan Ward, Esq., Second Lieut.-Colonel; Edward Ba[r]nes, Esq., Major; and Mr. Luke Denny, Adjutant."

The same account notes that the town of Marlborough (Middlesex County) joined in the choice of these officers and that the regiment (the Sixth, under the new arrangement) consisted of the inhabitants of Marlborough,[12] Westborough, Shrewsbury, Southborough, Northborough, and Grafton: the first of the county of Middlesex, and the others of Worcester County.

Despite Gage's proclamation, ninety Representatives arrived in Salem on or before October 5. They convened on the sixth, and on the following day adopted resolutions declaring that the governor could not legally dissolve the General Court before it met; that his proclamation was therefore unconstitutional; and that its statements were unjust and disrespectful and proof of his "disaffection" toward the province. They followed this by resolving themselves "into a Provincial Congress, to be joined by such other persons as have been or shall be chosen for that purpose, to take into consideration the dangerous and alarming situation of public affairs in this province, and to consult and determine on such measures as they shall judge will tend to promote the true

[12] Marlborough (Marlboro), being in Middlesex, had not been listed in the Worcester County convention's rearrangement of the militia, but it had for geographical reasons formed part of a Worcester County regiment under the old arrangement and it continued so to constitute itself under the new conditions.

interest of his majesty and the peace, welfare, and prosperity of the province."

The Representatives then formally organized as a "Provincial Congress" and adjourned to meet at Concord on the following Tuesday (October 11).

Arriving at Concord, the Representatives met the special delegates sent by a number of the towns. Ward was one of the first of the delegates to arrive. His associate from Shrewsbury was again Representative Heywood.

The Congress assembled in the court-house, but, finding that it needed larger space, moved thence to the meeting-house (the "Old Third"), and there opened its proceedings with the election of John Hancock as president.

The gathering included a goodly number of men who helped to make history—military and civil—in the following years. It contained a large proportion of fighting men: a full majority of those of middle age had seen service in the French and Indian wars, or had garrisoned the province frontiers.

The country members already harbored the thought that the time had arrived for throwing off allegiance, and the more careful had difficulty in restraining them. John Pitts wrote that the Boston representatives were "by far the most moderate" men there.

Some of the radically aggressive had conceived, and freely expressed, the theory that Great Britain's wealth and power rested chiefly on her American colonies, and that disunion, by shifting trade advantages to European competitors, would relegate the empire to insignificance.

Representing the opposite view was much propaganda designed to affright. Typical is a printed broadside addressed "To the Provincial Congress," a copy of which was delivered to every member. It warned of an overwhelming army of fifteen or eighteen thousand Canadians and Indians ready to be let loose on both Massachusetts and Connecticut at a moment's notice.

"Now, gentlemen," it continued, "Coolly recollect our weak and defenceless State, and you will easily perceive how impossible it will be for us, to resist even one Third of such Force. Seriously and honestly call to Mind how compleatly miserable will then be our Situation, by being exposed to all the Cruelties and Barbarities of an implacable and Savage Enemy. When I cast my Eyes on my innocent and helpless Wife and Children, and recollect how soon they must fall into the Hands of Savages full of inveterate Hatred and Revenge, my very Soul is overwhelmed with Agonies, far beyond the narrow Limits of Description:—Place yourselves under the same shocking Incumbrances, and you will quickly feel the Horrors of Despair and Anguish unutterable. . . . To paint the tragical Scene with its various and multiplied Miseries, but in a faint Light, requires more Time than is proper for a Letter. If you have any Pity, if any Compassion, if any Humanity, you will not, you cannot expose such Innocents to Torture and Death. . . . However you may now flatter yourselves, this Truth I am compelled to sound in your ears, that whatever Lives are lost, by your Indiscreet or rash Conduct, sooner or later must be, by you accounted for. . . ."

The writer's threats and forebodings troubled Ward so little that he employed the reverse of his copy of the broadside for the writing of non-importation agreement forms and militia resolutions.

Ward was a member of both initial committees of the eleventh and also of the committee appointed on the twelfth "to take into consideration the state of the province." With him on the latter were Hancock, Joseph Warren, Joseph Hawley, Dr. Benjamin Church, Elbridge Gerry, James Warren, William Heath, and others.

The committee next day reported an address to Gage declaring that the convening of the Congress had been rendered "indispensably necessary" by the "distressed and miserable state of the province occasioned by the intolerable grievances and oppressions to which the people are subjected"; and citing the Port Act, the Regulating Act and that labeled for the "Impartial Administration of Justice," and the hostile preparations in Boston—the increase in the number of troops, and the fortress on Boston Neck.

It continued, "Permit us to ask your excellency whether an inattentive and unconcerned acquiescence [in] such alarming, such menacing measures, *would not evidence a state of insanity;* or whether the delaying to take every possible precaution for the security of the province, would not be the most criminal neglect in a people heretofore rigidly and justly tenacious of their constitutional rights?"

The address was accepted with only one dissentient vote, and Ward was placed on the committee appointed to deliver it to Gage.

On the following day, immediately prior to adjourning, the convention accepted a resolution of the Committee on the State of the Province which declared against the transfer of any province moneys to the provincial tax receiver. It also strongly recommended the payment of outstanding taxes to persons to be named by the towns and districts themselves.

Meeting again in Cambridge, October 17, the Congress received the governor's reply to its address. It was referred to the Committee on the State of the Province; as also were the letters of the Reverend Samuel Peters, who predicted "hanging work" (with the patriots for victims) as a quick sequence to the arrival of the additional redcoats on their way across the ocean.

Three days later came the naming of a new committee (Ward a member) to consider "what is necessary to be *now* done for the defence and safety of the province."

The final amended report of this new committee was accepted October 26. It established a Committee of Safety with duties of watchfulness, and power to call out and direct the militia "whenever they shall judge it necessary for the safety and defence of the inhabitants of this province"; a subordinate Committee of Supplies; and General Officers to command.

It also urged the prompt officering of the militia in towns that had not already so organized; that any inhabitants of the province, not already supplied, immediately provide themselves with arms and ammunition; and the preparation of "a well digested plan for the regulating and disciplining the militia, placing them in every respect on such a permanent footing as shall render them effectual for the preservation and defence of the good people of this province."

The next morning saw the election of the Committee of Safety; and the afternoon following, that of the Committee of Supplies.

"It was then moved, that the Congress proceed to the choice of three General Officers" to command the militia in the event of its being called out by the Committee of Safety. And Jedediah Preble, Artemas Ward, and Seth Pomeroy were elected, to rank in the order named.[13]

The appointment of these men is a high tribute to the esteem in which they were held by the province representatives. Massachusetts was preparing for war, if need be, against one of the world's great powers. A New York writer had voiced the thoughts of many when he expressed it as the "maddest of all possible Quixotisms to think of making an hostile opposition" to the army and navy of Great Britain,[14]—but that is what the leaders of Massachusetts were deliberately planning, unless the English government should grant the province everything but nominal independ-

[13] The career of Artemas Ward (now 47 years of age, lacking one month) we have already considered in these pages.

Jedediah Preble, 67 years old, had seen a variety of service in the French war and had risen to the rank of brigadier-general in the provincial service.

Seth Pomeroy, 68 years old, had as major been present at the capture of Louisburg, 1745 (chiefly in charge of a corps of gunsmiths), and ten years later had, as acting-colonel of Ephraim Williams' regiment, commanded in the hottest part of the fierce battle of Lake George, which resulted in the utter defeat of the French and Indian forces and the capture of Baron Dieskau, the French commander-in-chief in Canada. He was a delegate to both the First and Second Provincial Congresses.

[14] *American Archives*, 4th, I, 289, note.

ence. They prayed, and believed, that in the day of trial they would be upheld by the other colonies, but their belief held no assurance that the other colonies would carry support to the point of open warfare. And they knew that on the courage, patriotism, and integrity of the men chosen as general officers, largely depended the fate and future of the province, the political freedom they cherished so highly, and their own lives, if, as rebels, they should fail to make good their defiance of England.

On the day of the election of the general officers, and the day following (October 27 and 28), the Congress demonstrated its desire to adhere as closely as possible to the charter government by requesting, individually and collectively, the attendance of all members of the Council elected and accepted in the spring, "that this body may have the benefit of their advice upon the important matters that may then come under consideration." These councilors had been officially superseded by the mandamus councilors appointed by the King under the obnoxious new Regulating Act, but this supersession was ignored. The intent is plain to continue the recognition of the Council elected in conformity with the charter: Gage's vetoes were respected—none of the thirteen whom he had refused as councilors were invited to sit as such, though several of them were present in the Congress; and the only omission from his list of fifteen acceptances was of Danforth, who had been sworn in as a mandamus councilor.

Among the final acts of the session were the appointment of Henry Gardner as Receiver-General, accompanied by the recommendation that all province moneys be turned over to him; and the reading and acceptance of the reply, prepared by the Committee on the State of the Province, to the governor's communication of October 17.

Gage had sought to justify his fortification of Boston Neck, blamed the patriots for "open and avowed disobedience" to English authority, declared that by convening as a

Provincial Congress the delegates were "subverting the charter," and demanded that they "desist from such illegal and unconstitutional proceedings."

The Congress reply was strong and spirited. It reminded the governor that not only was the Boston Neck fortress both a continuous threat and a continuous annoyance to the town of Boston, but that the very presence of the troops in the province without the consent of the Representatives, was illegal. It ridiculed the charge that the Provincial Congress was a violation of the charter, and asserted that, on the contrary, its convening had been "directed by the principles of the constitution itself; warranted by the most approved precedent and examples, and sanctioned by the British nation at the revolution; upon the strength and validity of which precedent the whole British constitution now stands, his present majesty wears his crown, and all subordinate officers hold their places."

The session terminated on the same day (Saturday, October 29).

The following Wednesday the Committee of Safety held its initial meeting. Its first recommendation to the Committee of Supplies was for the purchase of pork, flour, rice, and peas. Next, for "arms and ammunition" and "large pieces of cannon." Later, came those for spades, pickaxes, cooking-pots, etc.

The Provincial Congress gathered again at Cambridge on November 23.

It heartily approved the "bill of rights" and enumeration of grievances drawn up by the Continental Congress, and its non-importation, non-consumption, and non-exportation resolutions; and it elected representatives to the Second Continental Congress.

It counseled the encouragement of every provincial industry and particularly advised the manufacture of saltpetre and gunpowder. Its resolutions declared gunpowder to be "an article of such importance, that every man among us who loves his country, must wish the establishment of manufactories for that purpose." It spoke of "the ruins of several powder mills, and sundry persons among us who are acquainted with that business," and it recommended "encouragement by repairing one or more of said mills, or erecting others" and renewing the industry "as soon as possible."

It added John Thomas[15] and William Heath[16] to the staff of general officers: Thomas as fourth, Heath as fifth.

On the morning of its last day, December 10, it called upon the committees of correspondence to obtain and report the names of those who had signed or who might sign the tory "Association" started by Timothy Ruggles. The Ruggles covenant pledged its members to oppose the "authority of any Congresses, committees of correspondence, or other unconstitutional assemblies of men," and "if need be" to "repel force with force."

Immediately after the adoption by the Congress of its tory association resolution, the Committee on the State of the Province (of which General Ward continued a member) reported an address to the inhabitants of Massachusetts Bay. It was ordered printed in the Boston newspapers and in handbills, and forwarded to all towns and districts. It reminded the province that the men of Massachusetts were "placed by Providence in the *post of honor,* because it was the *post of danger";* and counseled enforcement by each town of strict adherence to the plans of the Continental and Provincial Congresses.

It continued with advice concerning the equipment and pay of the "minute-men":

[15] John Thomas was about 50 years old. His first army service had been as a surgeon. Later, in 1758, 1759, and 1760, he was colonel of expeditionary regiments which saw duty in Nova Scotia, and at Crown Point, Montreal, etc. In 1760 his regiment formed part of the army which compelled the surrender of Montreal. He was a delegate to the First and Second Provincial Congresses.

[16] William Heath was 37 years old. He had seen no active service but he had achieved local prominence as a militia officer. He had served several years as a Representative, and was a delegate to the First and Second Provincial Congresses and a member of the Committee of Safety.

"We now think that particular care should be taken by the towns and districts in this colony, that each of the minute-men, not already provided therewith, should be immediately equipped with an effective firearm, bayonet, pouch, knapsack, thirty rounds of cartridges and balls, and that they be disciplined three times a week, and oftener, as opportunity may offer. To encourage these, our worthy countrymen, to obtain the skill of complete soldiers, we recommend it to the towns and districts forthwith to pay their own minute-men a reasonable consideration for their services; and in case of a general muster their further services must be recompensed by the province. An attention to discipline the militia in general is, however, by no means to be neglected."

The committee next submitted, and the delegates adopted, resolutions dissolving the Congress because it had already sat longer than the people of the province had anticipated, but earnestly recommending the election of delegates to a new Congress.

Meantime, Charles Lee had joined the Annapolis convention of Maryland county deputies and he found there wide scope for his energy. He helped to inspire the gathering to vigor, furnished plans for a new organization of the Maryland militia, and personally superintended the arrangements for mustering companies.

The first quarter of 1775 was rich with happenings. Novanglus and Massachusettensis disputed; the drilling and arming continued.

The Worcester County convention met again on January 26 for another two-day session. General Ward acted as chairman and also served on a committee appointed to "take into consideration a plan for this county to adopt respecting the non-consumption covenants of the Continental and Provincial Congress."

The committee recommended the signing of non-consumption covenants by everyone who had not already done so;

presented a covenant which "heartily approved" the form drawn up by the Continental Congress and amplified by the Provincial Congress; and pledged the members of the convention to strict adherence to its every article and clause.

On the second day Ward was on *four* committees, the most important being one to "take the affairs of trade into consideration, and to remonstrate against riots and routs."

The committee's report declared that the enemies of America's cause were "assiduously endeavoring" to provoke the patriot party to acts of violence, so that they might "have a pretence" to represent them as the aggressors; and advised great care "in discountenancing and suppressing all acts of violence, except so much as is necessary to carry the resolves of the Continental and Provincial Congress into execution."

It continued that, confident of the justice of their cause, they were determined "firmly and religiously to support and maintain" their rights—"*even to the loss of our lives and fortunes.*"

The second Provincial Congress opened in Cambridge on February 1. Ward, this time alone as Shrewsbury's representative, became again a member of a committee "to take into consideration the state and circumstances of the Province."

A tory handbill distributed a few days later (February 6) warned of the fate of Wat Tyler, and advocated the seizure of the patriot leaders. It continued: "Never did a people rebel with so little reason; therefore our conduct cannot be justified before God! Never did so weak a people dare to contend with so powerful a State; therefore it cannot be justified by prudence. It is all the consequence of the arts of crafty knaves over weak minds and wild enthusiasts, who, if we continue to follow, will lead us to inevitable ruin. Rouse, rouse, ye Massachusetians, while it be yet time!" [17]

February 9, the Congress adopted a new commission

[17] *American Archives,* 4th, I, 1216.

(drawn up by the Committee on the State of the Province) for the Committee of Safety, specifically defining its "business and duty" as the prevention of any attempt to apply either the Regulating Act or that for the "Impartial Administration of Justice."

It next took up the choice of general officers—reëlecting those voted by the First Congress: Jedediah Preble, Artemas Ward, Seth Pomeroy, John Thomas, and William Heath—again to command in the order named.

As a result of the precedence thus confirmed, General Ward became commander-in-chief of the Massachusetts forces at the very outset of armed resistance, for Preble, elected to the first place, did not act upon his appointment.

On February 9, also, Ward was named on a committee "to bring in a resolve directing how the ordnance in the Province shall be used."

February 11, he was, with Samuel Adams, Joseph Warren, Hancock, Hawley, Robert Treat Paine, and Tyng, appointed to draw up "a resolve purporting the determination of the people, coolly and resolutely, to support their rights and privileges at all hazards."

The afternoon of February 15, he was on a special committee to call upon a committee that had arrived from Connecticut; and in the evening he conferred with them as a member of the Committee on the State of the Province.

The same day, John Whitcomb[18] was added to the list of general officers.

[18] John Whitcomb, about 61 years old, was colonel of the minute-men of the Second Worcester regiment. In the Ticonderoga expedition, 1758, he had been lieutenant-colonel of Bagley's regiment; and he held the command of a regiment at the capture of Montreal, 1760. He had served many years as a Representative, and was one of the "Glorious Ninety-Two." He was elected to the Council in 1773, but preferred to stay in the House.

The Whitcomb Family in America, 194, and Henry S. Nourse, *American Antiquarian Society Proceedings,* New Series, VII, 97, say that Whitcomb was in the Lake George battle, September 8, 1755; but accounts of the battle have no mention of his (Willard's) regiment: the only Massachusetts regiments cited are Williams', Ruggles', and Titcomb's. Whitcomb had probably not arrived by September 8. He was in Deerfield August 30 and was expected to start out the next day.—Letter of Jonathan Ashley, *New England Historical and Genealogical Register,* IV, 87. He was perhaps in the reinforcements which arrived shortly after the battle.

The Congress adjourned on the following afternoon and Ward returned to Shrewsbury.

Meanwhile, the Committees of Safety and Supplies added to the patriot stores of ammunition, food, etc., making Concord and Worcester the chief depots.

February 21, the Committee of Safety voted that the Committee of Supplies should "purchase all kinds of military stores, sufficient for an army of 15,000 men to take the field." Next day, that it buy tents, lead balls, etc., and employ men to make thirty rounds of cartridges for the entire force.

On the twenty-third, the committees voted the sending of two field-pieces to each regiment.

Unfortunately, it was easier to vote the purchase of "all kinds of military stores" than to obtain them. The Committee of Supplies worked industriously, but the result fell far short of the needs anticipated—and later severely experienced.

As spring approached, Gage sent out his spies. Among them were Captain William Browne, of the Fifty-second Regiment of Foot, and Ensign Henry de Birniere,[19] of the Tenth Regiment, who together reconnoitered the route from Boston to Worcester. De Birniere's account of their experiences has become a classic.

It was in Framingham, on their return trip, that the two Englishmen, gazing through the windows of Buckminster's tavern, witnessed the drilling of a company of militia.

"After they had done their exercise," wrote De Birniere, "one of their commanders spoke a very eloquent speech, recommending patience, coolness and bravery (which indeed they much wanted); particularly told them they would al-

[19] Histories print the ensign's surname variously: as, *De Berniere* or *D'Berniere* (with or without an accent on the penultimate "e"), *De Bernicre* or *D'Bernicre*. I have avoided all these forms, following instead that of the English *Army Lists*, which record the name both with and without the prefatory "de," but are consistent in always spelling it (both in print and in script) with an "i" as the first vowel (*Birniere*).

I have taken the same authority for the addition of a final "e" to the Captain's surname.

ways conquer if they did not break, and recommended them to charge us cooly and wait for our fire, and everything would succeed with them—quotes Caesar and Pompey, brigadiers Putnam and Ward, and all such great men; put them in mind of Cape Breton, and all the battles they had gained for his Majesty in the last war, and observed that the regulars must have been ruined but for them."[20]

While Browne and De Birniere were spending Sunday (February 26) in semi-concealment in Worcester, Lieutenant-Colonel Leslie's battalion was making its abortive attempt to secure the cannon held by the patriots near Salem. These cannon worried Gage, for they were suspected to be new brass field-pieces smuggled in from Holland. In reality they were only old iron 12-pounders, relics of the French war, but even old cannon were hugely valuable to the patriots, for they possessed and could obtain very few of any age or calibre.

Scarcer still were available artillerymen. Ward's letter of February 27 to David Cheever, a member of the Committee of Supplies, notes that there was not one man in his district competent to teach the handling of the two cannon to be delivered for his regiment. He adds: "There is a person in this town who understands the Exercise but has of late discovered such Sentiments in Political matters that I dare not trust him."[21]

The last remark is typical of the soul-racking uncertainty of the period. The dividing lines of American and English nationality have now for generations been so clear and strong that, despite the labors of modern historians, many people find it difficult to realize that the Revolution held much of the anguish of civil war.

Symptoms of insurrection were showing everywhere throughout the province, but Gage held back from any de-

[20] *Massachusetts Historical Society Collections*, 2d, IV, 209-210; and elsewhere.
[21] Original letter, *Massachusetts Archives*, CXLVI, 2.

cisive move to check its rise. Across the sea came word from the English government advising the arrest and imprisonment of the principal members of the Provincial Congress. It would be better, declared Lord Dartmouth, that the conflict be thus brought on, than in a riper state of rebellion. But Gage and his associates feared—or did not think it politic—to take the step.

At the next session of the Provincial Congress, opened on March 22, the members were instructed to give to the Committee on the State of the Province all information which had "fallen within their knowledge" concerning the number of field-pieces in the province, irrespective of their ownership, and also concerning the number of men "acquainted with the business of making firearms."

A few days later (March 30), the committee "reported a resolve, relative to what movements of the troops should make it fit to call the militia together."

On the following day it brought in a resolution (passed) urging upon towns and districts the immediate and compulsory transfer of all province money in the hands of tax collectors and constables who had refrained from paying it over to the Provincial Congress Receiver-General. The resolution also recommended that the towns "without delay" collect any unpaid taxes; and concluded by counseling that they "vigorously exert themselves to suppress every opposition to measures recommended by the Continental and Provincial Congresses," as they esteemed "the freedom and happiness of themselves and future generations."

Immediately thereafter came a resolution that "if there is any town which does not incline to pay their public moneys to Mr. Gardner, they are desired to give their reasons for such refusal to this Congress."

The next morning the committee reported an encouraging and laudatory address to the Stockbridge Indian minutemen, and introduced a resolution (passed) to purchase a blanket and a yard of ribbon for each of them.

April 2, came word that left no doubt of the passage of a bill which was to lay excessive restraint on colonial commerce and to ban American ships from fishing on the Newfoundland Banks. Further, that England had declared the province in rebellion and had ordered reinforcements to subdue it, sending also instructions for the shipping of the patriot leaders to England. To the old-style English tory, there was grim joy in the anticipation of a London display of the severed heads of American rebels.

Later, there arrived the report that the hangings would take place in Boston.

Stiles noted[22] that Parliament's declaration depressed "some timid persons," but that "in general the Friends of Liberty are hereby exasperated and declare themselves ready for the Combat, and *nothing is now talked of but immediately forming an American army at Worcester and taking the Field with undaunted Resolution.*"

The Congress quickly reacted to the new challenge. Militia plans no longer seemed sufficient. On April 8 the Committee on the State of the Province brought in a resolve for the raising and establishment of a provincial army; and for the appointment of delegates "to repair to Connecticut, Rhode Island, and New Hampshire" to tell them of this determination by Massachusetts, and "to request them to co-operate . . . by furnishing their respective quotas for the general defence." The Congress adopted the resolution by a vote of 96 to 7.

It followed this (April 8 and 10) with instructions to the committee to "take into consideration what number of men . . . will be necessary to be raised by the four New England governments for their general defence"; and "to draught such instructions as they shall think necessary to be given to the delegates appointed to repair to the neighboring governments."

April 10, the committee "reported a resolve, relative to

[22] *Literary Diary of Ezra Stiles,* I, 530, April 4.

exercising the minute-men in battalions, and that they be paid out of the public treasury." After a long debate this resolution was defeated.

April 12, the committee brought in a resolve (passed) arranging for county committees "whose business it shall be to receive from the committees of correspondence in their respective towns, a state of the conduct of the towns and districts with respect to their having executed the continental and provincial plans," and to lay their reports before the Congress at its next session, "that any neglect of such towns and districts in executing such plans may be speedily and effectually remedied."

April 13, the committee introduced a resolution (passed) providing for six artillery companies "to immediately enter on discipline, and constantly be in readiness to enter the service of the colony," and that the Committee of Safety "draw on the public treasury for paying said companies a suitable consideration for their services."

April 14, the committee reported a plan for officering the proposed provincial army. It was immediately accepted by the Congress, and the Committee of Safety was instructed "to apply to a suitable number of persons, to be in readiness to enter the service of this colony, to act as field officers: such field officers, in conjunction with the committee, to apply to proper persons as captains, and they to determine on such subaltern officers as may be necessary for each regiment, when an army shall be raised; the committee and officers *caeteris paribus* to give the preference to persons who have been chosen officers in the regiments of minutemen." But events broke too quickly for the plan to be matured, and the militiamen—both the "standing militia" and the minute-men—went into war under officers of their own choice and election.

On the following day the Congress adjourned. It had been a very full and hard-working session for General Ward. He had been continuously a member of the Committee on the State of the Province, and it was this committee which had led and directed the Congress.

Three days later, the Committees of Safety and Supplies awoke to the danger of concentrating so large a proportion of their scant but very valuable war supplies at Concord, and a joint meeting directed that the ammunition be distributed among nine towns. It also made various other arrangements for the safer and more convenient custody of provisions, equipment, etc.

Some cartloads were removed that same day (April 18), but before the work was well started the curtain was rung up on the first battle of the Revolution. Gage had got wind of the depots and caches at Concord, and that night a detachment of English grenadiers, light infantry, and marines set out to destroy them.

The story of Lexington and Concord—of the Battle of April 19—has been depicted by a thousand writers. The riding of Revere and Dawes and Dr. Prescott—and many other less famed messengers—to arouse the country. The village green at Lexington in the early morning, and the firing of the first shots of the war of the American Revolution. The confident tramp of the Englishmen on to Concord. The swelling tide of the militia. The sharp contest at the bridge. Then—the retreat of the British regulars, "driven before the Americans like sheep"; running the gauntlet of Yankee muskets, every furlong rendering its quota of dead or wounded. So hot the pace that when they met Lord Percy and his relief brigade the survivors threw themselves on the ground, "their tongues hanging out of their mouths."[23] And the continued retreat of the united English forces—nearly two thousand of the proudest infantry of the Old World.

In the speed and stress of that running twenty-mile fight, many of the militia companies disintegrated into pursuing individuals or small changing groups only intermittently co-

[23] Stedman, *History of the American War*, I, 133.

hesive—but even so they persisted, mobile and in deadly earnest, an irresistible "moving circle" of musketmen, and pursued the enemy up to Charlestown Neck.

Here, in the dusk of the evening, the fighting ceased. General Heath and other American leaders called a halt. The English troops were permitted to enter the city without further molestation, but "the rebels," wrote De Birniere, "shut up the Neck" and "placed sentinels there. . . . So that in the course of two days, from a plentiful town, we were reduced to the disagreeable necessity of living on salt provisions, and fairly blocked up in Boston."[24]

English troops and English authority were bottled in the capital, and Massachusetts never again acknowledged either.

It was learned that two could play at the sport of blockading. The English government had willed a water blockade of the capital on June 1, 1774. American militiamen established a land blockade on April 19, 1775.[25]

[24] *Massachusetts Historical Society Collections,* 2d, IV, 218.

[25] The rallying of Massachusetts' men on April 19 was very different from the disordered rush toward Boston in the preceding September. Every man carried a musket and he set out with his neighbors in company formation. Companies meeting at cross-roads joined in battalions and thus pushed on in substantial strength. Though formation was speedily lost by many of those who took part in the fighting, it was retrieved after the halt at Charlestown Neck and the occupation of Cambridge and Roxbury directly subsequent.

For the great improvement in organization achieved by a majority of the townships, the credit must be variously divided—among the militiamen themselves, and the various bodies and individuals who inspired and directed their reconstitution and training. To the minute-men and the standing militia rank and file is, however, due the largest share of the special honors earned on April 19—the chief credit for the sudden effectiveness with which the English troops were driven back, and their startling transformation into a beleaguered garrison. The Provincial Congress had empowered the Committee of Safety to call out the militia, and the general officers to command and direct it if it should be thus called out; but neither the minute-men nor the standing militia had waited for the call of either the Committee of Safety or the general officers—or even, in many cases, of their regimental officers. Immediately on word that the English were coming out, or of the firing at Lexington—and long before any general order could have reached them—the men had come together in their town companies and marched to meet the enemy.

CHAPTER V

April 20–June 15, 1775: Age 47

General Ward takes command of the army besieging Boston. His Council of War plans to fortify Dorchester Heights. The difficulties in organizing an army and the peril of anarchy. Benjamin Church's early attempt to betray his country. Ward commissioned as Commander-in-chief of the Massachusetts forces. General Gage determines to occupy Dorchester Heights and to follow this with the seizure of the Charlestown peninsula. The Committee of Safety recommends the occupation of Bunker Hill. The Council of War resolves to occupy both Bunker Hill and Dorchester Heights. The final decision for Bunker Hill alone. Colonel Prescott given the command of the detachment.

GENERAL WARD lay ill in bed when the express rider galloped through Shrewsbury with news of the clash at Lexington. But next morning at daybreak he mounted his horse and set out toward Boston, joining and passing company after company of the militiamen filling the roads as they also hurried eastward to the capital.

From Shrewsbury to Cambridge is now a pleasant motor trip, but on horseback over the rough highway of the year 1775 it could have been no holiday jaunt for a middle-aged man afflicted with bladder-stone. Yet Ward unhesitatingly journeyed it to direct the dangerous enterprise of rebellion against the world-famed power of Great Britain.

Those men of New England who thus unflinchingly accepted duty's call to leadership, and, leading, dared, arms in hand, to oppose the authority of the King and Parliament of England, risked a fate far more bitter than death on the battlefield. They dared also the hangman's gallows—and, beyond, perchance the horrors of the severed head and limbs rotting by the roadside. Such things have been impossible in England for a century or more—but they were not impossible then. Nor did they seem so to Ward and his associates, for they had been young men grown at the time of the Jacobite hangings and beheadings of 1746.

The risk of punishment for treason was much greater when Ward assumed the leadership than when Washington took hold. Behind Ward, and the other early leaders of the Revolution, were only the forces of New England—indeed, at the first challenge, only the forces of Massachusetts. When Washington was appointed, he had the patriot element of thirteen colonies at his back.

On Ward's arrival at Cambridge he took command of the besieging forces and called a council of war—the first Revolutionary council of war.[1] Three general officers were present—Ward himself, William Heath, and John Whitcomb; six colonels, including William Prescott of Pepperell—later "of Bunker Hill"; and six lieutenant-colonels. Samuel Osgood acted as aide-de-camp to General Ward and Joseph Ward as secretary.[2]

[1] The council probably met in Jonathan Hastings' house, which from an early date (perhaps from the first day of the siege) served as headquarters for both Ward and the Committee of Safety. The house is portrayed on the page opposite. The lower sketch is of the main entrance hall, that to the south (on the right of the upper illustration), opening into the southeast room, Ward's office. The Committee of Safety met in the rear room adjoining. To the left of the west entrance was the "long, low dining-room" in which Ward entertained Washington on his arrival at Cambridge. The house is best known as the "Holmes House," for it achieved nineteenth-century fame as the birthplace and residence of Oliver Wendell Holmes. Later it became the property of Harvard College and was torn down in the spring of 1884, following the completion of Austin Hall Law School nearby. Its site is marked by a stone memorial.

[2] Joseph Ward, a schoolmaster by profession, a man of thirty-eight years, and General Ward's second cousin once removed, had been enrolled in the forenoon by Heath, fifth general officer, who had exercised the command until Ward's arrival.

Until my special study of the pre-Revolutionary period brought unpleasant disclosures, I had always held Joseph Ward as a shining star among the descendants of William Ward of Sudbury, ranking him in my esteem as next only to Artemas Ward. But in the MSS. of the Earl of Dartmouth I came upon evidence that convicts him of nauseous double-dealing: posing as a radical patriot and at the same time offering information so obtained (or that he pretended to have obtained) as part of the price of a crown position.

At the very time that the storm over the Hutchinson-Oliver letters was brewing (page 48), Joseph Ward was writing to Lord Dartmouth praying for the position of Secretary or Lieutenant-Governor of New Hampshire—or "any other commission in civil government

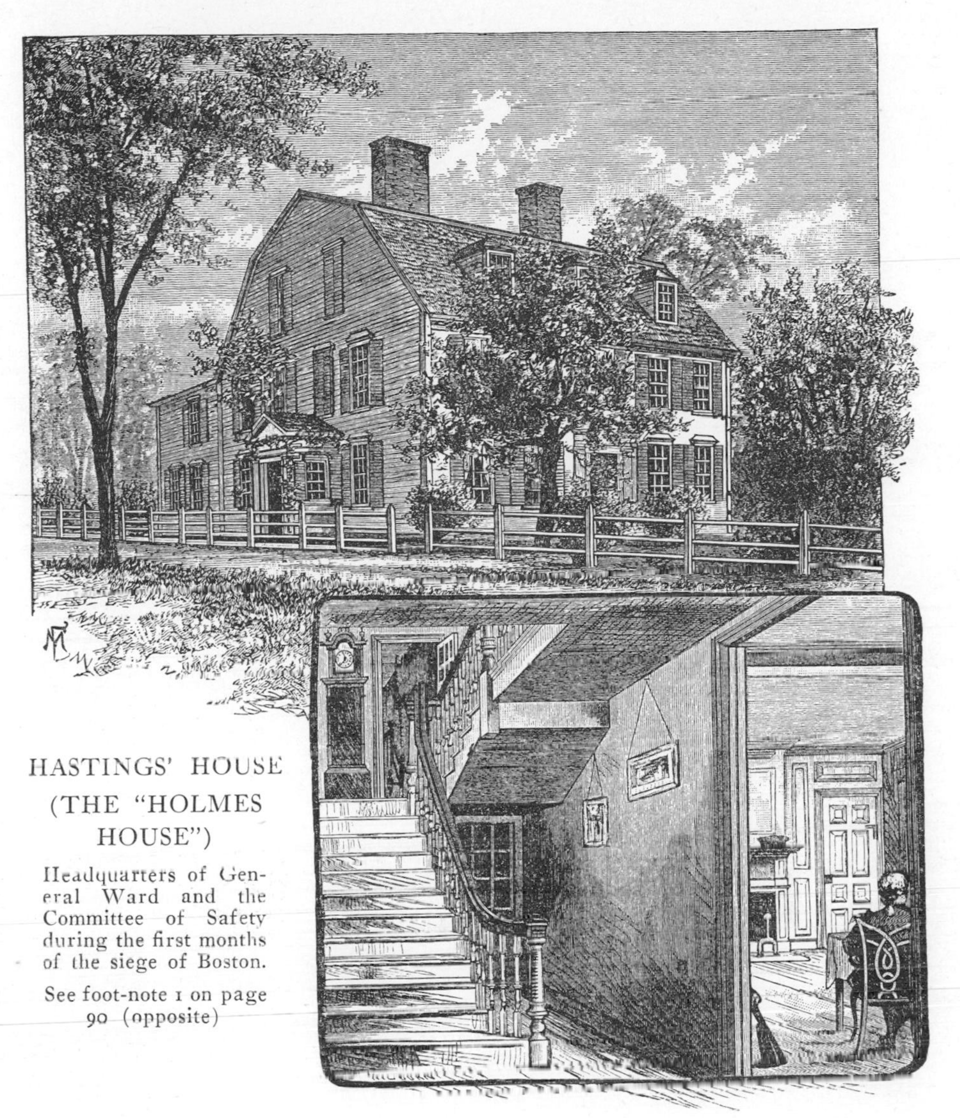

HASTINGS' HOUSE (THE "HOLMES HOUSE")

Headquarters of General Ward and the Committee of Safety during the first months of the siege of Boston.

See foot-note 1 on page 90 (opposite)

From Justin Winsor's *Memorial History of Boston,* III, 108

The General Ward who took his place at the head of the council table was a man of medium height; clean shaven, of prominent features; too stout for his forty-seven years[3] and at the moment showing the effects of his recent illness, but well enough nevertheless to apply himself conscientiously to the duties to his hand. Dressed in the manner of the times—hair in a powdered wig; a long coat with silver buttons; a figured neckcloth surmounting a ruffled shirt; a long waistcoat with big pockets; knee-breeches, and riding-boots. A "God-fearing" man, strongly believing in and living up to the religion he professed; quiet, thoughtful, and rather over-stern in demeanor; somewhat slow in speech and with a biblical turn to his conversation; inflexible in his ideas, and fully convinced that the Massachusetts Bay Colony was the land most approved by Providence, and that those of Massachusetts were the Chosen People.

It is a pity that Joseph Ward did not record the full proceedings of that council of war, but even if he had, it would probably have made most matter-of-fact reading. There was no time that afternoon for sentiment or rhetoric; nor to

in New England." He asserted that his "connections and acquaintance with the people in several Provinces" gave him "an opportunity of knowing all the measures which are pursuing to secure their independency." He declared that the colonists were only awaiting a favorable opportunity to break away; and he gave detail after detail of alleged patriotic plans, "as I apprehend it is uncertain whether your Lordship will be informed of some of those things in any other channel." He did not neglect to ask secrecy concerning his communications, as they "might give offence to my countrymen if known."—Original letters: December 3, 1772; January 6, 1773; February 18, 1773; March 20, 1773; May 8, 1773: *MSS. of the Earl of Dartmouth.*

It required a good deal of mental effort to resist the temptation to suppress this disclosure; but to have yielded would have been unfair to students, who are entitled to the whole truth from writers who present the results of historical research. It would also have been unjust to the memory of the true patriots of the Revolution to have longer permitted Joseph Ward's name to be classed with theirs.

It is comforting to be able to conclude this distasteful foot-note with the statement that, to the best of my knowledge and belief, Joseph Ward "played the game straight" after the actual outbreak of hostilities. He acquitted himself well as secretary to General Ward; and, later, as Commissary of Musters, he won Washington's commendation. It was his post as Commissary of Musters which gave him the rank of colonel.

[3] It has been asserted that Ward was "unable to get on horseback," that he was "so infirm that he was not fit to appear in public on horseback," etc. This is incorrect and misleading. When several years older he readily traveled the several hundred miles to and from Philadelphia on horseback, the detailed record of his journey to the (then) national capital showing that he could make nearly as good time on the road as Washington himself.

discuss high military or political topics. Instead, the imperative essentials were to place, house, and feed the army that had suddenly sprung into being, and was being further swelled by men marching in from the western counties, and from Connecticut and New Hampshire, and, later, from Rhode Island.

The Massachusetts militiamen had driven the enemy back into Boston. They had caged the lion, but could they hold him prisoner?

That first day—and the next few following—were full of feverish activity and grave anxiety. Guards were posted and earthworks hastily thrown up to bar the roads leading north, west, and south from Boston, and to protect the central position at Cambridge. And messages were sent widespread for gunpowder, for supplies—for all the paraphernalia of war.

The greatest anxiety was felt concerning the American right—at Roxbury, south of Boston Neck.

General Thomas had taken stand in Roxbury, throwing a hastily gathered division across the route by which the enemy was most likely to try to force his way out. On the second day Ward ordered General Heath to reinforce him with the Prescott, Learned, and Warner regiments, but Thomas called for yet more men, and on the twenty-second David Green's regiment also joined him.

On the same day the American lines were extended on the north to Chelsea.

The militiamen thus completed a girdle of Boston harbor—stretching in a semicircle of twelve miles across and around hills and valleys, rivers and marsh.

Within its arc were the three peninsulas which controlled the thoughts and strategy of the siege. The center peninsula was Boston; with the Charlestown peninsula to the north, and Dorchester Neck (as the Dorchester peninsula was then called) to the south. The Charlestown and Dorchester peninsulas dominated Boston, and both lay open as prizes of

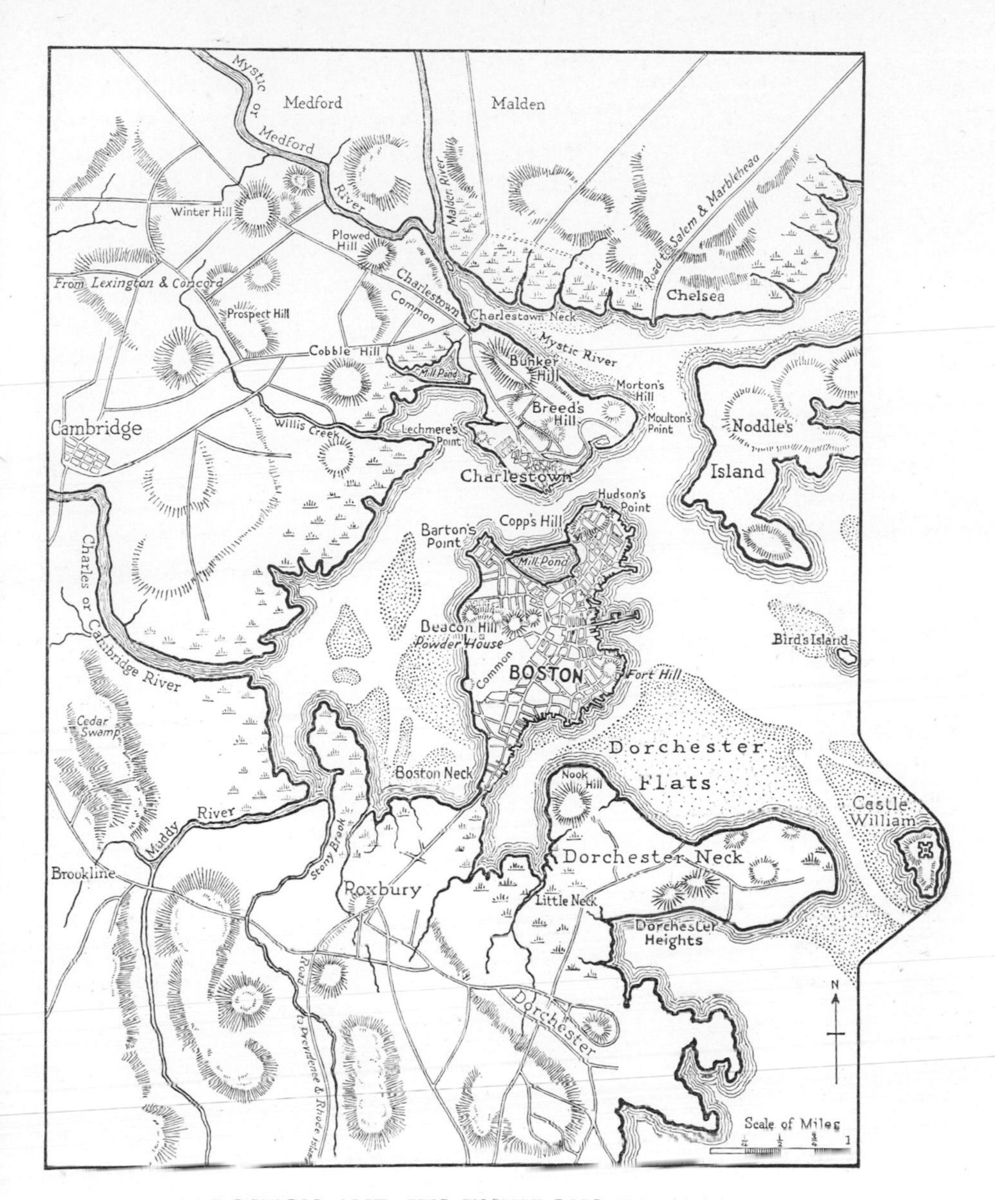

BOSTON AND ITS ENVIRONS IN 1775

Note the three peninsulas—Charlestown, Boston, and Dorchester Neck. They constituted the strategic heart of the siege of Boston.

war for whichever contestant should first feel himself able to seize them and prove himself able to retain them.

An admirable choice were the positions that the besiegers so quickly took. Despite the meager American equipment—the old-fashioned musket[4] and the scant artillery—and the lack of discipline, that first cordon was never broken.

There quickly arose, though, need for decisive action by the provisional government. The siege had been clapped on with dramatic force and suddenness by the militiamen themselves. The task of maintaining it passed to the provincial leaders—particularly the leaders of Massachusetts, for on that province rested the chief burden and responsibility.

Both by law and tradition it had become the duty of the Massachusetts militia to turn out on an alarm—to the last man if need be—and to march at a moment's notice to "repel," "pursue," and "destroy" whatever enemy had put the province—or the township—in peril. But neither law nor tradition expected the militia, as such, to keep the field. To conduct a campaign, men were drawn (by voluntary enlistment or by impressment) from its local ranks in their home towns (so and so many from each township or company) and reassembled in special regiments and brigades.

The Committee of Safety saw the opportunity to form an army on the spot, in place of this customary but slower method of gathering quotas from townships scattered all over the province, and on the second day (April 21) it resolved to enlist 8000 men from those around them—but a large part of the besieging force melted away before the resolve was translated into action.

The men, having answered the alarm and pursued the enemy as far as pursuit had been deemed feasible by their officers, felt no obligation to remain any longer than their own and their companions' estimates of the necessities of the

[4] The musket was generally the personal property of the man who carried it, but sometimes it was a "Province" or "King's" arm, furnished by his town selectmen or local military committee, or one lent by a neighbor or "forcibly taken from a Tory."

situation; or than suited their own needs, or desires, or conscience. As the entire force was a body of their own building and officering, and they had come out on their own initiative, they felt that, instead of awaiting permission to return to their homes, they could stay or go according to their own volition.

They had dropped everything on the alarm, many of them marching in the clothes they had been wearing in the fields, and without a farthing in their pockets. After a few hours in camp they began to think of their unfinished work, their untilled fields; and many of them decided to go home—for a while at all events. Each one reasoned that there was no imperative necessity to remain, for the redcoats displayed no indication of coming out;—and that, anyway, there were plenty of his fellows who would stay! The especially conscientious private arranged with some one else—generally a relative or townsman—to take his place before he left camp, but a great deal more frequently this precaution was overlooked.

The same thoughts and impulses affected the Connecticut troops.

Ward was the central figure of command, but until the Provincial Congress or the Committee of Safety should act, he was without authority to enlist the men around him, or to pay them, or to hold them in any way.

On the fourth day (April 23) he wrote to the Provincial Congress imploring immediate action.

"My situation is such," he declared, "that if I have not enlisting orders immediately, I shall be left all alone. It is impossible to keep the men here, excepting something be done. I therefore pray that the plan may be completed and handed to me this morning, that you, gentlemen of the Congress, issue orders for enlisting men."[5]

[5] I have not come across the original of this letter, but William Lincoln stated that it was in existence at the time (1838) of the publication of the *Journals of each Provincial Congress of Massachusetts,* and that it was dated April *23,* 1775. *American Archives,* 4th, II, 384, gives the date as April *24,* 1775. The minutes of the Provincial Congress

Thus prompted, the Congress declared for the raising of an army of 13,600 (instead of the Committee of Safety's 8000) and shortly followed its resolution by issuing "beating orders"—authority to whom issued to enlist men; commissions in the new army being contingent on success in obtaining the required totals. In order to retain in field service as large a proportion as possible of the officers who had come to the siege, the company size was reduced to fifty-nine men, including officers, and a regiment was limited to ten such companies. Enlistments were to the end of the year.

The "beating" system was hallowed by custom, but it did not fit the emergency. Its greatest defect was that the men enrolled did not, under the conditions of the siege, except by their own voluntary action, become reliable effective members of the army until the completion of their companies—or regiments—and their "mustering in" (inspection and swearing in by specially appointed officers known as "muster masters"), which meant, in many cases, a delay of several weeks.

Under its circumstances the rank and file continued to perplex the general officers with frequent unheralded changes both in strength and personnel. The passing of day after day with no new formation definitely evolved and the old formation in a constant state of flux, the conflicting rumors of what both they and the enemy were doing and were about to do: these things not only accentuated the natural restlessness of the young single men—they also left undiminished the homeward pull of farm and family felt by the large number of married men in the ranks. Patriotism of the highest order had brought them to the siege ready for a life-and-death conflict. They were not in camp for the "glory" of war or pride of regiment, but solely to fight for the defense of what they considered their rights, and against the violation of their

apparently confirm the Lincoln date, and suggest that this letter, instead of one concerning the New Hampshire troops, should have been cited in the sentence preceding the resolution for an army of 30,000 men. See *Journals of each Provincial Congress,* 148, April 23, and note.

homes and the country they had developed. To be ready to give their lives for their homes, and at the same time to neglect those homes entirely in the busy farming season, would have seemed foolish to the logical New England mind —hence the tendency of the Massachusetts militiamen, with or without permission, to return to their families at any moment's impulse to attend to some farm work—or because of the sickness of wife or child.

The problem was intensified by the competition between officers with beating orders, and their excessive deference to their men's demands. An officer who was strict might find it impossible to fill his beating order and would thus lose his eligibility for a commission.

It is nevertheless a serious mistake to presume, as many have done, that the lack of military discipline and the prevalence of informal furloughs signified also an army of lethargy or idleness. Those first two months in the American camps were filled with much earnest labor by men and officers alike. "The Army is employed thus," wrote a private in the Cambridge lines, "a large number is upon guard night and day; another party is upon fatigue, or labour, & ye rest perform Duty on the Common from 10 o'clock to 12 o'clock & from 4 o'clock to Sunsett."[6]

There is some woeful contemporary testimony to the profanity of the camp talk—but a certain quantity of rough language is to be expected wherever men assemble in the absence of their womenfolk. There was, withal, a strongly religious atmosphere—the troops attended daily prayers and joined fervently in the singing of psalms. A high code of morality was enforced. A "bad woman" received short shrift: sometimes being "doused" in the river and then "drummed out of town."

Blended with the camp profanity, mosaicking it with peculiar effect, were the many scriptural phrases current in daily speech—the result of much Bible reading and discussion.

[6] Original diary of Joseph Meriam, *Chamberlain Collection,* Boston Public Library.

Scriptural language lent weight also to the invectives which the Americans let loose upon the heads of their enemies. Biological, social, and political epithets such as dogs, lobsters, butchers, cannibals, unnatural enemies, parliamentary tools, etc., had their uses, but they did not convey the weight and relish of such phrases as "red-coated Philistines," "uncircumcised heathen," etc. One private always referred to General Gage as that "Crocodile and Second Pharoe," and there are many diary entries which bear testimony to the prevailing sentiment that the "God of Israel" was on the American side.

We have, further, been told that the New Englanders thus gathered together were most distressingly careless of their personal appearance and that they apparently used little soap—in other words, that they were disgracefully dirty! It would have been strange if it had been otherwise. Several thousand men so closely crowded that they filled every house and every barn to overflowing, covering every inch of floor space as they slept at night—after digging trenches, throwing up earthworks, and doing all manner of camp chores by day. No running water or bathtubs in the houses in which they were quartered (private bathtubs were unknown then and for many years to come), and still fewer facilities for cleanliness in their other improvised shelters: in motley boat-sail tents and hastily constructed huts of boards or stone or turf: or as they bivouacked without any protection at all. They would have been the most particular of men if—again in the absence of their womenfolk—they *had* paid much attention to their personal appearance.[7]

The post of general officer in this army presented many peculiar problems—superimposed on days unceasingly crowded by consideration of military plans and dangers. Casual contemporary references show Ward one day at Roxbury; on another reconnoitering Lechmere's Point; again,

[7] In many cases the men were not to blame. Soap was not always readily obtainable. Lieutenant-Colonel Storrs writes in his diary (June 9): "My company uneasy for want of beer, and soap for washing."—*Massachusetts Historical Society Proceedings,* XIV, 85.

reconnoitering Dorchester Neck; and, next, riding over the Charlestown peninsula. He was fortunate in having the energetic coöperation of a number of able officers—chief in authority among them during the first weeks being General Thomas of the Massachusetts forces, the Connecticut Generals Putnam and Spencer, and Colonel Stark of New Hampshire—and also the valuable assistance of Joseph Warren, whose popularity gave him great influence among the troops; but lack of experience and precedents, and of qualified assistants, added greatly to the labors of every commanding officer, and it does not surprise one to read Jedediah Huntington's statement that both Ward and Putnam had "too much business on their hands."[8]

And there was lack of gunpowder, bayonets, horses, cooking utensils, and clothing; of everything except courage and food—the only two products of which Massachusetts at that time had any surplus.

Ward's insistent demands for much-needed equipment and materials were on at least one occasion hotly resented by the Committee of Supplies. In a letter to the Provincial Congress they complained of his impatience at the delay in supplying him with muskets and planking. They declared that they should "expect an explanation" from the general when the affairs of the colony were "a little settled."[9]

Of food, happily, there was plenty for all. Fresh meat was bountifully provided by the cattle in the vicinity or raided from the islands in the harbor; and every day, big carts rolled in from the neighboring towns laden with farm produce. There was no thought of the semi-starvation from which the Continentals later suffered in the lukewarm central provinces.

Reserve stocks were quickly reported to headquarters.

"I am informed that there are not less than 5 or 6 hundred bushels of peas at Newburyport," Ward writes, for example, to the Committee of Supplies. He wishes that they may be

[8] *Massachusetts Historical Society Collections,* 5th, IX, 495.

[9] Lincoln, *Journals of each Provincial Congress,* 557.

obtained for the soldiers. He also calls for all the "vinegar that it is possible for us to have." "Vinegar," he adds, "is a most important article." He had evidently not forgotten his classics and their references to the *posca* of the ancient Romans—the vinegar and water that served as the standard beverage of Cæsar's legions.

In the midst of all the other demands on his attention, Ward found time to ensure proper treatment of the English prisoners of war. Shortly after the battle of April 19 he sent word into Boston that the "wounded were taken every possible care of; that they were attended by the most skillful surgeons," but that "if General Gage chose to have any surgeons of his own appointment to attend them, he was at liberty to nominate them, and they should be permitted to give their attendance."[10] He also issued a general order in which he commanded that the "officers of the guards who have the care of the prisoners take the best care of them, and treat them in the kindest manner, and procure good surgeons to take care of the wounded." [11] Supplementing this, he wrote to Colonel Barrett in Concord, to which town some of the prisoners had been moved, "Pray keep them from any Infection that may arise from putting too many in one room

[10] In an article by a London writer reprinted in *American Archives,* 4th, II, 950.

[11] *Ward's Order Book,* April 21, 1775. The original Order Book, April 20, 1775–March 20, 1777, is (1921) owned by Mrs. A. Ward Lamson, Dedham, Mass. It is a tome of 350 pages, 8 × 12½ inches, originally parchment-bound. It is chiefly in the handwriting of Joseph Ward, but some entries are by aides-de-camp Samuel Osgood and Peleg Wadsworth, and a few are by General Ward himself. Photostat copies are in the Artemas Ward House, Shrewsbury, Mass., and the Artemas Ward MSS. A manuscript copy of all of the "Cambridge Orders" (April 20, 1775, to April 3, 1776), and of the "Roxbury Orders" from July 29 to October 20, 1775, is in the Adjutant-General's Office, Boston.

"Fenno's Orderly Book" (MS., two small books, April 20, 1775, to September 6, 1775.—Massachusetts Historical Society) has been freely quoted in the belief that it was kept by John Fenno, and that John Fenno was Ward's secretary, but neither of these points is correct—it was not kept by Fenno, and Fenno was not Ward's secretary. It is a copy (with some changes and additions) made by Joseph Ward of part of the original Order Book described above. It presumably owes its title of "Fenno's Orderly Book" to the pencil memorandum, "Kept by John Fenno, Secretary to the Commander-in-chief," which appears on the inside of the front cover of the first volume. This incorrect statement is of later addition and is not in the handwriting of either Joseph Ward or John Fenno.

. . . provide every thing needful for their comfortable subsistence."[12]

Reports of this reaching England did much to offset the untrue and highly colored tales of American atrocities on April 19. The London writer chronicling Ward's attitude, added, "The public will hardly believe that so fair and generous an enemy could be guilty of barbarity and cruelty."

Ward's indignation was, however, roused by Gage's violation of the agreement governing the exodus of the Boston patriots, and his council of war recommended that the reciprocal resolution of the Provincial Congress be suspended "until they are fully satisfied that the agreement is punctually fulfilled, and in the meantime to arrest and intern all Crown officers and known enemies to the liberties of the colonies."[13]

There were, too, rifts in the quick strong loyalty which had overnight beleaguered Boston. We find letters to Ward and the Committee of Safety from outlying towns telling of

[12] April 26, 1775.—Original letter, *Massachusetts Archives,* CXCIII, 70.

[13] May 12, 1775.—Original resolution, *Massachusetts Archives,* CXXXVIII, 48.

Gage had promised that any of the inhabitants of Boston who deposited their arms in Faneuil Hall should receive permission to leave the town and take with them their families and effects. But the number applying for passes was so large that the tories of the capital became alarmed and so far prevailed upon Gage that he threw many obstacles in the path of the exodus—resulting in much additional hardship and sometimes in the separation of families.

Many of those who were permitted to come out were entirely destitute, the abnormal conditions after the closing of the port having exhausted their meager resources.

The Provincial Congress took these poor people under its protection and allotted them to different towns, requiring the towns to provide for them—the province later to foot the bills.

The Congress added a resolution that the "inhabitants of Boston thus removed shall not in future be considered as the poor" of the towns to which they were allotted. This was interpreted even by the well-informed Frothingham (*Siege of Boston,* 95) as a "delicate" resolution to guard the feelings and sentiments of those to be thus publicly assisted and supported, and the idea has been adopted by lesser writers.

The resolution had, however, nothing whatever to do with "delicacy" or sentiment. On the contrary: instead of being a protection for the feelings of the refugees, it was passed *to protect the towns from being burdened with them.* It supplemented the preceding resolution providing for the payment of town expenses in caring for the refugees, and it signified that after the special war exigency (thus provided for) had passed, the towns should be under no obligation to support them—as they would have been if the refugees *had been* considered as their "poor." It was because of this obligation to take care of their own poor that Massachusetts towns were so careful to warn away strange would-be residents who, in the opinion of the selectmen, might become a burden; and to put under bonds any resident harboring a stranger.

men believed to be in communication with the English authorities. The vein of anti-patriot sentiment thus disclosed, and everywhere interwoven, was sometimes heroic, sometimes nauseously venal. Though not suspected until several months later, it reached even into the Committee of Safety in the person of Benjamin Church, a prominent member and frequently its chairman. From what date his double-dealing extended, no man knows, but he went through the lines into Boston and was whispering treachery with the British commander before the siege was forty-eight hours old. Fortunately, as six years later in the case of Benedict Arnold, the English profited little therefrom.

The besieging lines were at their leanest during the last week of April and the first days of May. Most of the men had returned to their homes—some to get additional clothes and to arrange farm and family affairs because they had enlisted or because they intended to; others, because they had decided that camp life was not to their taste. On April 26 a considerable body of men who had encamped in Watertown and Waltham were called into Cambridge and Roxbury, but they served only as a temporary stop-gap, for they also had begun to melt away. There was a special scarcity of officers—they had gone back not only on personal missions but also to try to fill their beating orders from among the men who had left the camp without signing on.

On May 8, while the camps were in this dangerously weakened condition, Ward received another of a succession of warnings that the English were planning the seizure of Dorchester Neck, and confirmatory reports apparently left little doubt that the enemy was preparing a capital stroke.

The situation had become desperate. The Provincial Congress debated a partial retreat from the American position, and on the morning of May 10 directed a committee to confer with the Committee of Safety on moving the whole or part of the cannon and stores back into the country. A plan much urged was the evacuation of Cambridge and the posts to the north, retaining only the Brookline and Roxbury positions.

But Ward and his fellow officers at Cambridge viewed matters from a more aggressive standpoint. There was no symptom of weakening in their council of war. Instead, they planned a strong counter-move. They unanimously resolved (May 9) to call in additional militiamen—not only to strengthen Roxbury, but also to forestall the enemy by themselves seizing and fortifying the dominating heights of Dorchester Neck: "Dorchester Hill," as the resolution reads; "Dorchester Heights," as they are best known to history.

No narrative of the siege records this episode, for it was submerged by the rush of events which followed within the next few weeks, but the page opposite bears a facsimile of the resolution signed by Samuel Osgood, General Ward's aide-de-camp.[14]

The resolution was immediately followed by a request to the Committee of Safety for 2000 men to reinforce Thomas, and "that if possible the reinforcements be brought to camp the ensuing night."

The Committee of Safety responded with a resolution ordering the militia officers of the towns of Dorchester, Dedham, Newton, Watertown, Waltham, Roxbury, Milton, Braintree, Brookline, and Needham, immediately to muster one half of their standing militiamen and all their minutemen, and to march them forthwith to Roxbury.

The order was, at the direction of the Provincial Congress, changed on the next day to a call *for all the men enlisted in the entire province* to march to Cambridge, and the following letter was dispatched to recruiting officers throughout the country:

[14] S. A. Drake happened on the original, or a copy of it, and mentioned it in his *Historic Fields and Mansions of Middlesex,* 260–261 (also, same page numbers, in the same work later published as *Old Landmarks and Historic Fields of Middlesex* and *Historic Mansions and Highways around Boston*), but it sank out of sight again and for many years lay buried in the autograph collection of John Mills Hale. It was released only so recently as February 14, 1913, when the Hale Collection was sold by Henkels in Philadelphia. It is now among the Artemas Ward MSS.

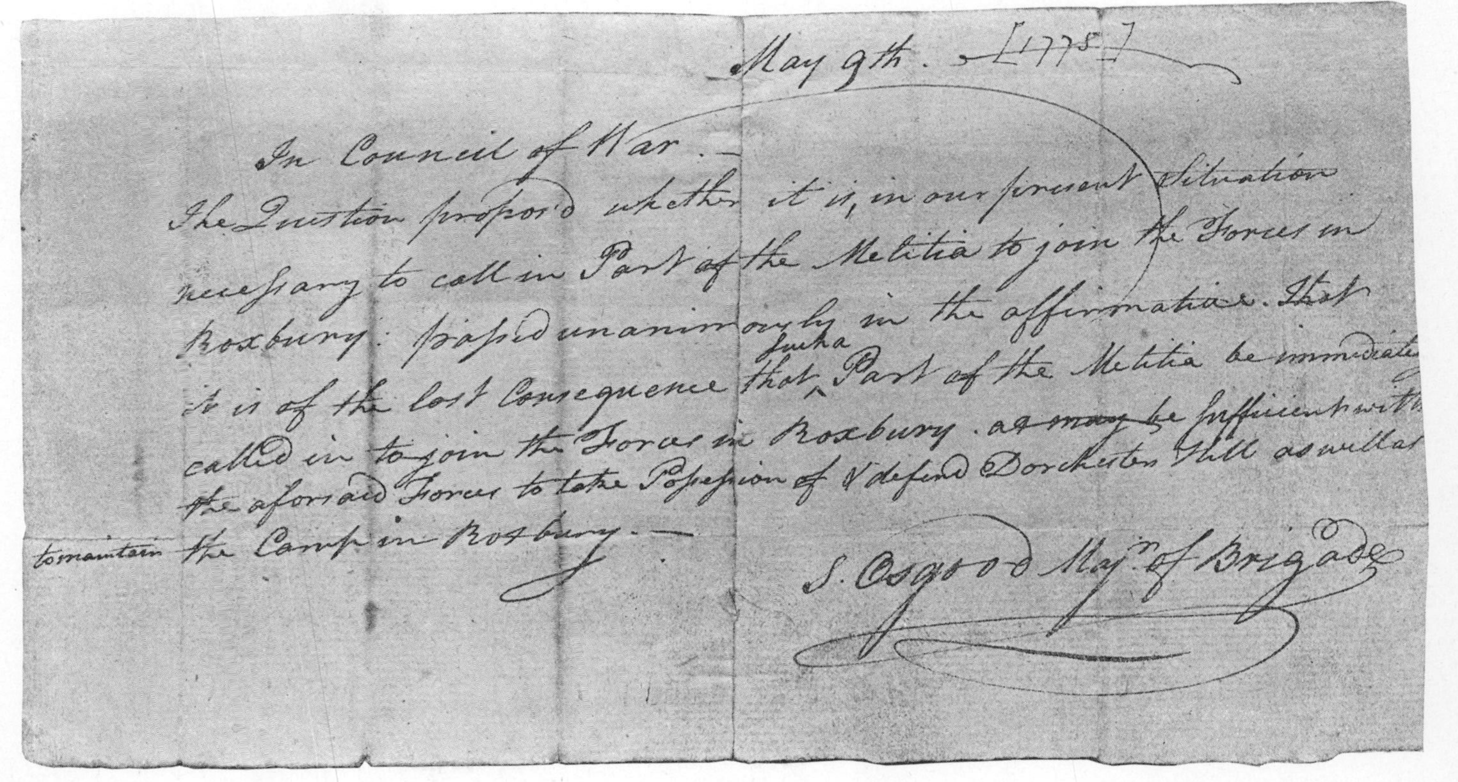

May 9th. [1775]

In Council of War.—

The Question propos'd whether it is, in our present situation necessary to call in Part of the Militia to join the Forces in Roxbury: pass'd unanimously in the affirmative. That it is of the last Consequence that such a Part of the Militia be immediately called in to join the Forces in Roxbury as may be sufficient with the aforesaid Forces to take Possession of & defend Dorchester Hill as well as to maintain the Camp in Roxbury.—

S. Osgood Majr of Brigade

From the original in the *Artemas Ward MSS.*

THE FIRST AMERICAN RESOLUTION FOR THE SEIZURE OF DORCHESTER NECK

"In Committee of Safety, Camb., May 10, 1775

SIR:

As we are meditating a Blow against our restless Enemies—We therefore enjoin you as you would Evidence your Regard to Your Country, forthwith upon the Receipt of this Order to repair to the Town of Cambridge with the Men inlisted under your command.

We are, etc.

BENJA CHURCH, JUNR.
Chairman."

The letter was intended by the Committee of Safety only for officers in outlying towns, but a copy, both written and signed by Benjamin Church himself, was sent to Thomas.[15] This may have been merely a blunder—the possibility is suggested by the superscription "To General Thomas of Plymouth"—but whether or not, and despite its address, the letter was promptly delivered to Thomas at Roxbury.

Thomas did not take the letter as unintentional. He read it as a direct order intended for his compliance. He was, however, too alert to withdraw his men from the post entrusted to him, even at the command of the head of the Committee of Safety, without special confirmation of the order. He could not complain to Ward, for the Committee of Safety was superior to all military officers. The only higher authority than Church, as the head of the Committee of Safety, was the Provincial Congress itself. So, refusing meanwhile to move his men, he immediately sent a message of inquiry to Joseph Warren as President of the Congress.

Warren's answer was prompt and decisive:

"I have this moment received your letter, the Contents very much surprised me, as I had been absent from the Committee of Safety all Day I could not at first understand the

[15] Original letter, *Emmet Collection,* New York Public Library.

matter, but upon Enquiry I find the Committee gave Orders that all recruiting Officers should repair to Cambridge with the Men they had enlisted, but the sending the Order to your Camp was certainly a very great Error, as it was designed only for those Officers who are in the Country, absent from Camp.

"Your readiness to obey Orders does you great Honor, and your prudence in sending to Head Quarters upon receiving so extraordinary an Order convinces me of your Judgment."

If Warren, who "had not the greatest affection for" Church,[16] had lived to see him arrested for maintaining an illicit correspondence with the enemy, he might have better understood the "very great error" of "so extraordinary an order."[17]

It does not require much imagination to discern the great danger in which the American forces would have been placed if Thomas had obeyed the Committee of Safety order. An English detachment rushed into Roxbury—the enemy commanding an open road into the country—the American center at Cambridge immediately untenable; and no alternative but a pitched battle under the most disadvantageous conditions, or a hurried—and surely disorganized—retreat.

Ward's Dorchester Heights project of May 9 was not fulfilled,—probably because Thomas decided that the seizure of the peninsula was too hazardous a project for his division even if reinforced. We have his letter of a few days later saying that he "much despaired of defending" Dorchester Neck, had he "ever so many men on the spot," unless it could be strengthened by "Regular Intrenchments" and furnished

[16] Goss, *Paul Revere,* I, 207.

[17] This incident is found in no other account. The three individuals most closely associated with it had been long dead when the first American history of the Revolution was written. Warren and Thomas had laid down their lives for their country—Warren at Bunker Hill, Thomas a year later in Canada; and the proscribed Church had lost his life at sea. The letters which illustrated it lay buried in England for many years—until the auction of the collection of the Reverend Thomas Raffles of Liverpool, England, at Libbie's, Boston, February 3–5, 1892—and modern writers have overlooked them since their recovery.

with cannon and "persons to take the proper direction of them" to offset the land and sea batteries that the English could bring into action.[18]

Nor did Gage make his expected move. Instead, he held his troops within his lines, and American conditions took an upward turn as militiamen in considerable numbers came into both the Cambridge and Roxbury camps.

The attention of the American commanders turned next to their left. A joint committee appointed by the council of war and the Committee of Safety "for the purpose of reconnoitering the highlands in Cambridge and Charlestown," advised, May 12, the raising of breastworks near Prospect Hill on both the north and south sides of the road from Cambridge to Charlestown (the north breastwork to be on the side of Prospect Hill); and redoubts on Winter Hill (in place of the guard-house standing there) and Bunker Hill, the latter being the highest point of the Charlestown peninsula. The report concluded with the statement that "when these are finished, we apprehend that the country will be safe from all sallies of the enemy in that quarter."

The committee's recommendations resulted in a breastwork being thrown up near the base of Prospect Hill to guard the Cambridge-Charlestown road, but the Winter Hill and Bunker Hill plans were temporarily set aside.

"On the most important measure, that of occupying Bunker Hill, there was much difference of opinion. General Putnam, Colonel Prescott, and other veteran officers, were strongly in favor of it, and chiefly to draw the enemy out of Boston on ground where he might be met on equal terms. . . . Generals Ward and Warren were among those who opposed it, and chiefly because the army was not in a condition, as respected cannon and powder, to maintain so exposed a post; and because it might bring on a general engagement, which it was neither politic nor safe to risk. It was determined to

[18] To the Honorable Gen. Ward, May 18, 1775.—*Thomas Papers,* 1774–1776, 29, Massachusetts Historical Society.

take possession of Bunker Hill, and also of Dorchester Heights, but not until the army should be better organized, more abundantly supplied with powder, and better able to defend posts so exposed."[19]

Ward and his council planned also the equipment of a fleet of "batteaux" and whale-boats[20] in Charles River and other waters of the vicinity[21] and made various attempts to burn the English shiping by means of blazing "fire-boats."

And still an army held together largely by moral suasion! A full month after the outbreak of hostilities, and not an officer commissioned, nor a man mustered.

A variety of circumstances had delayed the filling of the regiments. Very mischievous in effect had been the action of the Committee of Safety (possessed by its initial fears that enlistments would fall short) in giving out more beating orders than were needed to enlist the number of men authorized by the Provincial Congress; and in giving them out somewhat indiscriminately. Many orders were only partly filled, and some were out on which the committee had no information whatever. The men estimated to have enrolled fell considerably short of the 13,600 desired, yet the number of orders in circulation made the committee afraid to give enlisting authority even to enterprising officers with men ready to sign with them. This not only left such officers outside the army establishment, but also their men, unless they chose, as generally they did not, to enlist under strange officers. One entire regiment was thus affected because its colonel had not applied for beating orders with sufficient promptness.[22] On

[19] Frothingham, *Siege of Boston,* 116.

[20] There is little whale-fishing now done from the shores of New England, but in those days it was still an important industry. Whale-boats served the Americans as war vessels in their harbor forays and figured as transports in plans for storming Boston. And when spears were called for, it was noted that they could "easily be obtained from the whalemen in the vicinity."—*Massachusetts Archives,* CXCIII, 396.

[21] Committee of Safety resolution, May 10.—Lincoln, *Journals of each Provincial Congress.*

[22] This was Colonel Woodbridge, who had "been in the camp with his minute-men doing duty ever since the battle [of April 19], but did not apply to this committee for

the other hand, some officers had indulged in sharp practice—deliberate fraud was charged in one flagrant case—to obtain them.

The situation was rendered the more unsatisfactory because no action of any kind had been taken even on orders which had been completed. The army hung between heaven and earth—the men feeling themselves only provisionally enrolled and the officers not yet sure of their rank.

This condition could not continue indefinitely and Ward again wrote to the Provincial Congress, calling most emphatically for attention: asserting it to be "absolutely necessary that the regiments be immediately settled, the officers commissioned, the soldiers mustered and paid, agreeable to what has been proposed by the Congress—if we would save our country."[23] His letter, addressed to Joseph Warren, is reproduced opposite page 108.

The Congress responded by deputing James Warren to wait "on the Committee of Safety for a List of such colonels and other Officers as they shall report to be prepared for receiving their Commissions."

The immediate result was meager—only two regiments being reported as "full" and recommended for commissions. Next day, one more was certified as "full"; and a fourth a few days later as "nearly full." But Ward's protests were bearing fruit, and Friday, May 26, brought a new list of eleven "full," or "nearly full," or in "good forwardness."

Additional delay had arisen from disputes over field-officers' commissions. In Ward's own regiment were two aspirants for the post of lieutenant-colonel: Joseph Henshaw, who had marched to Cambridge as head of the minute-men battalion; and Jonathan Ward, who had brought down

enlisting orders, until the committee had issued orders sufficient to complete the army, and therefore the committee did not give him orders, but promised they would recommend him if there should be a vacancy."—Committee of Safety, June 10 (Lincoln, *Journals of each Provincial Congress*).

[23] In the *American Archives* copy of this letter, 4th, II, 647, May 19, 1775, the word "numbered" should be corrected to read "mustered."

the remainder of the regiment. The same circumstances had bred similar claims and disputes in other regiments.[24]

The privates, too, were quick to resent any arrangement which did not suit them—nor were they always careful in the language used concerning officers. For example, twenty-seven privates petitioned Ward against being shifted from one regiment to another. "We . . . beg that your Excellency[25] would be pleased to continue us in the regiment we engaged to serve in, and not to be removed for the future *only to serve the malevolent disposition of our Captain.*"

Meanwhile, on the afternoon of May 20, the Provincial Congress had resolved "that the president be desired to deliver to General Ward the commission[26] prepared for him as general and commander-in-chief of the Massachusetts forces."

Thus Ward formally received his commission, Samuel Dexter of Dedham having first "administered the oath" to him.

The nominal strength of the Grand American Army, as the newspapers styled it, was at this period about 16,000 men. Of those from beyond the borders of Massachusetts, only the New Hampshire troops came under Ward's direct authority, but the Connecticut and Rhode Island forces also paid him a voluntary obedience.

But now a new and ugly danger had raised its head.

There had been no constitutional government in Massachusetts for nearly a year, and during this interim, and

[24] James Warren blamed much of the Provincial Congress embarrassment in officering the army on the establishment of minute-men and declared he wished "it had never taken place."—May 7, 1775, to John Adams, *Warren-Adams Letters,* I, 47.

[25] Ward, while in command at the siege, was variously addressed and referred to as: *Your Excellency, His Excellency General Ward, Honorable General Ward, General Ward, Honorable Artemas Ward, Esq., The General Officer of the Army of This Colony, The Commanding Officer of the Colony Forces,* and *Captain-General.* The last title was the official military designation of the royal governors of Massachusetts.

[26] The preparation of General Ward's commission had been entrusted, May 17, to a committee consisting of Colonel Jedediah Foster of Brookfield, James Sullivan of Biddeford (Maine), and Captain Michael Farley of Ipswich. Amory's *Life of James Sullivan,* I, 381, says that the actual work was done by James Sullivan.

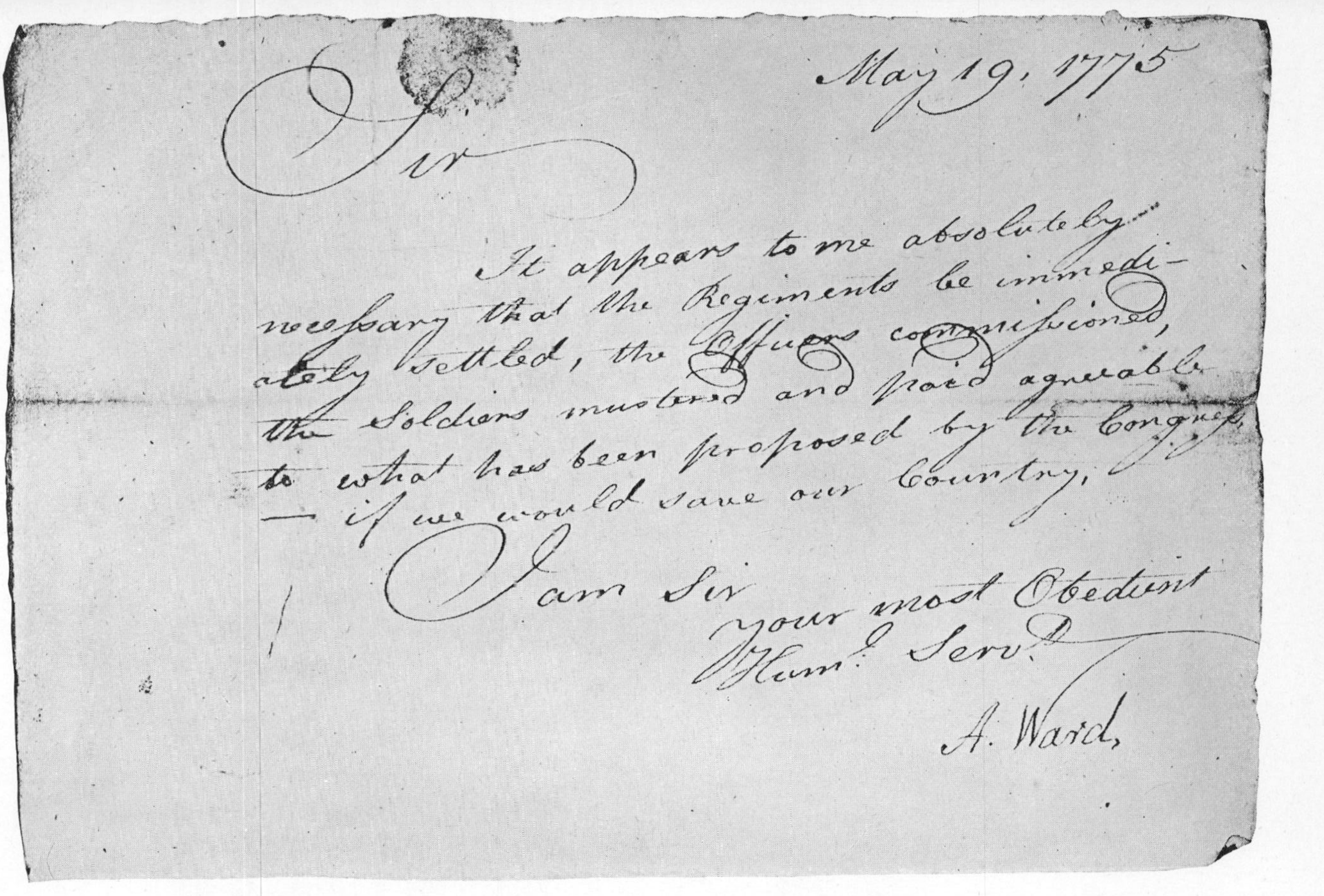

May 19. 1775

Sir

It appears to me absolutely necessary that the Regiments be immediately settled, the Officers commissioned, the Soldiers mustered and paid agreeable to what has been proposed by the Congress, — if we would save our Country,

I am Sir
your most Obedient
Hum.l Serv.t

A. Ward,

From the original (8 × 5½) in the *Massachusetts Archives*

WARD'S LETTER TO PRESIDENT JOSEPH WARREN URGING THE PROVINCIAL CONGRESS TO ACTION

The Congress of the Colony of the

Massachusetts-Bay.

To The Honorable Artemas Ward Esq. Greeting

We, reposing especial Trust and Confidence in your Courage and good Conduct, Do, by these Presents, constitute and appoint you the said Artemas Ward to be General and Commander in Chief of all the Forces raised by the Congress aforesaid, for the Defence of this and the other American Colonies ——

You are therefore carefully and diligently to discharge the Duty of a General in leading ordering and exercising the Forces in Arms, both Inferior Officers and Soldiers, and to keep them in good Order and Discipline; and they are hereby commanded to obey you as their General, and you are yourself to observe and follow such Orders and Instructions as you shall from Time to Time receive from this or any future Congress or House of Representatives of this Colony, or the Committee of Safety so far as said Committee is impowered by their Commission for the Defence of this and the other Colonies; And to demean yourself according to the Military Rules and Discipline established by said Congress, in pursuance of the Trust reposed in you ——

By Order of the Congress

Jas Warren President P.T.

Dated the 19th Day of May A.D. 1775

Saml Freeman Secy P.T.

From the original (12½ × 15¼), owned by the Massachusetts Historical Society

WARD'S COMMISSION AS COMMANDER-IN-CHIEF OF THE MASSACHUSETTS FORCES

for some years preceding, the most influential brains of the province had emphasized and enlarged upon the rights of the people, and by their reasoning and protests had highly sharpened the Massachusetts wit and appetite for political controversy and individual independence which had been bred by generations of town-meetings.

The result suddenly assumed an alarming aspect. The militiamen encamped in their thousands around Boston found many topics to debate and to discuss, and soon—free of the restraining influences of their home towns—they experienced no difficulty in proving to themselves and to each other that they need obey only what and whom they pleased—for was it not true that there was no longer any law or court or government in Massachusetts?

What was this Provincial Congress, and by what authority did it or its committees or its appointees presume to dictate? True, the delegates, many of them, had been elected in the ordinary manner, but they constituted nevertheless only an irregular assembly which had no place in the charter of the province. The Provincial Congress could *recommend*, and it could appoint committees and *they* could recommend; but on what did it, or they, base their right to *order?*

They, the soldiers, knew their duty to their country and were ready to do it—but they did not intend to submit to anybody's arbitrary regulations, nor to be censured or punished for violations of rules to which they had not agreed and which nobody else had a right to make!

The variations on the topic were manifold and continuous, and the discussions developed a spirit of active violence that threatened to demolish the already attenuated social fabric.

A comfortable measure of prosperity had been widespread throughout the province,—in no part of the world had there been less want,—but inequalities of condition inevitably showed themselves in every township, and, as in all lands and in all ages, there were in every company the discontented, the envious, the shiftless, and those of incendiary heart. Such men now had a clear field for argument, and they speedily corrupted a large part of the army, the virus infecting each new corps that came in and spreading far and wide throughout the country as the men went back and forth. The abnormal conditions everywhere besetting, the strange new era into which the colonies had suddenly plunged, and the recourse to arms and bloodshed to resist old and long established authority—these things raised new thoughts and questions of *other* rights and wrongs: of the respective merits of law and force, and of existing tenures of property and the distribution of property: that for a time swept hundreds of normally steady-going men perilously close to the vortex.

Spread before them were all the possessions of the province, save only those under the protection of the redcoats in Boston: all of the bigger and more prosperous farms which dwarfed their own possessions; all the material wealth in every form that Massachusetts had developed in a hundred and fifty years: and between this wealth and them, no barrier but a very shadow of a government.[27]

[27] *May 4, by the Committee of Safety* (Lincoln, *Journals of each Provincial Congress*):

"Resolved, . . . that the public good of this colony requires that government in full form ought to be taken up immediately."

May 16, the Provincial Congress to the Continental Congress:

"We tremble at having an army, although consisting of our own countrymen, established here, without a civil power to provide for and control it."

May 26, Joseph Warren to Samuel Adams:

"I see more & more the Necessity of establishing a civil Government here and such a Government as shall be sufficient to control the military Forces, not only of this Colony, but also Such as Shall be sent to us from the other Colonies. The Continent must Strengthen & support with all it's Weight the civil Authority here, otherwise our Soldiery will lose the Ideas of right & wrong, and will plunder instead of protecting, the Inhabitants. This is but too evident already; & I assure you *inter nos,* that unless some Authority Sufficient to restrain the Irregularities of this Army, is established, we Shall very soon find ourselves involved in greater Difficulties than you can well imagine. . . . My great Wish therefore is that we may restrain everything which tends to weaken the Principles of Right & Wrong, more especially with regard to *property*. . . . I hope Care will be taken by the Continental Congress to apply an immediate Remedy, as the Infection is caught by every new Core that arrives . . . For the Honor of my Country, I wish the Disease may be cured before it is known [to the public] to exist."—Original letter, *Samuel Adams Papers,* New York Public Library; a copy, edited to modern capitalization, spelling, etc., is in Frothingham's *Joseph Warren,* 495–496.

May 27, in the Provincial Congress—reported by the committee appointed to bring in a resolve for the regular administration of justice:

"Whereas, it appears to this Congress, that a want of a due and regular execution

It was the good fortune of Massachusetts (and of the Revolution) that the chief command of this restless, seething army was in the hands of a man whom the troops esteemed and respected. Had Ward held less of their respect and affection, the much discussed "disorder" might have become *disaster*.

It had been the sound judgment of the provincial delegates which had placed Ward above all of the general officers except Preble. His attributes had not included seniority—for he was the youngest of the general officers who had seen service; but neither was he appointed because of greater possible activity—for by that standard Thomas would have outranked him. His military record, though not from any personal fault, was less brilliant than that of Pomeroy, or Thomas, or Whitcomb. And he had neither wealth nor high position to enhance his standing. But he had been tested and tried in the political storms of many years, and he stood as a recognized champion of the patriot cause and, as such, an inspiring commander for the patriot army.

He was not a "regular general," nor blessed with a great political following, but for a full twenty-four years he had been in the closest contact with the typical Massachusetts life: meeting his home neighbors and those of greater distance throughout Worcester County as justice of the peace and judge of the Court of Common Pleas; as selectman and church moderator, as representative and councilor, and as militia officer—and he thoroughly understood the men and their manner of thought. The molding of his character

of justice in this colony, has encouraged divers wicked and disorderly persons, not only to commit outrages and trespasses upon private property and private persons, but also to make the most daring attacks upon the constitution, and to unite in their endeavors to disturb the peace, and destroy the happiness and security of their country: and, whereas, this Congress conceive it to be their indispensable duty to take effectual measures to restrain all disorders, and promote the peace and happiness of this colony, by the execution of justice in criminal matters:

"Therefore, Resolved, That a court of inquiry be immediately erected, consisting of seven persons, to be chosen by this Congress, whose business it shall be to hear all complaints against any person or persons, for treason against the constitution of their country, or other breaches of the public peace and security."

and the ripening of his experience during those twenty-four years now stood his country in good stead.

Some there were who thought him over-lenient to offenders, and that he held the reins too loosely; but when the point was raised, both friend and enemy among the leaders of Massachusetts realized that to put another in his place might overnight destroy the province. It was not possible to enforce rigid discipline, and until a regularly constituted government could be reëstablished there was always the danger that the army might get out of hand no matter who was in command, but Ward filled his most difficult post with so substantial a degree of dexterity that even his most bitter detractor—James Warren, of Plymouth—feared the result of making a change and, in the following month, testified "we dare not superceed him here." A severe or arbitrary or unpopular general would have been defied, and the defiance might have kindled the flames of armed anarchy. An ambitious general might have torn authority from the Congress and set up a military standard. Either calamity would have alienated the sympathies of the other colonies and, rousing and confirming their dormant suspicions of Massachusetts, would have destroyed the Revolution in its cradle. And either would have brought a grim aftermath to the patriots of Massachusetts: with confiscation and hangings to mark the penalty for unsuccessful rebellion.

There were other able men in Massachusetts, with more military experience and, some of them, with stronger ideas of military discipline. But there was none other whom Ward's contemporaries dared to trust at the helm while there threatened a return to elemental passions.

Discipline indeed remained lax, and the camp slipshod. How could it be otherwise, with men continually coming and going, shifting and changing like the sands of the sea? It *was* a loose command, and of a kaleidoscopic army, but nevertheless it achieved its first main purpose—the siege was maintained, and the enemy kept within the town.

The Provincial Congress pressed the Continental Congress for advice on, and continental authority for, the establishment of an orthodox form of provincial government. Because they feared to make the attempt without it, the Massachusetts leaders awaited the sanction or mandate of the "Continent," despite the increasing dangers of the political situation. But Joseph Warren warned that if a new civil government were not speedily come into, a military government would of necessity evolve—and every Massachusetts instinct recoiled at the thought of that possibility.[28]

The Provincial Congress suggested also the continental adoption and general direction of the Revolutionary armies. In this it was deemed necessary to move with great caution in order to avoid offending the soldiers. It would

[28] There are many examples of the American revolutionists' determination to preclude the possibility of military dictation whether by English arms or their own forces. They quickly resented anything that savored of encroachment on civil power.

On June 26 the Provincial Congress had:

> "Resolved, that all the small arms that are or may be procured . . . be delivered to the Committee of Safety, at Cambridge, they to give their receipts for the same to the person from whom they receive them; that the same be delivered out to such officers as shall produce orders therefor from the Hon. General Ward, they giving receipts for the same to the said committee of safety, to be returned in good order, unless lost in service of the colony."

On June 28 Ward, acting on this resolution, ordered:

> "that the commanding officer of each regiment make application to the committee of safety for so many fire-arms as their respective regiments stand in need of; each commanding officer to give his receipt for the fire-arms he may receive, and the committee of safety are hereby ordered to deliver out arms to such commanding officers as make application to them for the same."

The words "the committee of safety are hereby ordered" acted like the proverbial red rag on the members of the committee, and they immediately forwarded an indignant protest to the Provincial Congress.

They pointed out with much detail that the Provincial Congress resolution did not "impower the General to order them to deliver said arms, but only to order his officers to receive from this Committee such arms as they are ordered by the honorable Congress to deliver on the general's orders to his officers," and they apprehend "that it is of vast importance that no orders are issued by the Military or obeyed by the Civil powers, but only such as are directed by the honorable representative body of the people, from whom all Military & Civil power originates."

. . . . . .

Again, in Braintree, Mass., Abigail Adams records the town's refusal to permit any soldier to vote. "Newcomb insisted upon it that no man should vote who was in the army. He had no notion of being under the military power; said we might be so situated as to have the greater part of the people engaged in the military, and then all power would be wrested out of the hands of the civil magistrate. He insisted upon its being put to vote, and carried his point immediately."—*Letters of Mrs. Adams,* I, July 16, 1775.

have been indeed a serious matter if the armed men of the New England provinces had challenged the continental authority as at times they threatened the provincial. Dr. Warren wrote Samuel Adams that this was a matter to be handled with "much delicacy," as otherwise, despite even the weight of the united continental authority behind either a committee of war or a new "generalissimo," dangerous dissensions might arise in the army, for "our soldiers, I find, will not be brought to obey any person of whom they do not themselves entertain a high opinion."

Further heightening the perturbation of the American leaders throughout that feverish month of May were the continued warnings of the British determination to occupy Dorchester Neck and to break through the American lines at Roxbury. To guard against surprise, Thomas kept outposts near Dorchester Neck by day, and stationed pickets upon it at night—facing them toward both Boston and Castle William and supporting them with parts of two regiments within easy call.

The English movements lent color to the reports, for they included the fortifying of flat-boats and other vessels to cover landing parties, but Gage was not yet ready to try his steel again, and the month closed with exultation over the successful issue of a brush which developed from a raid on Hog and Noddle's islands (now Breed's Island and East Boston).

The raid had several important results—the destruction of an enemy schooner mounting sixteen pieces of cannon, the bringing of hundreds of sheep into the American camps, and, finally, the influencing in (then) far-off Philadelphia the continental vote for Putnam as major-general—"Old Put" having assumed the command when the affair developed into a land and water engagement between the English on their vessels and on Noddle's Island, and the Americans on Chelsea Neck. Joseph Warren also joined the detachment, serving as a volunteer.

The edible outcome proved so satisfactory to the American commissary that night visits to Pettick's (Peddock's) and Deer islands quickly followed and with almost equally profitable returns.

Other minor encounters, preceding and following, also served to keep both sides on the alert.

But always, incessantly, increasingly imperative was the need for gunpowder. Letter after letter by Ward calls for it. Especially impressive in its extreme earnestness and courageous confidence is the address to the Continental Congress that he signed on June 4, together with Joseph Warren (as chairman of the Committee of Safety) and Moses Gill (chairman of the Committee of Supplies). They convincingly set forth the danger to which the province is exposed by the scarcity of ammunition, but they dwell on the bravery of the New England troops, "whom we think we can without boasting declare are ready to encounter every danger for the preservation of the Rights and Liberties of America." They ask only for "arms and ammunition"—feeling that thus supplied, even if otherwise unassisted, they may "with the Common blessing of Providence baffle the designs of the enemy and be greatly instrumental in bringing our present dispute to a happy issue."

Two days later, American attention was again directed to Dorchester Neck, and Generals Ward, Thomas, Spencer, and Heath, with a number of other officers, surveyed the heights with a view to their occupation. The English "fired three times at them with their Cannon, but did no harm."[29] But again the project was deemed too hazardous.

Looking next toward the north, Ward on June 12 moved Reed's New Hampshire regiment close in to Charlestown Neck, the short isthmus connecting the Charlestown peninsula with the mainland. Reed's men are stationed on the mainland side of the Neck, with sentries reaching onto

[29] Samuel Bixby's Diary, June 6, 1775.—*Massachusetts Historical Society Proceedings,* XIV, 286; James Cogswell, aide to General Spencer, June 13, 1775, to Levi Hart.—Winsor, *Proofs and Corrections,* VI, 130 verso, Massachusetts Historical Society.

Bunker Hill. In their rear, at Medford, is Stark's New Hampshire regiment.

Then quickly approached a climax to all the threats and counter-threats. The English had received the greater part of the reinforcements for which they had been waiting. Well equipped, well disciplined, well officered, and headed by a galaxy of famous generals, they felt that their turn had come, and they decided that the time was ripe to raise the siege. Their first move was to be—on Sunday, June 18—the seizure and fortification of Dorchester Neck. This to be succeeded by the occupation of the Charlestown peninsula, for it "was absolutely necessary that we should make ourselves masters of these heights."[30]

News of the English decision reached the besiegers. A crisis impended. With the English army moving out of the town, no man could certainly foretell the issue if, unchecked, it should push forward over either or both peninsulas to an attack upon the American lines. A successful English onslaught might break up the only American army and throw the colonies and their cause into confusion and helplessness. For the safety of America the English must be held in Boston.

The Committee of Safety, June 15, addressed the Provincial Congress, pressing for an immediate augmentation of the army, an immediate remedying of the deficiency in arms, an immediate commissioning of additional officers, and the ordering of all the militiamen in the colony to "hold themselves in readiness to march on the shortest notice"; and made the session historic by passing its famous "Bunker Hill" resolution:

"Whereas, it appears of Importance to the Safety of this Colony, that possession of the Hill, called Bunker's Hill, in Charlestown, be securely kept and defended; and also some

[30] General Burgoyne to Lord Stanley, June 25, 1775, *American Archives,* 4th, II, 1094. See also General Howe to General Harvey, and to his brother, Lord Howe, both of June 12, 1775, *Proceedings of the Bunker Hill Monument Association,* 1907, 111, 115.

one hill or hills on Dorchester Neck be likewise Secured. Therefore, Resolved, Unanimously, that it be recommended to the Council of War, that the abovementioned Bunker's Hill be maintained, by sufficient force being posted there; and as the particular situation of Dorchester Neck is unknown to this Committee, they advise that the Council of War take and pursue such steps respecting the Same, as to them shall appear to be for the Security of this Colony."

All histories have it that the result of the action of the council of war on this resolution of the Committee of Safety was Ward's order to fortify Bunker Hill—and the resolution and order have been variously interpreted: as a step of almost blind recklessness, a desperate hazard, occasioned by the urgent necessity to do something to check the British plans to raise the siege; as a move to offset the British intention to take Dorchester Neck; as an act of defiance calculated to bring on a general engagement; as the first step in the contemplated expulsion of the English from Boston.

But the determination at which the council of war of June 15 actually arrived was of a character much bolder—no less than a sudden tightening of the lines around the British forces by the simultaneous fortification of *both Bunker Hill and Dorchester Neck*.

Facing the next page (118), there printed for the first time, is a facsimile of the record of this decision in the handwriting of Ward's secretary.

At earlier meetings, Ward and Joseph Warren had opposed the fortification of Bunker Hill until the American forces could be better equipped. But the English onslaught, long threatened, long deferred, was at last imminent, and resolve ran high to drive boldly forward to block it.

The supply of powder was still very low, but the army had been acquiring regimental form as company after company filled up, and it had achieved a little military experience in the skirmishes of the preceding weeks; so now that the Committee of Safety had placed the issue before them, recommending the occupation of Bunker Hill but leaving the matter of Dorchester Neck to their discretion, the council of war with true New England courage unanimously decided on occupying *both.*

The Bunker Hill project alone had seemed rash a month earlier, but now twice as bold a movement was accepted without a dissenting voice, and a joint committee of the council of war and the Committee of Safety rode at once to Roxbury to consult with Thomas and his staff.

No previous history has told this because there was no record of the resolve to the historian's hand at the time that most histories of the Revolution were written, and when twenty-nine years ago the original manuscript came to light at the sale of the Thomas Raffles Collection, the history of the siege had settled into such a well-defined mold that later historians have overlooked that ancient piece of writing. Even iconoclasts have found opportunity only in new or multiplied criticisms of strategy, tactics, or personalities.[31]

Histories in general state, or leave the impression, that Ward advised against the fortification of Bunker Hill, confusing his objections of an earlier date with the council of war of June 15. The resolution of the council of war of June 15 is proof that he approved the project. A council divided against Bunker Hill, with the chief character opposed,

[31] It is possible that some students failed to remember that the title "Dorchester Neck" was at that time applied to the Dorchester peninsula, not (as in the maps found in most histories) to the isthmus connecting it with the mainland. The isthmus, the modern "Washington Village," was then known as the "Little Neck."

A "Neck" may be either a peninsula or an isthmus. In some cases, a change in popular usage has shifted a "Neck" title from a peninsula to an isthmus. "Boston Neck" is a good example of such a shift: it had first been employed to signify Boston, the peninsula (the deposition of "John Odlin and others," and the Indian deed of 1685, etc.), but later it came to mean instead the isthmus connecting Boston, the peninsula, with the mainland. "Charlestown Neck" also signified an isthmus. But "Dorchester Neck" was never employed up to the time of Bunker Hill, except to signify the Dorchester *peninsula*—and it adhered as the official title of the peninsula for another twenty-nine years, when annexation to the City of Boston brought its present title of South Boston.

Head Quarters 15 June 1775

Resolved in Council of War to take immediate Possession of Bunker's Hill, and Dorchester Neck.

J Ward Secry

In Committee of Safety.

Cambridge June 15 1775

Whereas it appears of Importance to the Safety of this Colony, that Possession of the Hill called Bunker's Hill in Charlestown, be securely kept, and defended; & also some one hill or hills on Dorchester be likewise secured. Therefore Resolved Unanimously that it be recommended to the Council of War, that the above mentioned Bunker's Hill be maintained by sufficient force being posted there; and as the particular situation of Dorchester Neck is unknown to this Committee they advise that the Council of War, take and pursue such steps respecting the same, as to them shall appear to be for the security of this Colony.

Benja White Chairman

Col. Joseph Palmer }
Capt. Benja White } Sub Committee from Committee of Safety

Genl Putnam }
Col. Ward } Committee from Council War
Col. Gerrish }

The above Committees are appointed to consult with the Commanding Officers at Roxbury respecting the expediency of carrying the above Resolutions into Execution

J Ward Secry

From the original (6¼ × 7¾), owned by the Boston Public Library

THE RESOLUTION OF THE COUNCIL OF WAR, JUNE 15, 1775, TO OCCUPY BOTH BUNKER HILL AND DORCHESTER NECK

Read *first* the center resolution headed "In Committee of Safety." This is a copy, by Ward's secretary, of the Committee of Safety resolution which recommended the fortification of Bunker Hill, but left the matter of Dorchester Neck to the judgment of the Council of War.

Read *next* the top section—the resolution of the Council of War to take possession of both Bunker Hill and Dorchester Neck.

Read *last* the bottom of the manuscript—the record of the committees appointed to go to Roxbury to consult with General Thomas and his officers.

It is possible that the manuscript should be read straight down from top to bottom, thus giving the Council of War credit also for initiating the resolution, but the form of the resolution, considered with the minutes of the Committee of Safety, makes it almost certain that the above sequence is correct.

could not have unanimously agreed to double the risk by taking Dorchester Neck also.

Thomas and his Roxbury council evidently voted against the occupation of Dorchester Neck, for again the plan was set aside. One may dream a great variety of dreams as to the result of the simultaneous fortification of Bunker Hill and Dorchester Heights by the Americans on the night of June 16. Perhaps, if Thomas had acceded, it would have been June *15*—note the *"immediate"* of the council of war resolution.

The Roxbury decision did not, however, dampen the ardor of the headquarters generals. They held to their determination to fortify Bunker Hill, and on the following day (June 16) Ward issued his orders for the movement.

Colonel Prescott was given command of the detachment. His force: the greater part of his own, Frye's, and Bridge's regiments; Samuel Gridley's artillery company; and about two hundred of Putnam's Connecticut men—a total of about 1200. His instructions: to proceed that evening to Bunker Hill, build fortifications to be laid out by Colonel Richard Gridley, and defend them until he should be relieved.

The coöperation of the right division at Roxbury being impossible, and the center division at Cambridge being incapable of heavy withdrawals without weakening it to a dangerous degree, the decision to take Bunker Hill was a step bold to the point of rashness. It meant that Ward, with only 5000, or fewer, effectives,[32] including Putnam's Connecticut men,

[32] Ward's center division numbered during the week preceding Bunker Hill about 7500 rank and file, including the Connecticut men and Sargent's small command, but the "fit for duty" proportion at that period—*i.e.*, the regimental strength after deducting the sick and the absent and those necessarily held "on command"—seldom averaged more than two-thirds and generally fell below it. Hence the above estimate of "5000, or fewer, effectives."

The main body of the division consisted of sixteen Massachusetts regiments, returning a total strength of 6063 privates in a General Report of June 9 preserved in the *Massachusetts Archives* and printed in Frothingham's *Siege of Boston,* 118, note. (Frothingham's figure for Gridley's regiment should be corrected to 379 and the "Drummers, etc." line to read, "officers, drummers, fifers, &c.") I have found no general report closer to June 17. There are in the *Massachusetts Archives,* CXLVI, separate returns of several of the regiments dated after June 9 and before June 17, but the net change they effect in the total is not important.

must hold his center secure from attack and support his left while fortifying a dangerously exposed eminence within the range of both the English land and water artillery.

At noon, Ward and a number of other officers went out on Charlestown peninsula to reconnoiter Bunker Hill and its surroundings.[33]

Charlestown peninsula was at that time of the general shape of a conventional isosceles triangle, set a trifle south of southeast from its neck. It was a little more than a mile in length, and less than a mile in width at its base, the angles of its base pointing south and east.

The Mystic River flowed down its northeast side; a mill-pond and a small bay bounded it on the west. On the south, the passage to the, larger, "back bay" separated it from Boston.

The easterly side of the peninsula was laid out chiefly in hay fields and pastures: their strong dividing fences—of stone and timber—were on the following day to prove a serious obstruction to the English troops.

The westerly side was devoted in large part to orchards and gardens.

Covering the south point, stood Charlestown itself—save one, the oldest town of the Massachusetts Bay Colony.

The northerly face of Bunker Hill commenced its rise a little distance south of Charlestown Neck and presented an easy incline of about 350 yards to its smoothly rounded summit, 110 feet in maximum height and roughly elliptical in form, its long axis extending about 500 yards southeast by east. On both sides (easterly and westerly) it sloped toward the water. Southerly, it was connected by a stretch of high ground with the smaller hill called Breed's Hill.

Breed's Hill attained a maximum height of seventy-five feet. Its southerly slope reached to the houses of Charlestown, and its summit, about 600 yards from the shore, looked

[33] The Narrative of Major Thompson Maxwell, *Essex Institute Historical Collections*, VII, 107.

across a ribbon of water onto the Copp's Hill section of Boston.

Easterly of Breed's Hill were clay pits and brick kilns, and both northerly and easterly was a good deal of sloughy ground.

The two peninsulas (Charlestown and Boston) faced each other like miming marionettes (see map facing page 92). The water separating them was only about a quarter-mile in width.

CHAPTER VI

June 16–17, 1775: Age 47

Prescott's detachment for the fortification of Bunker Hill. Arrangements for its relief. The change to Breed's Hill. The battle told from headquarters standpoint. The day after the battle—the depression in Boston, and the excitement and apprehension in the surrounding towns. The English decision to abandon Boston.

A FEW short hours after Ward's return to headquarters from Bunker Hill, Prescott's men paraded on Cambridge common.

Pens of all kinds—well informed and otherwise—have told of the assembling of the detachment and its evening march for the Charlestown peninsula: two sergeants with dark lanterns leading the way; then the tall form of Prescott at the head of his men; and, in the rear, the carts loaded with intrenching tools. Instead of recounting the story in the coldness of the printed black and white, let us conjure it up in the warmth of living thought. Let us hope that we all possess sufficient imagination to picture those brave men as they went silently on their way. Uncover and bow your head with reverence as they pass, for on the morrow many of them will die in the bloodiest of all of the battles of the American Revolution.

Prescott's detachment was to be relieved the following evening by a force of about equal strength—the Nixon, Little, and Mansfield regiments, and 200 Connecticut troops. This relief party "with two days provisions and well equipped with arms and ammunition" to be on "parade at five o'clock ready to march."[1]

At Ward's headquarters—an evening and a night of

[1] The relief order, recorded in the orderly book kept by Nathan Stow, sergeant of Abishai Brown's company, Nixon's regiment, is an important addition to the history of the battle, for previous accounts have left the subject of relief or reinforcement vague and contradictory.

Frothingham's *Siege of Boston,* 122, cites Brooks and Swett as authority for the statement that "it was understood that reinforcements and refreshments should be sent to Colonel Prescott on the following morning." On a later page (127)—with "Brooks' Statement; Swett's History; Prescott's Memoir" as authorities—it says that Prescott told his men "that he would never consent to their being relieved." Thus it would seem that though *reinforcements* were expected (in the morning), Prescott did not expect or want *relief* (in the morning). The two expressions "relief" and "reinforcement" are, however, so loosely used that it is not safe to attach great importance to their comparative meanings or positions.

At an earlier date (March, 1818, 256) the *Analectic Magazine,* in citing "Particulars respecting the action," collected from Brooks and others, had stated that "There was some diversity of opinion as to the course to be pursued and what message should be sent to the commander-in-chief at Cambridge." Relief was urged by some, but Prescott said "No." . . . "It was determined to request the other three companies of Bridge's regiment to be sent as a reinforcement."

The "Prescott MS." (Butler's *History of Groton,* 337; and elsewhere) deposes that General Ward stated "that the party should be *relieved* the next morning." Also, however, that, next morning, Prescott refused to "request the commander to relieve them"—but said he would send for reinforcements.

The "Judge Prescott Account" (*Massachusetts Historical Society Proceedings,* XIV, 68; and elsewhere) contains in different form the same ideas: "The officers . . . urged him to send to the Commander-in-chief and request him to relieve them according to his engagement or at least to send a reinforcement. . . . The Colonel at once told them that he would never consent to their being relieved . . . but he would send for reinforcements and provisions."

Prescott's own account has nothing on the subject.

The Stow record clears away the mist and presents a clearly defined plan—Prescott's detachment to be relieved on the following evening (Saturday, June 17) by a new force of equal strength.

Though agreed upon at the time of planning the occupation of Bunker Hill, the relief orders were not issued until the following morning, for the enterprise was a close secret.

Putnam signed the orders for the Connecticut men. At least two examples survive: one in the orderly book by Moses Fargo, William Coit's company, *Connecticut Historical Society Collections,* VII, 22 (the hour for the parading of the relief party given as 6, instead of 5 P.M.); the other in that of Captain John Chester (?), *Massachusetts Historical Society Proceedings,* XIV, 91.

Nathan Stow died April 15, 1810, and his wife, Abigail, four days later. His estate descended by inheritance and purchase to two sons, Nathan and Cyrus. Nathan died November 10, 1831, and the homestead and its contents became the property of Cyrus. Cyrus died September 8, 1876, and his widow, Matilda, March 13, 1878. As they had no children, their family effects were sold at auction. The old papers in the attic were bought by a junkman, and by him sold for a nominal sum to Albert E. Wood, a well-known resident of Concord. Among them Mr. Wood found Sergeant Nathan Stow's Orderly Book.

Albert P. Putnam in 1896, and earlier, quoted the June 17 entries in letters to the Danvers (Mass.) *Mirror.* In 1901 he reprinted his 1896 letter, with a number of others on the Putnam-Prescott controversy, in a pamphlet "Gen. Israel Putnam and

anxious thought. Will Prescott succeed in fortifying the hill without arousing the enemy? If attacked before the works are strong enough to shield his men, what will be the fate of his little army? And if the defenses *are* completed without disturbing the English sentries—what next? What will be the English counter-move? An attack on Prescott's position? A drive at the American center by way of Lechmere's Point or Willis Creek? Or . . . Dorchester Neck? Will the American occupation of the Charlestown peninsula cause the English to change their plan to seize Dorchester Neck, or will they carry it out nevertheless, and, thence, try to raise the siege by attacking the Roxbury lines?

Meantime happened that midsummer night's madness:—that protracted officers' conference near the foot of Bunker Hill which resulted in as bold a case of gauntlet-throwing as history anywhere relates—the substitution of Breed's Hill for Bunker Hill[2] and Gridley's deliberate marking out of a redoubt on the lower hill directly facing Boston.

The fortification of Bunker Hill would have held Charles-

the Battle of Bunker Hill." He pointed out the new light shed by the June 17 entries but used them chiefly to aid his claim for Putnam preëminence.

The orderly book was published in 1893–4, in Eben Putnam's *Monthly Historical Magazine,* Salem, Mass., a periodical devoted principally to genealogy. In a prefatory letter in the issue of March, 1893, A. P. Putnam directed attention to the entries of June 17 with the remark that everything appearing on that day is of interest, but he apparently did not realize their specific importance.

The orderly book was evidently unknown to otherwise well-informed writers of histories published several years after A. P. Putnam's use of it. This is probably due to the obscure mediums in which it was given space—a local newspaper; a small pamphlet of reprints from the same paper devoted to the interminable Putnam-Prescott controversy; and a local genealogical magazine.

The original is now in the Public Library, Concord, Mass.

[2] The majority weight of circumstantial evidence supports the generally accepted opinion that the fortifying of *Bunker Hill* was ordered and that the change to Breed's Hill was made after consultation on the ground.

Prescott's letter of August 25, 1775, to John Adams (Frothingham, *Siege of Boston,* 395) speaks of his orders to fortify "Breed's Hill," but this, though followed in Bancroft's *History of the United States,* is usually taken as an unintentional mistake. The letter was written many years before Bunker Hill discussions and arguments became popular, and, hence, Prescott may be forgiven for not having employed the care in differentiating the two hills that would have been exercised by a writer of later date.

Both the "Prescott MS." and the "Judge Prescott Account" have *Bunker Hill* as the original order, but both also state that the two hills were at that time generally covered by the one name of "Bunker Hill"—the title "Breed's Hill" for the southern elevation being of only local usage.

The Committee of Safety report says that Breed's Hill was fortified "by some mistake."

General Orders June 17th 1775

Parole Deerfield
Countersign Conaway

Field Officer of the Day Lt. Mason
Col Greift

Field Officer of the Picquit to Night
Majr Wood

Field Officer of the Main Guard
Lt Col. Baldwin

Ajutant of the Day

General orders Head Quarters June
17th 1775 That Col Nixon Col
Little Col Mansfield with their
Regts & 200 Connecticut Troops
with 2 Days provision and well
equipted with Armes & Ammunition
march to relieve Col prescot
Col Fry & Col Bridge's Regts
Charlestown that the provisions
be well Dressed before they march
from camp & that they be on the
parade at 5 o Clock ready to march

Regimental Orders
That the several Companies
in my Regt parade prefisely
at five o Clock this afternoon
at our alarum posts with 2 Days
provision well Dressed their armes
& ammunition in Good order
ready to march in agreeable to
night Orders John Nixon Col

From *Nathan Stow's Orderly Book* owned by the Concord (Mass.) Public Library (slightly reduced)

WARD'S ORDER FOR THE RELIEF OF THE BUNKER HILL DETACHMENT

town Neck fairly safe against an enemy attempt to land there to cut off the detachment, for the Neck would have lain between the double protection of Prescott's men on the hill and Reed's regiment on the mainland. Breed's Hill could have been occupied later, if Bunker Hill had proved defensible, just as, in the following March, Nook Hill was fortified after Dorchester Heights had been secured. Moving forward to Breed's Hill on that night of June 16 greatly increased the danger of the detachment, for it left an unoccupied commanding height between it and the Neck.

The choice is made, however, and picks and spades set immediately to the task—plying hurriedly but most efficiently.

Gridley's lines call for a rectangular redoubt about 130 feet square, with projecting angles to the south. The ramparts to be about six feet high.

A few short hours of whispered earnest labor—and then the day breaks. The redoubt is nearly finished!

As the English discover it, they rub their eyes in amazement. Yesterday evening, an empty hill; at dawn, a fortified enemy position: and the work done under the very muzzles of their cannon without a sentry having been alarmed.

The English ships and forts open fire, but the Americans keep steadily at work.

In Cambridge, hard upon the firing of the *Lively* (the first English ship to bark), Putnam calls at headquarters to consult Ward before riding out to view the result of the night's labors which are to make Prescott's men world-famous.

It is still early in the morning when he returns to make his report. He urges the sending of reinforcements.[3] Ward orders forward two hundred men of Stark's regiment (on the left at Medford),[4] but decides against drawing any more

[3] Despite this request for additional men, Putnam fully agreed with Ward on the necessity of strongly guarding the Cambridge position against attack. His forenoon instructions to his lieutenant-colonel were *not* immediately to bring his men onto the peninsula, but to get ready for the later relief decided upon. (See extract from Storrs' diary on page 128, note 10.)

[4] Stark's letter to the President of the New Hampshire Provincial Congress, June 19, 1775.—*New Hampshire Provincial Papers,* VII, 522.

men from his Cambridge force until able to judge the British intention, for he has long center lines and the military supplies of the province to defend, and now fewer than 4000 effective men for the purpose.

After the conference with Putnam, Ward leaves headquarters to see if preparations are under way for the relief detachment.[5]

At ten o'clock Major Brooks arrives at Cambridge to press for reinforcements, but Ward declines to add to the order just dispatched to Colonel Stark.

The Committee of Safety is next to urge additional troops; and Devens, a prominent member, goes to Ward and demands that they be sent.

Ward refuses to change the disposition of his forces or to weaken his center by even so much as a corporal's guard until the English plans are shown.[6]

[5] Colonel Daniel Putnam's Letter, *Connecticut Historical Society Collections,* I, 240.

[6] The conventional method of telling the story is to say that at "about 11 o'clock" or "later in the morning," Ward ordered forward Reed's and (the main body of) Stark's regiments to reinforce Prescott; but Reed's and (the main body of) Stark's regiments were not ordered forward until the time of the general "alarm"—between noon and 1 P.M. The best authority on the movements of Stark's regiment is Stark's letter (already cited—page 125, note 4) to the President of the New Hampshire Provincial Congress, written on the second day after the battle while details were fresh in his mind. In it, Stark records Ward's morning instructions to send 200 men to Prescott's assistance, and the detailing of Lieutenant-Colonel Wyman with a force of that number. He then adds that "about 2 o'clock in the afternoon express orders came for the whole of my regiment to proceed to Charlestown to oppose the enemy who were landing on Charlestown point." This agrees considerably better with the arrival of the regiment on the battlefield than do the conventional accounts. "About 2 o'clock"—between 1 and 2 o'clock—any time after 1 o'clock (Dearborn stated that the regiment marched at "about 1 o'clock")—is when one might expect a message to get through to Stark if dispatched when (between 12 and 1 o'clock) the news was received at Cambridge of the first English landing. Numerous stories of the battle have told (in conjunction with accounts of the supposed "11 o'clock" or "later in the morning" order) that Stark was delayed by the necessity to make up his ammunition and it is assumed that this explains why many of the men marching on the "noon" to "1 o'clock" alarm got to the field before he did. The making up of the ammunition is apparently well attested, but it also fits in with the "about 2 o'clock" order, for when, in the morning, Stark found that part of his regiment was ordered into action, it is not unreasonable to presume that he began making preparations against further orders and was ready to march promptly on their receipt.

As Reed's and Stark's regiments are always coupled in these orders, and in their movements on June 17, it is probably correct to state that Reed's regiment also was not ordered forward until the time of the general alarm. Otherwise, because of its proximity to the battleground, its long delay in reaching the field would have required a great deal of explaining.

Ward has been charged with hesitancy and indecision on the day of the "Battle of Bunker Hill"—the irrevocable title of the action despite the change to Breed's Hill. If those who disagree with his judgment had accused him of being *stubborn*,[7] they would have assumed a defensible position. But "hesitating and "indecisive"!—the witnesses prove that such statements are very far from the truth.

Ward was again suffering from a severe attack of calculus, and his condition lends an element of the dramatic to his stand on that fateful morning—the "sulky" man whom Hutchinson had tried in vain to bribe, now in a day of sickness, as commander of the rebel forces, inflexibly holding to what he believes to be right in the face of entreaty, arguments, and demands, and successfully maintaining it in the face of all opposition.

In Boston, is much stir and discussion. Short of moving to raise the siege, the English officers have no choice but to dislodge the Americans on Breed's Hill, for another day may see heavier cannon mounted, with Boston as a point-blank target. There is, though, difference of opinion as to the tactics to be employed.

General Clinton and other officers want to cut the Americans off by taking them in the rear, but General Gage opposes this.

The English officers decide to carry the post by storm—they will "take the bull by the horns"—and "teach the impudent Yankees a lesson"!

Then to Cambridge between twelve and one o'clock[8] comes news of the landing of the British troops on the peninsula! The alarm is sounded: bells ring, the drums beat

[7] This adjective was applied by one critic—Curtis Guild, Jr., in his address at the 1910 meeting of the Bunker Hill Monument Association.

[8] Captain Chester (Spencer's regiment) is the authority usually quoted to fix the time that the alarm was given: he says "about 1 o'clock" and "just after dinner." The testimony of Jesse Smith (Nixon's regiment) was similar to that of Chester.—Frothingham, *Siege of Boston*, 132, note. Lieutenant-Colonel Storrs (Putnam's regiment) says "at noon" (see diary extract, page 128, note 10). Caleb Haskell, fifer in Captain Lunt's company (Little's regiment), states that the army "set out" after news that the "enemy were landing at Charlestown."—*Caleb Haskell's Diary*.

to arms. The English commander has at last shown his hand—and Ward orders a strong force forward to meet him. All available men of nine Massachusetts regiments, part of Gridley's regiment of artillery, and one of the remaining companies of Bridge's regiment set out at once for the battlefield. And an express rider gallops to Charlestown common and thence to Medford to summon Reed's and Stark's New Hampshire men to the fray.[9]

At the same time Captain Israel Putnam, Jr., brings word from his father, and orders forward his own company and the center contingent of Spencer's men.[10]

Ward's center division is now reduced to the Jonathan Ward and Gardner regiments; rather more than half of Putnam's Connecticut men; Sargent's small command (posted at Lechmere's Point); and two companies of Bridge's regiment. It is guarded on the left by Patterson's regiment, held at the breastwork near Prospect Hill.

The Jonathan Ward regiment is marched to Lechmere's Point to join Sargent's men as a vanguard to meet any attempt of the British to attack via Willis Creek.

[9] See foot-note on page 126, note 6.

[10] Frothingham (*Siege of Boston,* 188) refers to a statement that all of Putnam's regiment was in the action, and also says (132), "General Putnam ordered on the remainder of the Connecticut troops"—giving Chester's letter (July 22, 1775, *Siege of Boston,* 389) as authority. Chester's letter suggests the idea, but the diary of Storrs, lieutenant-colonel of Putnam's regiment, and the casualty list show that the instructions to the Connecticut men were limited as I have given them above.

Following is Storrs' entry for June 17 (*Massachusetts Historical Society Proceedings,* XIV, 85–86):

"At sun rise this morning a fire began from the ships, but moderate; about 10 went down to Gen. Putnam's post who has the command. Some shot whistled around us. Tarried there a spell and returned to have my company in readiness to relieve them; one killed and one wounded when I came away."

"About 2 o'clock there was a brisk cannonade from the ships on the battery or entrenchment. At noon orders came to turn out immediately, and that the regulars were landed at sundry places. Went to headquarters for our regimental. Received orders to repair with our regiment to No. 1 and defend it. No enemy appearing, orders soon came that our people at the entrenchment were retreating and for us to secure the retreat. I immediately marched for their relief, the regulars did not come off from Bunker's Hill, but have taken possession of the entrenchments, and our people make a stand on Winter Hill and we immediately went to entrenching; flung up by morning an entrenchment about 100 feet square. Done principally by our regiment under Putnam's directions, had but little sleep the night."

Gardner's regiment is sent to join Patterson, taking the place of Doolittle's regiment, which is marching to Charlestown.

The Putnam men are drawn in toward Cambridge.

The two companies of Bridge's regiment are posted for the immediate protection of headquarters.

At Roxbury, also, all was activity. The English commander might attempt a diversion by a drive from the Boston Neck lines. Every man was ordered to arms, and Colonel Learned marched his regiment to the meeting-house and thence to the burying-yard, which was the alarm-post, and there placed his men in ambush with two field-pieces "placed to give it to them unawares, should the regulars come."[11]

At Cambridge, the noise and excitement died down as regiment after regiment passed on. The town, says David Townsend, a young man studying medicine under Joseph Warren, was "quiet as the Sabbath." Breathless tension succeeded the hurry of forming and marching troops. American and English forces were for the first time opposed in formal battle. Prescott's men had challenged; Gage had accepted the challenge; and all that Massachusetts stood for was at stake.

Ward had done the utmost that lay in his power. His center was carved lean of troops and stripped all but bare of powder.

He was again out (presumably on a tour of inspection) when Townsend called at headquarters.[12] The only man there was Dr. Warren, just appointed Massachusetts' second major-general, also indisposed that day and taking a much needed rest.

On Townsend's arrival Warren rose and left the house, riding direct to the battlefield on which before the sun set he was to lay down his life. When he reached the redoubt he cheered Prescott's men—all of them fatigued, some

[11] Samuel Bixby's Diary, *Massachusetts Historical Society Proceedings,* XIV, 287.

[12] *New England Historical and Genealogical Register,* XII, 230.

of them hungry and thirsty[13]—by telling them that 2000 additional troops would be with them in twenty minutes; that he had passed them on the way.

The English complete their debarkation at Moulton's Point without mishap or interruption, but Howe, who commands them, sees that the American position is stronger than it had appeared and he sends word for additional troops. He awaits their arrival before beginning the attack.

Back in Cambridge, when Ward learns that the English troops on the Charlestown peninsula are being reinforced, and that there is consequently little danger of a raid on Cambridge via Willis Creek,[14] he orders Sargent and Jonathan Ward[15] also on to Charlestown.

[13] The orders to Prescott's detachment required "provisions for 24 hours," but some—perhaps a considerable number—of the men had failed to husband their supplies. Efforts were made by Devens and others to send fresh supplies, but horses were scarce. A few wagons crossed, but the cannonade frothing over the Neck, though not very dangerous, was effective in checking vehicular traffic. The want most keenly and most generally felt was for liquid refreshments. This fact has been translated into pathetic accounts of the longing for drinking water: "and, the greatest want of all, they lacked the delicious draught of pure, cool water for their labor-worn and heat exhausted frames" (*Ellis*); "during the whole day they received not even a cup of cold water" (*Bancroft*); and, similarly, with variations, many other writers. But what those New England farmers were awaiting was their *rum, beer,* or *cider.* If the men had merely wanted *water,* they could have obtained plenty of it from the houses along the main road and from the wells in Charlestown. Charlestown was in their undisputed possession during the entire morning. Contemporary depositions state that some barrels of beer were received (Frothingham's *Siege of Boston,* 133, note; Winsor's *Narrative and Critical History of America,* VI, 137), and in the Boston Public Library is the order signed by Joseph Ward, as secretary, for two barrels of rum "for the Troops at Charlestown." But the quantities that reached the men were not sufficient to meet their needs or desires.

[14] About the same time he also perhaps received word from Colonel Sargent, at Lechmere's Point, that the schooner Sargent mentioned in his letter of long after had given up the attempt to make a landing by Willis Creek. "A large schooner, with from five to six hundred men, attempted to gain the landing, but the wind against her and the tide turning, she returned. About 4 P.M., General Ward permitted me to march my regiment with one called his own to Charlestown."—Paul Dudley Sargent to S. Swett, December 20, 1825 (Frothingham's *Command in the Battle of Bunker Hill,* 10).

[15] Washburn's *History of Leicester,* 304, and A. H. Ward's *History of Shrewsbury,* 55, have the story of the halting of Jonathan Ward's regiment on the mainland side of Charlestown Neck by a horseman who declared (Washburn's *Leicester*) that "orders had been sent that no more troops should go into action." Part of the Jonathan Ward regiment, nevertheless, in defiance of the order, marched across the Neck and toward the battlefield in time to help cover the retreat from the redoubt. According to tradition the horseman was Benjamin Church, but other circumstances make this doubtful.

Shortly after, Gardner, too, sets his regiment in motion, drawn in the same direction.[16]

Meanwhile, what of that first main force dispatched to Prescott's assistance?

After leaving Cambridge, there is a great deal of confusion, for the men are not yet experienced soldiers. They start out as companies and regiments, but many units lose formation and become inextricably tangled. Some troops fail to cross Charlestown Neck; others halt on Bunker Hill instead of pressing forward. Some do not reach the firing line until the battle is almost over; many do not reach it at all.[17]

The American positions are nevertheless fairly well manned by the time the English are ready to attack. And, in one form or another, they all but span the peninsula.

The redoubt and its breastwork extension running north-by-east down the hill, are held by Massachusetts men under Prescott's direct command. As also, with one company of New Hampshire men, is the short impromptu line to the right.

The breastwork is about 300 feet in length and reaches to a piece of sloughy ground that has been mentioned so often that it has become known as "the Slough."

In the redoubt is Dr. Warren. He has set aside his high

[16] Gardner's instructions had been to assist Patterson in holding the position later known as Fort No. 3, but inactivity within sight of the first pitched battle of the siege galled him because of what he considered a stigma on his reputation the sudden dispersal of his command in the battle of April 19.

[17] Of the nine Massachusetts regiments ordered forward in force between 12 and 1 o'clock, five (Brewer's, Nixon's, Little's, Doolittle's, Woodbridge's) were represented on the firing line at the time of the first attack—about 3 P.M. The additional company of Bridge's regiment also was there, and one new company of Gridley's artillery. Later in the action, two other regiments were represented on the field—Asa Whitcomb's and Gerrish's (the latter by Adjutant Febiger's detachment); and Trevett brought on his company of Gridley's artillery in time to do good service. The other regiments and parts of regiments failed to be represented because their commanders misconstrued or disobeyed orders and halted at other points: on the wrong side of the Neck, as Mansfield's regiment, Major Scarborough Gridley's companies of Gridley's regiment, a part of Gerrish's regiment under Captain Mighil, and Scammon's regiment (Scammon's regiment did cross the Neck but not until the fighting was over); or on Bunker Hill proper, as part of Gerrish's regiment under Colonel Gerrish.

military appointment and is serving as a volunteer in the ranks.

Behind the "rail fence"—that famous hay-stuffed double fence, and its stone wall extension—starting from a point near the base of Bunker Hill and reaching across to the shore of the Mystic River, are Colonels Stark and Reed with their New Hampshire regiments; Captain Knowlton with the original Connecticut detachment, and some Massachusetts men.

The weakest point of the line is between the slough and the rail fence. It is only slightly protected by short stretches of fence or hedge. Part of the time it is defended by the few American cannon brought on.

A second line of defense—of earth breastworks—has been commenced on Bunker Hill.

The English reinforcements land at about three o'clock.

There is no longer any sign of life in the redoubt. The English officers begin to fear that the Americans have retreated and that there will be no fight.

But the Americans are there—coolly awaiting the enemy.

Their officers have ordered them to lie low and hold their fire until the English are within sixty yards.

The redcoats advance in two divisions—one under Howe to flank the American position by turning or breaking through the rail fence; the other, under Pigot, to storm the redoubt and breastwork.

They move slowly, for they are burdened with full knapsacks, hindered by the field fences, and sweltered by a hot June sun. But they feel unbounded confidence in their strength and expect an easy victory.

The English draw near to the American positions.

The Americans receive the order to fire!

A sudden hail of bullets stops the English advance and mows down the ranks.

A few minutes the redcoats hold firm—then they fall back in full retreat!

The American farmers have won the first round against the famed soldiers of Great Britain!

A short breathing space—then the English rally and advance again.

Charlestown meantime had been set ablaze, completing an extraordinarily spectacular panorama of war and destruction:

An earth-fort set upon a hill; further back, a fragile fence line stretching to the shore. A brilliantly accoutered army advancing over their dead comrades to the assault. Shells and cannon-balls belching from ships and land-batteries; flames coursing the streets of Charlestown and curling up its church spires. Hundreds of spectators on the surrounding hills and the roof-tops of Boston.

The English are within thirty yards of the American lines when the militiamen receive the order to fire.

Again their bullets tear through the enemy's ranks with terrible effect.

The English press forward a few steps in the face of the storm—but it is too deadly—and again they retreat, this time precipitously and in blank disorder.

There is a longer interval now, and some on both sides think, and hope, that the fighting is over for the day.

Instead, the English general is making new plans. He has learned that it is not always easy to "take the bull by the horns," and for this third assault he adopts new tactics.

He trains his artillery, hitherto misplaced and ill-handled, so that the cannon-balls penetrate the end of the breastwork and scour its length, driving its defenders into the redoubt; then concentrates his attack on the redoubt, telling his men to hold their fire and take the position at the point of the bayonet.

As Howe moves his men forward for a third assault, Prescott realizes that his position is desperate. His powder is almost exhausted, and cannon-shot come crashing into the redoubt through the north passageway.

But he has no thought except to fight to the last moment! His men reserve their fire until the English are within twenty yards. But this time the enemy push forward without returning it—the American fire slackens for want of ammunition and the Englishmen crowd up to and over the parapet.

The Americans fight their way out of the redoubt and through the two divisions closing in on them.

The English attempt to flank in force, but are held back by the men at the rail fence and a few gallant companies of late arrivals descending Bunker Hill. The American death toll is heavy here; and—unhappy day for his beloved Massachusetts—Joseph Warren is among those who fall.

The Americans retreat over Bunker Hill. On its brow Putnam tries to make another stand—but the projected breastworks are not half built and the position is too exposed, so the retreat continues over Charlestown Neck.

The English have won the battle, but they have been so severely handled that Howe fears the risk of following the Americans onto the mainland.

Instead, the two shaken armies settle themselves on opposite sides of the Neck and feverishly begin throwing up protective works: the English on Bunker Hill facing the mainland; the Americans on Prospect and Winter hills.

And thus the sun went down on the bullet-riddled fences and the blood-stained fields, and the long summer evening brought to a close the most eventful day in American history.

The officers on both sides were glad of the respite from active hostilities, but there was no truce in the hearts of the venturesome of the American rank and file. Darkness had scarcely fallen when a number of them were, as individuals, trying to carry the fight back to the enemy, sniping from the cover of isolated houses and creeping toward the English advance lines on the Neck in search of enemy targets.[18]

[18] Martin Hunter, later a general of His Majesty's Forces, then ensign of the 52d Regiment of Foot, recorded that attacks on his regiment were made all through the

Nor did the coming of darkness bring any pause in the American labor on the new lines—picks and shovels plied unceasingly to make ready for the redcoats if they should follow up their advantage by a night assault.

Once only during the night did the work stop—and that when shortly before dawn there came an alarm that the English were sallying out from Bunker Hill with artillery and light horse. Every man was ordered to drop his tools and stand to his arms.

But the redcoats came not. And within an hour of daybreak Ward had strengthened the new Prospect Hill post with a thousand Massachusetts and Connecticut men drawn from the Roxbury division.[19]

The Sunday that dawned saw in the American camps none of the peace-time New England Sabbath calm. Bullets had

night.—Moorsom, *Historical Record of the 52d Regiment,* 9. Hunter had fought in the battle and was on the following day promoted to lieutenant.

Lieutenant-Colonel Stephen Kemble (Journal, *Kemble Papers,* I, 45) also complained that "All this night the Rebels kept a popping fire on our Advanced Posts, from Houses on the opposite side of Charles Town Neck, wounded several Men, and Killed one officer."

[19] Histories give the impression that the works built on Prospect and Winter hills represented, during the first two or three days following, only the labor of the men who had stopped in the vicinity after the retreat from Breed's Hill. The first reinforcement noted by Frothingham (*Siege of Boston,* 211) is an order of June 20 for one-half of eight Massachusetts regiments to be drafted daily to relieve the troops on Prospect Hill. But they were strengthened in part much earlier—at least as soon as the very early morning after the battle. General Greene tells of the marching of 1000 men from the Roxbury division on the night of June 17 (*Sparks Papers,* XLVIII, f. 68 verso, Harvard College Library); and Samuel Haws of Joseph Read's regiment records (*Military Journals of Two Private Soldiers,* 58, 59) that his regiment was "ordered to cambridge to asist our forces and we reached their about twelve o'clock at night and Lodged in the mēting house"—then at daybreak (18th) marched to Prospect Hill, "expecting to come to an ingagement." Noah Chapin, Jr., ensign of Solomon Willes' company, Spencer's regiment, has much the same story to tell—of marching "in hast" to Prospect Hill, reaching there "a Little after Sun Rise."—Original diary, State Library, Hartford, Conn.

About noon, a new "alarm" caused additional reinforcements to be sent to the hill from the center division.—*Caleb Haskell's Diary,* 6.

As no engagement developed, Read's men were at "about 4 o'clock" ordered back to Roxbury and "arived their about sunset very weary." The Connecticut contingent was also back in Roxbury "a little before night."

On the day following (June 19), one-half (by companies) of seven Massachusetts regiments of the center division and half of the Connecticut forces were ordered to Prospect Hill.—*Nathan Stow's Orderly Book.*

These reinforcements were evidently very pleasing to Putnam, for Cook of Tiverton told Stiles (*Literary Diary of Ezra Stiles,* I, 574) that on June 19 he "saw General Putnam entrenching" on Winter Hill "and in good Spirits being fully reinforced."

to be "run" and cartridges to be made "in readiness for another battle";[20] and fatigue parties were everywhere busy —adding to the Roxbury and Cambridge defenses, as well as to the rapidly developing lines guarding the mainland side of Charlestown Neck—from this date a separate and important division of the besieging army.

It was thought that the enemy would quickly strike afresh to raise the siege.

The roads for miles around were again filled with excited travel—but this time it surged in opposing streams, mutually congesting and obstructing: militiamen hurrying toward the American camps, and women and children from the neighboring towns fleeing back into the country,[21] whole families loaded into big farm-carts, or on horseback, or afoot. And at Watertown the Provincial Congress ordered that a horse be held constantly ready so that the secretary could at a moment's notice ride away with his records. "It is expected that the English will come out over the Neck to-night," wrote Abigail Adams, "and a dreadful battle must ensue. Almighty God! cover the heads of our countrymen, and be a shield to our dear friends."[22]

But in Boston that Sunday no battle plan was contemplated. English cannon roared almost continuously—but it was the defensive roar of a sorely wounded lion, purposed to keep his enemy at bay. There was no thought of so soon retrying the issue with the sharpshooting New England rebels. Gage had driven the Americans from their hastily seized position, and all of the Charlestown peninsula had passed into his hands, but his army had sustained losses so heavy as to lower its morale and to cripple its offensive power. He had removed the immediate menace of Breed's Hill, but he was no nearer freedom of action than before the battle. He had stretched one of the walls of the jail, but the jail still

[20] *Caleb Haskell's Diary*, 6.

[21] James Warren, June 18, 1775, *Warren-Adams Letters*, I, 59.

[22] *Letters of Mrs. Adams*, I, June 18, 1775.

held him prisoner, and its bars now loomed before his eyes as murderously secure.

The battle just fought had indeed definitely decided the outcome of the siege of Boston. It was the direct and specific cause of the evacuation of the capital. The period of English occupation following June 17 constituted, consciously or otherwise, merely so many months of "marking time." Right up to the last dispatch received prior to the news of the Battle of Bunker Hill, official England had held no intention to relinquish Boston. On the contrary, Lord Dartmouth, writing July 1, tells Gage that the King trusts "that we shall soon hear" that the rebels surrounding Boston "have been dispersed, their Works destroyed, and a communication opened with the Country." It was further believed that even if the English force should be deemed inadequate "to advance further into the country," it was nevertheless large enough not only to hold Boston, but also to recover possession of New York, and perhaps, in addition, to seize and maintain a post on Rhode Island.

But Gage's report of the battle changed all this, and within five weeks of the official acknowledgment of its receipt, Lord Dartmouth received word from the King that he considered it not only advisable but "necessary to abandon Boston before the winter."[23]

[23] The story is easily and clearly read in the correspondence between Lord Dartmouth and the English commanders in Boston. At the beginning of the year (January 18, 1775), General Gage had written to Lord Dartmouth that "it's the opinion of Most People, if a respectable Force is seen in the Field, the most obnoxious of the Leaders seized, and a Pardon proclaimed for all other's, that Government will come off Victorious, and with less Opposition than was expected a few Months ago."—*Stevens Transcripts,* Library of Congress. And Lord Dartmouth on April 15 had said, "It is imagined that by the time this Letter reaches you, the army under your Command will be equal to any operation that may become necessary."—*Stevens Transcripts,* Library of Congress; Bancroft MSS., *England and America,* New York Public Library. No doubt then in his mind of the success of the King's army in Boston!

The events of April 19 roused indignation at "the rash and rebellious conduct of the Provincials," but they did not alarm official England. Gage sent his report of the "skirmish" (the report was received in London June 10) and Lord Dartmouth, replying, writes (as quoted above in the main text) that the King trusts "that we shall soon hear" that the rebels surrounding Boston "have been dispersed, their Works destroyed, and a communication opened with the Country." He continues, "Whether you have found it expedient or not to advance further into the Country will have depended upon your own judgement of the utility & propriety of such a plan of operation & upon the advice & opinions of the able Generals by whom you are assisted; but if from the probability of small advantage on the one hand, & great risk on the other hand, you should have desisted from such an enterprise or should have been of opinion that your Force is inadequate, in that case it is hoped that the defence of Boston, & the possession of the circumjacent posts necessary to that defence may be secured by a part of the Army & another part detached under the command of one of the Majors General to recover possession of New York, which is in every light a post of the greatest importance." Turning next to Rhode Island, Lord Dartmouth says, "It is not wished to encourage ideas of a separation of our Force into small detachments that may hazard the loss of the whole, & therefore I shall only observe that the insular part of the Colony of Rhode Island appears to me to be a post of very great advantage, not only from its situation in general but as it would keep open a communication between Boston & New York, & from which either might in case of exigency receive succour & support."—July 1, *Stevens Transcripts,* Library of Congress; Bancroft MSS., *England and America,* New York Public Library.

All such dreams faded after the arrival (July 25) of Gage's report of the battle of Bunker Hill. Lord Dartmouth, who had been so confident of the English position in Boston, quickly decided to relinquish it. In a long letter written a few days after the receipt of the report, he notes the possible necessity of quitting Boston and perhaps removing the entire force to Halifax and Quebec (August 2, *American Archives,* 4th, III, 7); and only four weeks later he sends to Howe (about to succeed Gage) the message (given in the concluding sentence of the main text of this chapter) that the King considers it not only advisable but *"necessary to abandon Boston before the winter"* (September 5, *American Archives,* 4th, III, 642).

Historians have noted the effect of the battle on conditions in Boston, and Gage's—and Howe's—consequent desire to evacuate it; its effect also on public and official opinion in England and elsewhere in Europe; and further that in November there arrived from England instructions to abandon the town: but the direct connection between the battle itself and the evacuation order has been obscured by the length of time required for sailing vessels to make a complete circuit of correspondence between the English commander-in-chief in Boston and the office of the Secretary of State in London. No wireless—no cable—no steamships then! Many students have failed to realize that Lord Dartmouth's letters of August 2 and September 5 were based on conditions of much earlier dates. The report of the battle of June 17 was, as noted above, not received in London until July 25. When Lord Dartmouth prepared his "abandon Boston" letter of September 5, he had in hand only the reports of conditions immediately following the battle. Even at the moment of signing, he was in receipt of no advice of later Boston date than July 26.

One sees also occasional reference to the advice of Lord Barrington, Secretary of War, so early as November 12, 1774, to Lord Dartmouth, that the troops be withdrawn from Boston as "a place where at present they can do no good, and without intention, may do harm."—*Political Life of Wm. Viscount Barrington,* 140. But this advice can have had little, if any, influence with Lord Dartmouth and his associates, for the general plan advocated was diametrically opposed to the royal and ministerial policy. Barrington's idea was to rely exclusively upon the navy to reduce Massachusetts to submission—by cutting off the fisheries, killing commerce, etc. He would have Gage withdraw all troops from the province—first moving them from Boston and then taking them back to England when "a proper juncture shall offer for their return." Barrington's idea of Massachusetts popular sentiment was ludicrously inaccurate. He would have Gage instructed that, on thus removing his troops from Boston, he should remind the people of Massachusetts that it was their own fault that he was abandoning them unprotected to the "tyrannical anarchy" which had come upon them!—that he must leave the colony to be the prey of its own "present distracted state, until it shall become disposed to co-operate in helping itself to a better."

CHAPTER VII

Criticisms of the Battle of Bunker Hill

IN the preceding chapter I have told the story of the Breed's Hill-Bunker Hill battle from headquarters' standpoint. It reads differently from other accounts because it is based in part on contemporary records hitherto overlooked, but I have been careful to avoid personal bias and have eschewed embellishment and partisan argument.

I have no quarrel with those who criticize either the conception or the execution of the battle.[1] There is room for honest disagreement on both, and hindsight can always find points on which to hang or by which to bolster an argument.

[1] The animadversions of James Warren, of Plymouth, are considered on pages 142, 162–163. See also the reference to Henry Dearborn, of New Hampshire, on page 142. Other criticisms are either milder or in their exaggeration hold an element of humor:

Lieutenant Samuel B. Webb could in his Connecticut enthusiasm find no good in any general officer except Putnam! He wrote, June 19, 1775: "For God's sake, to urge Gen. Lee and Col. Washington to join, head-officers is what we stand greatly in need of; *we have no acting head here but Putnam—he acts nobly in everything.*" This quotation is from an extract from an additional leaf of the Chester-Webb letter of June 19, printed in Frothingham's *Siege of Boston,* 416, Third and later editions. Neither the extract, nor any other part of the additional leaf, is given in Ford's *Correspondence and Journals of Samuel B. Webb.* The facsimile in the latter work of the main part of the Chester-Webb account also differs from the copyist's description in the *Siege of Boston.*

Colonel Paul Dudley Sargent, in his turn, could see only New Hampshire men! It was his retrospective opinion that if Ward had "marched the whole of his troops then in Cambridge to Charlestown not one of the enemy would have escaped, but instead of that he only walked Hasting's front yard the whole day." Then, continuing, he brushed to one side all Massachusetts and Connecticut fighters, to bestow the entire credit of June 17 on Stark's and Reed's New Hampshire men, for "those two regiments did all that was done that day, of any consequence."—Letter, December 20, 1825, to S. Swett. Another part of this letter by Sargent is quoted on page 130, note 14.

An unsigned report by an English government agent recorded a poor opinion of Ward as expressed by two French officers, then in London after a visit to America, whom he believed to be "in the service of the Rebel Americans." Their statements, though, cannot be taken very seriously, for they include very tall yarns of the devices which the "rebel chiefs" employed "to keep up" the spirit of the Americans, "some of which they themselves were witness to, such as making their own people put on English regi-

Some of the questions which have long engaged writers and controversialists can now be laid to rest, settled by the publication of new contemporary evidence and the better consideration of old. Of these are the viewpoints of the American military leaders at Cambridge concerning both the Bunker Hill project and the possibility of occupying Dorchester Neck; the original plan for the relief of the detachment; and lesser items, as the supply of "drinking water." Some others must still remain largely a matter of individual opinion.

Questioning the fundamental policy of the expedition, one may ask with much sapience why the Americans thought it necessary to occupy the Charlestown peninsula, when egress from Boston by that route could have been blocked, or checked, with much less risk by works on the mainland side of Charlestown Neck.

It was, perhaps, a move foolishly reckless, but it was also a move of high moral courage—and was rewarded by success far beyond all expectations: beyond, if you will, all merit! It had been projected to prevent the enemy from moving out of Boston onto the mainland, and it resulted in driving them out of Boston into the sea!

If the battle had not been fought, the English would, as their least exploit—and at little, if any, cost—have taken

mentals, & come into Camp in the character of Officers & soldiers deserting from his Majestys troops—& one man personated a Member of Parliament."—*Stevens' Facsimiles,* XIII, 1301.

Another spy said that the American army was incensed against Ward because he "never so much as gave one Written order that day."—Belcher, *First American Civil War,* I, 208. This idea has found lodgment in the minds of some writers, but (irrespective of its merits as an indictment if it were accurate) it is not based on either facts or probabilities. Ward's Order Book contains only one order of June 17—that to Thomas for ordnance to be sent to Cambridge (the separate MS. order is owned by the American Antiquarian Society—*United States Revolution,* IV, 15), but there can be no reasonable doubt that of the many others given, a number were reduced to writing. Several fugitive examples testify to the probability: two are in the possession of the Boston Public Library, and the copy of the relief order (page 123, note) tells of a third.

John Pitts wrote, July 20, 1775, of the confusion and lack of command, but his references apparently apply chiefly to the immediate vicinity of the battlefield, for his specific complaint is that "there were not officers enough to lead the men on."—Frothingham, *Siege of Boston,* 160.

possession of Dorchester Neck within the next twenty-four hours. Quickly following would have come their occupation of the Charlestown peninsula.[2] And thereafter, even should they have found it impossible to make any further advance, they could have safely and easily maintained the town and harbor as a base for operations against both New England and New York.

One comes next to Ward's judgment against large early reinforcement of Prescott's detachment, and his determination to hold his center in full strength until the enemy had displayed his choice of attack.

Whether we agree or disagree with him, the contingency upon which he based his judgment was at all events no fallacy, for the letters of General Howe—soon to replace Gage as English commander-in-chief—tell us that Cambridge *was* the main objective in his plan for raising the siege.[3]

It was impossible for Ward—or anyone else in the American camp—to divine what proportion, if any, of the British strength would be sent over the Charlestown peninsula in the face of the American intrenchments, and what proportion by way of Lechmere's Point[4] or Willis Creek.

An attack by way of Lechmere's Point or Willis Creek was a very real peril. Washington also so regarded it when, nine months later, the American forces undertook the occupation of Dorchester Neck. We find him carefully avoiding the danger of unduly weakening his center, though the American lines had by that time been greatly strengthened and Lechmere's Point had been converted into a strongly forti-

[2] General Burgoyne to Lord Stanley, *American Archives*, 4th, II, 1094.

[3] Howe's plan was, first to occupy Dorchester Neck and make an attack upon Roxbury. Then "to go over with all we can muster" to the Charlestown peninsula and thence "either attack the Rebels at Cambridge; Or perhaps, if the Country admits of it, endeavor to turn that post: . . . In either case, I suppose the Rebels will move from Cambridge; And that we shall take and keep possession of it."—General Howe to Lord Howe, June 12, 1775, *Proceedings of the Bunker Hill Monument Association*, 1907, 115. The same plan, in different words, appears in General Howe's letter to General Harvey, June 12, 1775. *Ibid.*, 111.

[4] See the quotation from Colonel Sargent's letter on page 130, note 14.

fied position, equipped with some of the heavy Ticonderoga guns.

I hesitate to refer to James Warren's criticism that Ward "never left his house" all day—repeated with variations forty-three and fifty years later by Dearborn[5] and Sargent[6]—for to me it has always seemed trivial. It has, though, been so widely quoted that it cannot be ignored.

One might indeed indict the sentence itself for malicious intent to deceive. To many readers it has suggested a condition which has no foundation in fact. That Ward "never left his house" all day, might or might not signify a measure of the "callous indifference" with which one hasty writer charged him, even if it meant that he had remained away from his post and stayed home to nurse the sickness which had seized him. But the "house" in which he stayed was both *his own army headquarters and also that of the Committee of Safety*—the very heart and center of the besieging force.

It happens that James Warren's statement was not literally true, for Daniel Putnam and David Townsend, calling at headquarters at different hours, both found Ward out on the military business of the day;[7] but I am quite willing to accept the statement that he was not away from headquarters for any considerable length of time on June 17, and I think that it can well be argued that headquarters was the proper and the very best place for him to be on that eventful day. It was essential that some one of high authority be there to receive reports and to give orders.

There was a deplorable amount of confusion among the troops on the Charlestown peninsula and in the vicinity (excepting always those holding the battle-line), but Ward, necessarily remaining in Cambridge until the landing of the English reinforcement had completed the disclosure of his opponent's plan of action, could not have reached the field in

[5] Dearborn, *An Account of the Battle of Bunker Hill.*

[6] See page 139, note.

[7] See pages 126 and 129.

time to have changed conditions there—even if (which is doubtful) he, or any other man, could have changed them to any great degree.

And if he had left headquarters before the English commander had displayed his intention, he would have been taking an entirely unjustifiable hazard.

All of which seems very plain, yet apparently some of Ward's critics would have liked to see him put the last keg of powder in a coach and drive over to the Charlestown peninsula in order to make a complete show for the spectators in Boston.

CHAPTER VIII

June 18–July 3, 1775: Age 47

The American camp after the Battle of Bunker Hill. The election of George Washington as Commander-in-chief of the American forces. Artemas Ward commissioned as First Major-General; Charles Lee as Second Major-General. The arrival of Washington and Lee at Cambridge.

THE sudden shock of battle and the menace of a renewed onslaught by the English redcoats had temporarily cleared the surcharged political atmosphere of the camps, but the spirit of insubordination was still rife and for some hectic hours was heightened by poisonous rumors charging treachery at Bunker Hill in some of the officers.[1] The accusations were, however, quickly discredited[2] and their venom as speedily dissipated, leaving a better feeling in their wake.

Further relief proceeded from the handbills sent broadcast by the Provincial Congress—with the authority, finally received, of the Continental Congress—for the election of representatives to a General Court to function "as near as

[1] Diary of Ezekiel Price, June 19, *Massachusetts Historical Society Proceedings,* VII, 191.—"An opinion prevails among the Continental Army, that treachery was in some of the Continental Officers. A suspicion also arises among them that sand was mixt with the powder, and that the cartridges and ball being thus sent was with design: all which creates great uneasiness in the camp."

Provincial Congress, June 20.—"Ordered, that Colonel Cushing, Major Perley, Colonel Prescott, Colonel Barrett, and Deacon Fisher, be a committee to inquire into the grounds of a report which has prevailed in the army, that there has been treachery in some of the officers; and that, if they find that such report is without foundation, they bring in a resolve for quieting the minds of the people, in respect thereof."

[2] Diary of Ezekiel Price, June 20.—" . . . all the reports of treachery were entirely without foundation, and propagated by the enemies to the cause, and weak, discontented men, and by some cowards who fled from the engagement and formed these lies to favour their escape from danger."

may be, to the spirit and substance of the [provincial] charter."

The spreading of this call for the resumption of provincial government had been shortly preceded by the news that Connecticut had formally placed her troops under Ward's command; and was quickly followed by word that the thirteen colonies represented in the Continental Congress had united in action and had adopted both the rebellion and its army; and, next, that Rhode Island had put her troops also under Massachusetts control.

These developments set increasingly strong checks upon camp malcontents, for they suggested and signified both a politically united New England and a politically united "Continent" behind those in authority. And, fortunately for Massachusetts and the Revolutionary cause, the flames of anarchy died down and burned themselves out. Indiscipline still flourished, but sedition had passed.

A new and confident military ardor also pervaded the ranks as a result of the battle.[3]

[3] Some writers have pictured the American forces as thrown into dismay by the loss of the Charlestown peninsula. To get oneself into the proper frame of mind to believe this, one must discard the testimony of the men who lived and fought in those days!

Both the project and its execution drew a certain quantity of censure, and there was hurry and fear among the non-combatants in nearby towns, but the typical American attitude was the very opposite of "dismay":

"We remain in good spirits as yet, being well satisfied that where we have lost one they lost three."—Colonel Stark, June 19, to the President of the New Hampshire Provincial Congress. *New Hampshire Provincial Papers,* VII, 523.

"Our Troops are in exceeding high spirits, & their Resolution increases, they long to speak with them again."—Wm. Williams, June 20. Frothingham, *The Battle-Field of Bunker Hill,* 42.

"The ministerial troops gained the hill, but were victorious losers. A few more such victories, and they are undone."—Wm. Tudor, June 26, to John Adams. Frothingham, *Siege of Boston,* 396.

"I wish we could sell them another hill at the same price. . . . Our people are in good spirits."—General Greene, June 28, to his brother Jacob Greene, Chairman of the Committee of Safety, Warwick, R. I. Johnson, *Sketches of the Life of Nathanael Greene,* I, 32.

"I am glad to hear that the Number of killed & wounded on the side of the Enemy amounts to so many more than 1000. I dare say you would not grudge them every Hill near you upon the same terms."—Samuel Adams to James Warren, July 2. *Proceedings of the Bunker Hill Monument Association,* 1898, 26.

"The Continental army . . . were in high spirits."—Diary of Ezekiel Price, June 20, *Massachusetts Historical Society Proceedings,* VII, 191.

Letters printed in the newspapers breathe the same spirit.

Other vital problems still remained, however, for the battle had emphasized the need for powder, artillery, tents, clothing, etc. On the day following, Ward wrote to the Committee of Supplies voicing his "immediate want" of "large Ordnance, a Quantity of powder, and small Musket Balls";[4] and on June 19 to the Provincial Congress saying, "I must earnestly entreat the Congress to furnish the train of artillery with a company of artificers immediately, as the army greatly suffers for want of them. This ought to have been one of the first establishments, and I hope the Congress will not delay the matter a day longer."[5]

Then again to the Committee of Supplies the very urgent reminder of the need for tents, blankets, etc., reproduced on the page opposite.

On the same day (June 24) the Provincial Congress ordered the dispatch of appeals to Connecticut, Rhode Island, and New Hampshire for an "immediate augmentation" of their troops. It declared that it had "the best grounds to suppose that, as soon as the enemy have recovered a little breath from their amazing fatigues of the seventeenth of June," and their "surprising losses" should be made up by the arrival of new troops, "which is almost daily taking place," they would make "the utmost efforts" to break the American lines and "strike general terror and amazement into the hearts of the inhabitants of the whole continent."

But the English generals never, during all their remaining sojourn in Boston, sufficiently recovered from the "amazing fatigues" engendered by the "seventeenth of June" to feel any desire to again force the American lines!

They did, however, hope to consummate their plan for the occupation of Dorchester Neck, and they set Friday or Saturday (June 23 or 24) for the purpose.[6] But Ward,

[4] *Artemas Ward MSS.*

[5] *American Archives,* 4th, II, 1028.

[6] "I may therefore safely predict, that with our present Force, the 2nd Divisn from Ireland not being yet arrived, we shall not do more than to possess these Heights [Breed's Hill and Bunker Hill] & the Dorchester-neck, wch Gen. Clinton will take

Cambridge June 24. 1775.

309

Gentlemen

If it is expected our lines be maintained & defended it is absolutely necessary the men be covered, there are many men that are ordered to the lines, which have nothing to cover them but the heavens. Men cannot be comfortable when they are both day & night without covering I must begg & pray that some covering may be this day provided for them. if not the men will get their deaths & there will be a universal uneasiness in the camp, such uneasiness as I shall not be able to lay

I am Gentlemen your humble servant

Artemas Ward

P. S. if our men must be in the rain without covering if we should be attacked Immediately after ye rain is over pray what are we to expect? Destruction

From the original (6¼ × 7¾) in the *Massachusetts Archives*

WARD'S DEMAND THAT THE TROOPS BE PROTECTED FROM THE WEATHER

learning their intention, reinforced Thomas's division, and Gage reconsidered his determination and renounced the project.[7]

This same Saturday (the twenty-fourth) brought news of the Continental Congress election (June 15) of George Washington (lately "Colonel Washington of Virginia") to the supreme command of the American forces; that (June 17) Ward had been made second in command, and Charles Lee, third.

On June 17, also, the lesser, but very important, post of adjutant-general had been given to another English officer—Horatio Gates, a retired English major who had settled in the Shenandoah Valley, Virginia, after the peace of 1763.

Advice of the appointments had been sent in letters by Hancock and others. Though intended for official information only,[8]

possession of, either to morrow or on Saturday."—General Howe to Lord Howe, June 22, 1775. *Stopford-Sackville MSS.*, II; *Proceedings of the Bunker Hill Monument Association*, 1907, 121.

[June] "23d. . . . great talk of some expedition tomorrow; the 63d regt and Batt. of Marines being order'd to Boston, and the flank companies of the 64th from the Castle."—Diary of a British officer, *Atlantic Monthly*, XXXIX, 551.

[7] June 24: "The expedition talked of was to attack Dorchester Hill, and was to have been today at 6 oclock in the morng. All the Troops on this side [Charlestown] were drawn out and paraded on the Hill [Bunker Hill] and some march'd into the road; this was to alarm the Rebels on this side and keep off their attention; but soon after we heard it was put off, the Genl hearing they had got intelligence and had reinforced that place with 4000 men."—Diary of a British officer, *Ibid.*

"Four days ago I received an order to command three armed vessels, and to put myself under the command of General Gage; as soon as I did I was ordered to be ready at six o'clock next morning to cover a part of some Troops which were to make an attack on the left side of Boston, and to flank a breastwork and a wood, which was supposed had a number of men in it; but about seven o'clock General Clinton sent to me not to proceed till farther orders from him. Some little time after I was ordered up to General Howe's camp to lie with the vessels on his right, where I last night left them, having been relieved, as I had not been in bed for four nights. I found, since I came down, the reason of the attack not going on was, that the rebels knew of our coming, and had seven or eight thousand men ready to receive us. I own I could have wished it had went on, as I had placed the vessels in such a situation as must have mowed them down, and done great execution."—Extract of a letter from a British officer in Boston, June 26, 1775, *American Archives*, 4th, II, 1107.

[8] "I am under a strict Injunction not to Communicate the Doings of Congress, but two or three Circumstances having Taken place in Congress which affected our Army, inducd me to ask Leave to mention them which I obtain'd with this positive Direction that at present they be not mentioned in the Newspapers which you will please observe."—John Hancock to Joseph Warren, June 18, 1775, *Proceedings of the Bunker Hill Monument Association*, 1898, 22.

it filtered through rapidly and became camp gossip within forty-eight hours.[9]

It is unnecessary to re-tell the story of the appointment of Washington as commander-in-chief.[10] Careful students no longer find in it any reflection upon Ward. They have read John Adams' testimony[11] and know that in the Congress which held the decision "the greatest number" were for Ward to head the continental armies, but that his title to first place was sacrificed by the New England statesmen to meet the overwhelming necessity of uniting the colonies.[12]

America's great good fortune was that, for once, the choice of expediency was also the best choice. During the first stages of the conflict Washington frequently proved his lack of military perspective and experience, but not all the seven years of the war developed another man as capable. He grew to great stature in the school of experience.

[9] "We hear a chief officer is appointed, Gen. Washington of Virginia, to supersede in the command of the troops here."—June 26, 1775, Diary of Lieutenant-Colonel Storrs, *Massachusetts Historical Society Proceedings,* XIV, 86.

[10] The choice of Washington satisfied the pride of the Southern delegates and dispelled their fear of a military Massachusetts dominating the other colonies. That was the preponderant motive underlying his nomination—but it was not the only one. The conclusion at which John Adams arrived was strengthened by several additional, and very important, points. To be acceptable to all of the provinces it was essential that the commander-in-chief selected be native-born, of proved courage, and of military prominence; or the troops of strange provinces might refuse to acknowledge him. He must be a man sufficiently aggressive politically to command the respect of the New England patriot leaders—civilian and other; yet he should also be moderate enough to ease the minds of the less ardent in the central colonies. It was desirable that he be of social importance, for the encouragement of the rather small proportion of the well-to-do on the patriot side. All of these requirements were combined with remarkable completeness in Washington's personality, character, career, and circumstances.

[11] *Works of John Adams,* II, 415–418; X, 162–165.

[12] John Adams and his companions fully realized how desperate was New England's need for the assistance of the other colonies. To continue unsupported the fight against Great Britain meant certain destruction. With the other colonies indifferent or (as perhaps some of them) actively loyal, the British forces—regulars and loyalist militia—could come to the attack from every side—and there was not enough powder in New England to carry the provincial armies through a single campaign.

There were then no powder mills in New England; and with the sea and surrounding country under English control, no powder could have been obtained from outside. All the patriotism of New England's sons would have weighed but little against empty casks and empty horns: and to learn the trade of making powder while defending themselves against an empire, would have required more than human strength and ingenuity.

A condition that, later, spelled serious danger for the united colonies would have meant the political annihilation of a detached group.

And Charles Lee—what were his thoughts when the Congress reached its decision? Disgruntled and disappointed he was without a doubt, for he had failed to achieve his dream of American leadership.[13] He had jockeyed himself so far to the front in popular esteem that a number of delegates had urged his name for the chief command; but not all his adroitness and ability had been sufficient to win that high prize. The Congress was filled with a superlative belief in his knowledge and skill, was anxiously eager to secure his services, and was imbued with sincere deprecation of colonial experience in the art of war; but a majority of the delegates drew back at the suggestion that the supreme command be placed in the hands of a foreign officer.

Lee had, next, played for second place, but that also eluded him. In harmony's interest and for the quicker welding of the colonies, the delegates had unanimously joined in the appointment of Washington as commander-in-chief, but, led by John Adams, those who had previously advocated Ward for that post refused to set his name aside again. Not even the magic of Lee's foreign service, nor their desire to gratify his demands, could prevail upon them to rank him above Ward.

For *third* place, that of second major-general, Lee received the vote of the Congress, so he brushed aside his ultimatum of "either second or nothing" and accepted the commission.

Two men between him and his ambition! But still no reason to lose hope of making his dream come true! It is seldom that the general heading an army at the inception of a war is in the saddle when it ends. There were many pitfalls ahead that were likely to prove disastrous to inexperienced riders. Charles Lee might yet confound his old enemies in England by confronting them as America's leader!

[13] In the month following the appointments, Lee declared that he might have considered *"at least* the preferment given to General Ward over me as the highest indignity."—To General Thomas, July 23, 1775, *Lee Papers,* I, 197. As Washington was the only other officer placed over him, the inference is plain.

On June 26 the Congress delegated Benjamin Church (still high in Revolutionary councils, still unsuspected) and Moses Gill as a committee to repair to Springfield, there to receive Washington and Lee "with every mark of respect due to their exalted characters and stations" and "to provide proper escorts for them, from thence, to the army before Boston."

Three days later Ward gave "Washington" as parole and "Virginia" as countersign. This started a fresh set of rumors which before night had spread through the lines into Boston, telling of "Colonel Washington's being expected this day to take upon him the Command of the Rebel Army."[14]

On the following day Ward received Hancock's two letters of June 22: one telling him of the appointment of Schuyler and Putnam as fourth and fifth major-generals, and of eight brigadier-generals; the other transmitting his commission as first major-general. The second letter is reproduced, together with Ward's acceptance, on the page opposite.[15]

Washington and Lee were on the same day met at Springfield by the Provincial Congress escort.

[14] Lieutenant-Colonel Kemble's Journal, *Kemble Papers*, I, 45.

[15] Ward's apprehension, expressed in his letter of acceptance, that some of the appointments might create "uneasiness" was fully justified. Washington was much troubled by the ill feeling they excited. He informed the Continental Congress that "General Spencer [5th brigadier-general] was so much disgusted at the preference given to General Putnam [5th major-general] that he left the Army without visiting me, or making known his Intentions in any respect." In consequence, Washington held back the other commissions until receiving further advice, for he feared that, in the appointments of the brigadier-generals, the "postponing of General Thomas to Pomeroy and Heath [the placing of Thomas as 6th, with Pomeroy as 1st and Heath as 4th], whom he has commanded, would make his continuance very difficult, and probably operate on his Mind, as the like Circumstance has done on that of Spencer."

Though the commissions were held back, the news of the appointments had become public property and it affected Thomas as Washington had anticipated.

Strong influence was brought to bear upon Thomas, for his resignation would have been a serious loss. Charles Lee was among those who urged him to remain in the service, invoking his patriotism in his country's hour of trial. It was in his exhortation to Thomas that Lee made his allusion to his being passed over in favor of both Washington and Ward that is quoted on the preceding page, note 13. Thomas remained, and very shortly after received the continental appointment as first brigadier-general "in the room of General Pomeroy, who never acted under the commission sent to him."

Congress Room Philada. June 22: 1775

Honble. Sir

In my last I inform'd you that this Congress had Appointed George Washington Esqr. General & Commander in Chief of all the Forces Rais'd or to be Rais'd by the United Colonies; that Gentleman takes his Departure to morrow morning from this City in order to Enter upon his Command, I the rather mention the Circumstance of his Departure, that you may Direct your Movements for his Reception —

I have the Honor to Transmitt you a Commission from this Congress appointing you First Major General & Second in Command of the Forces of the United Colonies, you will please to Acknowledge the Receipt of it.

I wish you the Divine protection, & Success in all your undertakings, and am with Respect, Sir, Your most Obedt. Servt.

John Hancock Presidt.

Honl. Major General Ward

From the original (7½ × 12⅝), owned by the Massachusetts Historical Society

PRESIDENT HANCOCK'S LETTER TRANSMITTING WARD'S COMMISSION AS FIRST MAJOR-GENERAL OF THE CONTINENTAL ARMY

(348)

Head Quarters Cambridge June 30th 1775

Sir. —

I have this Day rec.d your Favor of the 22. Inst. in which you are so kind as to inform me of the general Officers, that the hon.ble continental Congress have appointed. —

I wish, Sir, the Appointments in this Colony may not have a Tendency to create Uneasiness among us; which we ought, at this critical Time, to be extremely careful to avoid. —

I have, Sir, to acknowledge the Rec.t of the Commission of a Major Gen.l; & do heartily wish that the Honor had been confered upon a Person, better qualified to execute a Trust so important: — It would give me great Satisfaction, if I tho.t myself capacitated to act with Dignity, & to do Honor to that Congress, which has exalted me to be second in Command over the american Army. — I hope they will accept my sincere Desire to serve them; & my most grateful Acknowledgments for the Honor conferred upon me; & pray they may not be wholly disappointed in their Expectations. — I always have been, & am still ready to devote my Life, in attempting to deliver my native Country from insupportable Slavery. —

I am, Sir, with great Respect,

Your most obedient

Humble Servant

P. S. Col Gardner is wounded
I hope not mortally. —

Artemas Ward

From the original (7½ × 12) in the Library of Congress

WARD'S LETTER ACCEPTING HIS COMMISSION AS FIRST MAJOR-GENERAL OF THE CONTINENTAL ARMY

Two days later, on the morning of Sunday, July 2, they reached Watertown.

The Provincial Congress was ready for them with addresses of welcome prepared and adopted at the session of the preceding day. The glamour cast by Lee may be noted even here: the address to Washington lacked nothing in respect or cordiality, but that to Lee displayed more personal enthusiasm.

Upon James Warren as the new president of the Provincial Congress, succeeding Joseph Warren, who had died at Bunker Hill, devolved the chief honor of receiving Washington in the provisional capital of the province. It was an unhappy augury for the future relationship of two men so dissimilar as the Massachusetts Puritan and the rich planter from Virginia, that from *James* Warren, General Ward's detractor—instead of from Dr. *Joseph* Warren, his friend—Washington should receive an advance impression and an advance judgment of the man he was to succeed. If Joseph Warren had lived, Washington would have continued on toward the American camp with a very different and much truer impression of Artemas Ward and his works.

It was between twelve and one o'clock (some accounts say two o'clock) when Washington, weary from the journey and the ceremonies en route, rode quietly into the little town of Cambridge, which was to serve as his headquarters thenceforth so long as the British flag waved over the capital of Massachusetts.[16]

---

[16] Irving's *Life of George Washington,* First edition, I, 496 (different page number in other editions), says that "As he entered the confines of the camp the shouts of the multitude and the thundering of artillery gave note to the enemy beleaguered in Boston of his arrival." Lodge's *George Washington,* I, 134, also greets him with the "booming of cannon." Other old style historians have similarly indulged their imaginations.

All this is spurious. It is thus one writes of the arrival of the famed or conquering general—but Washington had not yet made the name or established the reputation by which we know him. The records of July 2, British and American alike, contain no reference to any cannonading at the time of Washington's arrival. The English firing (upon Roxbury) had ceased several hours earlier and there was none by the Americans.

Even without these disproofs one would naturally regard such statements with suspicion—Ward would not have ordered and Washington would not have desired the use of powder in complimentary salvos of artillery. The irreplaceable value of every grain

There is no record of how the newly arrived officers spent that Sunday afternoon and evening, but tradition has it that their first dinner at Cambridge—with Ward as host—was an affair of much joviality.[17] Ward welcomed his successor, the new commander-in-chief, in the same spirit of whole-hearted unpretentious sincerity with which he had received the news of his appointment.

The next day (which was "exceeding pleasant" in the morning, but "towards noon, very warm"[18]) Washington formally assumed the command.

No eye-witness recorded the occasion despite its high historic significance, but Ward had arranged that it should be "attended with a great deal of grandeur." The troops had been "turned out early in the morning" to be "got in readiness to be reviewed" and there were "one and twenty drummers," all especially drilled "respecting their duty," and "as many fifers, beating and playing around the parade."[19]

was in every patriot mind, and the Provincial Congress resolution of June 26 had explicitly echoed John Adams' admonition (to Elbridge Gerry, June 18, 1775, Austin's *Life of Gerry,* I, 90) against any such consumption.

[17] "In the long, low dining-room, fronting on the common, and separated from the parlor by a double vestibule, lighted by small heavily sashed windows on either side and opening out by another main door in that direction, Ward entertained Washington and the other generals soon after their arrival, the banquet, if not brilliant in its appointments, having been enlivened, tradition tells us, by patriotic songs."—Amory, *Old Cambridge and New,* 23.

"Washington . . . first dined at Cambridge with General Ward and his officers,—an occasion when all restraint appears to have been cast aside in the spontaneous welcome which was extended him. After dinner, Adjutant Gibbs, of Glover's, was hoisted (English fashion), chair and all, upon the table, and gave the company a rollicking bachelor's song, calculated to make the immobile features of the chief relax. It was a generous, hearty greeting of comrades in arms. Glasses clinked, stories were told, and the wine circulated. Washington was a man; we do not question that he laughed, talked, and toasted with the rest."—S. A. Drake, *Historic Fields and Mansions of Middlesex,* 262 (also, same page number, in the same work later published as *Old Landmarks and Historic Fields of Middlesex* and *Historic Mansions and Highways around Boston*).

[18] Diary of Ezekiel Price, July 3, 1775, *Massachusetts Historical Society Proceedings,* VII, 194.

[19] *Ward's Order Book,* July 2, 1775; *Paul Lunt's Diary,* July 3, 1775; letter of Lieutenant Joseph Hodgkins, July 3, 1775, *Ipswich Antiquarian Papers,* June, 1881.

Many historians and multitudinous orators have pictured the camp as full of enthusiasm on Washington's assumption of the command. All such statements may be set aside, for such writers and speechmakers are again self-deluded by a wrong perspective.

There was no such sentiment on July 3, 1775. It is probable that by that date every

New Englander had heard of "Washington of Virginia"—and that some of them had from a much earlier period held him admiringly in mind. Further, having discussed among themselves, town-meeting style, the political exigencies of the situation, the rank and file had accepted the action of their representatives in the Continental and Provincial Congresses and were ready to receive Washington with deference and fair cordiality.

But that is all one can say. There was no general enthusiasm—that was to come in after years when he had earned it by many long days and nights devoted to America's cause. No one was sufficiently impressed by his assumption of the command to send a letter to any newspaper, though events of much lesser moment were thus reported; no one seems to have described the ceremony in any letter to family or friends; and no diary recorded it.

There are the references already quoted concerning the preparations for music and parade, but—of authentic material—nothing more.

Most of the many diaries, memoirs, etc., that I have consulted pass both July 2 and 3 without any reference to Washington. Some diarists noted his arrival—as Jonathan Carpenter (Original diary, owned, 1921, by N. L. Boyden, Randolph, Vt.), Noah Chapin (Original diary, Connecticut Historical Society), Reverend David Avery (Original diary—in one of the volumes owned by Hannah C. Partridge, Hartford, Conn.), Caleb Haskell (*Diary*), General Heath (*Memoirs*), James Thacher (*Journal*), Ezekiel Price (Diary, *Massachusetts Historical Society Proceedings,* VII, 194), James Stevens (Journal, *Essex Institute Historical Collections,* XLVIII, 49), Ezra Stiles (*Literary Diary,* I, 582); but all of these nevertheless pass July 3 without speaking of his installation. Carpenter records that he "took the command," but this evidently refers to his arrival, for the entry is of July 2. Several diaries specifically testify that on July 3 there happened "Nothing new" or "Nothing remarkable" or "Nothing extraordinary": as those of Caleb Haskell, Samuel Haws (*Military Journals of Two Private Soldiers,* 60), John Kettell (Original diary, *Frothingham Papers,* 1630–1775, Massachusetts Historical Society), and James Stevens.

Simms' *Life of Nathanael Greene,* I, 33, states that "It was Greene who, according to the usage of the time, welcomed Washington to the army in a public address," but this statement is incorrect. Greene's own testimony in his letter of July *4,* 1775 (Geo. W. Greene's *Life of Nathanael Greene,* I, 99), is as follows: "I sent a detachment today of two hundred men, commanded by a colonel, lieutenant-colonel, and major with a letter of address to welcome his Excellency to camp. The detachment met with a very gracious reception, and his Excellency returned me a very polite answer, and invitation to visit him at his headquarters."

Lodge in his *George Washington,* I, 134, quotes Dr. Thacher to lend verisimilitude to his story of the installation: "The next day he rode forth in the presence of a great multitude, and the troops having been drawn up before him, he drew his sword beneath the historical elm-tree and took command of the first American army. 'His Excellency,' wrote Dr. Thacher in his journal, 'was on horseback in company with several military gentlemen. It was not difficult to distinguish him from all others. He is tall and well proportioned, and his personal appearance truly noble and majestic.'" *But* the quotation from Dr. Thacher is of an encounter of July 20, seventeen days later (Thacher's *Military Journal*).

In conclusion, one may read with some curious interest the following alleged recollection of the ceremony published, 1883, in Secomb's *History of the Town of Amherst, N. H.,* 371. The account had been given to the author forty or so years earlier by Andrew Leavitt, a very old soldier, then about ninety years of age.

"The officers placed their men in as good shape as they could, but they were a motley looking set, no two dressed alike. Some were armed with fowling pieces, some with rifles, others with muskets without bayonets. When all was in readiness, Washington and his staff advanced to the square prepared for their reception. He was a large noble looking man, in the prime of life, and was mounted on a powerful black horse over which he seemed to have perfect control.

"After a short address to the soldiers, he took from his pocket a Psalm book, from which he read the one hundred and first Psalm (another account says it was then sung by the soldiers to the tune of Old Hundred)."

CHAPTER IX

Criticisms of Ward as Commander-in-chief

I HAVE said that I have no quarrel with those who censure either the conception or the execution of the battle of Bunker Hill, and I make the most generous allowances for overheated and overstated assertions and insinuations inspired by it, whether of contemporary or later date; but I do most decidedly protest against the manner in which, concerning other periods of Ward's tenure as commander-in-chief, contemporary testimony has been distorted and misused to the disadvantage of his reputation.

Bancroft promulgated the theory that Ward was incompetent as commander-in-chief;[1] and it has been adopted by many historians, both American and English. But its foundations are fictitious, and examination crumbles them to nothing.

The witnesses marshaled by Bancroft were Joseph Warren, Elbridge Gerry, and James Warren. One finds that the first two did *not* testify against Ward; and that the third, though violently anti-Ward, became indirectly his best witness.

This is not the only instance in which Bancroft sacrificed historical accuracy to the zest of portraying a special viewpoint and nullified the value of his great historical labors by incorrectness of statement or quotation—but that fact has not saved Ward's reputation from being cruelly wounded.

The most serious injustice has been that wrought by Bancroft's declaration that Joseph Warren, one of the finest

[1] Bancroft's *History of the United States,* early editions, VII, 321, 388–389, 405; Centenary editions, IV, 541, 589–590, 602; "Author's last revision," IV, 173.

characters of his time, held but a poor opinion of General Ward as commander-in-chief: that he noted his inefficiency for the post, and advised his supersession. These statements have carried much weight because intimate association gave Warren full opportunity for judgment—but they are entirely, utterly untrue.

Especially insidious is the perversion of the Joseph Warren letter of May 17, 1775, to Samuel Adams which accompanied the Provincial Congress letter of May 16 to the Continental Congress (both of which letters I have cited in an earlier chapter).[2]

The Provincial Congress letter, also signed by Joseph Warren (as President pro tem.), was devoted chiefly to voicing the serious need for the reëstablishment of civil government in Massachusetts and the urgent Massachusetts desire for the advice and coöperation of the other colonies.

It concluded with the following request that the Continental Congress assume the direction of the army:

"As the Army collecting from different colonies, is for the general defence of the rights of America, we would beg leave to suggest to your consideration the propriety of your taking the regulation and direction of it, that the operations may more effectually answer the purpose designed."

It would be easy to expand on the numerous reasons—political as well as military—that rendered both desirable and essential the supreme control by the Continental Congress of the separate independent colonial armies raised, and being raised, in defense of a common cause; but, in so far as it affects the point under discussion, the important fact is that the Provincial Congress letter did not express any lack of faith in Ward's ability, nor did it request or suggest putting any one in his place. On the contrary, the Provincial Congress immediately followed it by preparing a formal commission for Ward as commander-in-chief of the Massachusetts forces. It is its *own* authority which it offers

[2] See page 110, note 27; also pages 113–114.

to surrender. It suggests that the Continental Congress (of all the colonies), instead of the Provincial Congress (of only Massachusetts), ought to be empowered with the general direction of the army.

This point being very clear, Bancroft had recourse to the Joseph Warren letter referred to—that of May 17 to Samuel Adams, which accompanied the Provincial Congress letter. Bancroft described Warren's letter as "interpreting" the conclusion of the Provincial Congress letter as a request that the Continental Congress take the command by appointing a generalissimo, and succeeded this by declaring that the generalissimo whom Warren (and others) desired was Washington.[3] These statements follow—are in the same paragraph with—his assertions that Warren had observed "the incompetency of Ward for his station" and that "every hour made it more imperative that he be superseded."

Nothing could be more completely inaccurate than the impression thus created. There is not in Warren's letter of May 17—nor in any other letter by him—any statement or suggestion, direct or indirect, that asperses in even the slightest degree either Ward or his ability; nor the expression of any wish for Washington or any other man to fill Ward's place. One finds, instead, direct testimony to Ward's hold upon the troops—for Warren fears that, despite its self-evident desirability, the assumption of the general direction of the army by the Continental Congress may cause trouble among the Massachusetts men, as they may object to having *anyone*—whether a continental committee or a continental generalissimo—placed in command over, or in place of, Ward; and so he sends the following warning:

"I would just observe that the application made to you

[3] Bancroft's *History of the United States,* early editions, VII, 388–389; Centenary editions, IV, 589–590. His "last revision," 1884, dropped his earlier citation of Joseph Warren, Gerry, and James Warren as witnesses to Ward's "incompetency," but it continued the charge (IV, 173) and carried a new inaccuracy—the direct assertion that (IV, 203) Joseph Warren's letter of May 17 interpreted the Provincial Congress letter of May 16 "as a request that the continent should 'take the command of the army by appointing Washington as its generalissimo.' "

respecting the taking the regulation of this army into your hands, by appointing a committee of war, or taking the command of it by appointing a generalissimo, is a matter, I think, must be managed with much delicacy."

Bancroft (and many of those following him) adopted from Warren's letter both the idea of the "delicacy" required, and the word itself—but they misapplied it. They have made it appear that Ward's "private virtues" constituted one of the chief reasons for using "delicacy" in superseding him. The context shows, however, that the "delicacy" advised had nothing to do with any possibility of reflecting upon his "private virtues" or reputation, or of hurting his feelings, but was essential in the choosing of either a committee or a generalissimo to assume from his hands the reins of chief command lest the troops should balk at the orders of such a committee or generalissimo and defy their or his authority. For, continuing, it was then that Warren remarked:

"Unless great care is taken, some dissentions may arise in the army, as our soldiers, I find, will not yet be brought to obey any person of whom they do not themselves entertain a high opinion."

With the complete letter before one,[4] there is no possibility of misunderstanding. Political conditions direct the offer of the supreme command of the army to the Continental Congress, but its assumption must be very "delicately"

[4] *Here is the full literal text of Joseph Warren's letter of May 17, 1775:*

"Yesterday Dr. Church was appointed to wait on the Continental Congress, with the address from this Congress, which renders it unnecessary for me to write so perticularly to you as I intended, as you will have from him an Exact state of Affairs, viva Voce. I would just observe that the Application made to you respecting the taking the Regulations of this Army into your Hands, by appointing a Committee of War, or takeing the Command of it by appointing a Generalissimo, is a Matter I think must be managed with much Delicacy. I am a little suspicious unless great care is taken, some Dissentions may arise in the Army, as our Soldiers I find will not yet be brought to obey any Person of whom they do not themselves entertain an High Opinion. Subordination is absolutely necessary in an Army; but the Strings must not be drawn too tight at first. The Bands of Love & Esteem must be principally relied on amongst Men who know not of any Distinction but what arises from some superior Merit. I know your Prudence and thorough Knowledge of our Countrymen, their many Virtues and their few Faults.—The matter of taking up Government I think cannot occasion much debate, if the South-

handled to avoid offending the Massachusetts men assembled under Ward's command.

That political conditions constituted the controlling impulse is further clinched by the fact that Warren's first reference is not to a "generalissimo" but to a continental "Committee of War" as the chief military executive.[5]

If he had meant more—if he had felt that the cause was suffering from Ward's continuance—he would not have hesitated to so express himself to Samuel Adams, for he and Adams were very close friends.[6]

Consider, next, Elbridge Gerry—another of the three men cited by Bancroft as having observed the "incompetency of Ward." His views and testimony on the army command and the military situation are in his letter of June 4, 1775, to the Massachusetts delegates in the Continental Congress. This letter has been widely quoted and misquoted, but not so heavily employed as Joseph Warren's of May 17, because it is improbable that it reached Philadelphia in time to have had any influence on John Adams' sudden determination to achieve the coup d'état which resulted in the election of Washington to the post of commander-in-chief.

An impartial reader vainly seeks in Gerry's letter for any reflection on Ward.

ern Colonies have any Apprehensions from the Northern Colonies, they surely must now be for an Establishment of *Civil* Government here, for as an Army is now necessary, or is taking the Field, it is obveous to every one, if they are without Controul, a *military* Government must certainly take Place; and I think I cannot see a Question with them to determine which is most to be feared, a *military,* or a *civil* Government.

I am Dear Sir with great Esteem, Your most Obedient Servant,

Jos. Warren."

The original (May 14–17, 1775) is among the *Samuel Adams Papers,* New York Public Library. A copy edited to modern capitalization, punctuation, etc., is in Frothingham's *Life of Joseph Warren,* 485.

[5] The manner of the Continental Congress's adoption and regulation of the army proved to be fundamentally different from a widely prevalent idea of a continental "Committee of War" or "generalissimo" which would permit the continued existence of the various colonial armies under their own commanders-in-chief. Under such a "Committee of War," Washington would have been commander-in-chief of the Virginian forces; Ward of the Massachusetts; Schuyler of the New York. Under the alternative, Washington would probably have held the double rôle of continental generalissimo and Virginian commander-in-chief.

[6] Wells, *Life of Samuel Adams,* II, 313–314; Frothingham, *Life of Joseph Warren,* 27, 525 note.

After emphasizing the lack of money and gunpowder, and the vital necessity for the reëstablishment of government, Gerry says:

"We want also a regular general to assist us in disciplining the army, which in twelve months' time, and perhaps less, by frequent skirmishes may be brought to stand against any troops, however formidable they may be, with the sounding names of Welsh fusileers, grenadiers, etc."

But this cannot be accepted as evidence against Ward unless one wishes to decry every colonial officer, including Washington himself. A "regular general"—*i.e.*, a professional soldier—must necessarily, at that time, have been of European training; and the man whom Gerry had in mind (as one discovers in his next sentence) was the Englishman *Charles Lee.*

A "regular general"—one versed in the training and disciplining of large numbers of men—was certainly needed; but not only during Ward's tenure as commander-in-chief. Such experience was as prime an essential under Washington as under Ward. Hence the great value attached to the services of Charles Lee and, even so late as the winter of 1777–1778, the impelling need for the organization and drill, instructions and reforms instituted by the Prussian general Steuben in Washington's headquarters army.[7]

It is *after* his reference to Charles Lee and his acknowledgment that "the pride of our people would prevent their submitting to be led by any general not an American," that

[7] A further reference to General Steuben, the conditions he found, etc., appears on pages 172–173, note 14.

It is important that the student bear in mind that slighting references by either contemporary or later writers should be regarded only so far as they are supported by facts. If unsupported statements are to be accepted, one may well be tempted to push the Revolutionary records from him with a sigh for the ability and character of the founders of the United States—for all of the leaders of that eventful period were subjected to scathing abuse.

The criticisms of Ward are matched by similar criticisms of Washington. We find Washington accused of lack of decision and initiative—the count made by several historians against Ward. We find the same charges against the discipline of the men under Washington that were made against the army under Ward—even to invidious comparison, praising by contrast a subordinate officer.

It has always been found easy to abuse the man in command!

Gerry makes his much-quoted reference to Washington—as follows:

"I should heartily rejoice to see this way the beloved Colonel Washington, and do not doubt the New England generals would acquiesce in showing to our sister colony Virginia, the respect, which she has before experienced from the continent, in making him generalissimo."

Thus we again sense the strong impulse for political unity. Gerry holds Washington in very high esteem, but the reason given for the New England commanders' expected acquiescence is neither the feeling of any imperative need for Washington as commander-in-chief, nor any dissatisfaction with Ward. It is a matter of deference to Virginia—showing to her "the respect which she has before experienced from the continent."

Gerry adds, "This is a matter in which Dr. Warren agrees with me." Here is, even at second-hand, Joseph Warren's only expression bearing upon Washington as generalissimo, and we find it presented as of political inspiration—not conceived by distrust of Ward's ability but having for its object the gratification of Virginia and the closer welding of the colonies.

Furthermore, in Gerry's letter, even the expressed great necessity for the reëstablishment of civil government, and the desire for a "regular general" and George Washington, are subordinate points—the chief need is for assistance by *ammunition* and *money*. If they could be furnished, the writer felt no doubt of the result, even without other continental aid. "A full supply of these," he declared, "would render Lord North and his myrmidons as harmless as they are infamous." [8]

[8] *Below is the full text of Gerry's letter of June 4, 1775 (edited to modern capitalization):*

"A public express for your honorable body gives me opportunity to hand you information of the affairs of this province. From the confusion, in which the engagement at Lexington threw the people, they are now beginning to recover, and I hope by the speedy assistance of some form of government that the measures, which will be necessary for defence, will not only be practicable, but executed here with success. The

So disappear the main foundations of the charge, so incorrectly reported and so carelessly perpetuated, that his contemporaries considered Ward deficient as commander-in-chief. One finds nothing of the sort by Joseph Warren,[9] nor

spirit of the people is equal to our wishes, and if they continue as they began, it will be as familiar to fight as to pursue the dangers of the ocean. We want assistance by ammunition and money. A full supply of these would render Lord North and his myrmidons as harmless as they are infamous. We have stripped the seaports of canvass to make tents; and it is of great importance to possess ourselves of about five hundred pieces of ravens duck to keep the soldiers in health. I should be glad if the bearer could obtain it on the credit of our vote, as we want all our specie to send out of the government for other purposes; but I am doubtful whether you can assist us in this matter although very important, as the great objects of your attention must take up your whole time.

"Government is so essential that it cannot be too soon adopted; and although no argument can be necessary to convince you of so plain a truth, yet it may not be amiss to hint a matter which can only be discovered by being where it has taken place. The people are fully possessed of their dignity from the frequent delineation of their rights, which have been published to defeat the ministerial party in their attempt to impress them with high notions of government. They now feel rather too much their own importance, and it requires great skill to produce such subordination as is necessary. This takes place principally in the army; they have affected to hold the military too high, but the civil must be first supported, and unless an established form of government is provided, it will be productive of injury. Every day's delay makes the task more arduous.

"We want also a regular general to assist us in disciplining the army, which in twelve months' time, and perhaps less, by frequent skirmishes may be brought to stand against any troops, however formidable they may be, with the sounding names of Welsh fusileers, grenadiers, etc. And although the pride of our people would prevent their submitting to be led by any general not an American, yet I cannot but think that general Lee might be so established as to render great service by his presence and councils with our officers. I should heartily rejoice to see this way the beloved Colonel Washington, and do not doubt the New England generals would acquiesce in showing to our sister colony Virginia, the respect, which she has before experienced from the continent, in making him generalissimo.

"This is a matter in which Dr. Warren agrees with me, and we had intended to write you jointly on the affair.

"The letter from our joint committees and the generals to the congress will come before you, and nothing further is necessary on this head."—Austin, *Life of Elbridge Gerry*, I, 77–79.

[9] It is of curious interest to note in how many different ways, and in what strained manners, the name of Dr. Warren has been used to detract from Ward's reputation despite the fact that in life the two men were warm friends and held each other in mutual esteem. For example:

Avery's *History of the United States*, V, 263, says: "Ward was not energetic enough to satisfy the provincial congress, and, on the fourteenth of June, the more active Warren was made the second major-general of the Massachusetts forces."

Viewed from a competent knowledge of the acts of the Provincial Congress, Avery's comment reads as an attempt to invent a piece of contemporary testimony against General Ward!

On June 13, an election was held with the understanding that the person named should be first major-general. But Dr. Warren was not chosen, the post going to John Whitcomb, a man fourteen or fifteen years older than Ward. The next day, the election for *second* major-general installed Dr. Warren.

By Avery's comment, one must judge that if a commander-in-chief is noticeably lack-

by Gerry, nothing beyond the universal Massachusetts desire for, and need of, continental support; to obtain which, one and all of those good Bay State patriots—Ward himself, Joseph Warren, the two Adamses—as others—were ready to sacrifice the pride of personal position; were ready to, and did, as occasion demanded, stand aside, or accept or resign responsibility: whichever way could best serve their country.

By elimination we have come to the head of the stream—James Warren of Plymouth, the only one remaining of the three men cited by Bancroft, and the true source and fountainhead. There is no mistaking James Warren's attitude. He was not only Ward's most malicious detractor—he was also an extremely successful detractor; for his calumnies[10]

ing in energy, the specific remedy is to appoint a *more elderly first*-assistant and an active *second*-assistant. Unless Ward's lack of energy became noticeable only between June 13 and June 14!

The truth is of course that some one had to be elected second major-general, whether or not Ward was energetic.

[10] *James Warren to John Adams, June 20, 1775:* "Had our brave men, posted on Ground injudiciously at first taken, had a Lee or a Washington instead of a General destitute of all military Ability and Spirit to command them, it is my Opinion the day would have terminated with as much Glory to America as the 19th of April. This is our great Misfortune, and is remediless from any other quarter than yours. We dare not superceed him here—it will come well from you, and really merits your attention." —*Warren-Adams Letters,* I, 63; and elsewhere.

James Warren to Samuel Adams, June 21, 1775: "Fine fellows you know our Countrymen are *and want nothing but a general of spirit and abilities to make them* a fine army. all our Efforts which are many cannot supply that defect. yours must do it. could you believe, he *never left his house on Saturday last;* I shall add no more. I wish that was the worst of it." The words italicized have been struck out, by a later hand, from the original letter in the New York Public Library (*Samuel Adams Papers*). The full text, in modernized form, is given in *Massachusetts Historical Society Proceedings,* XIV, 81; and elsewhere.

James Warren to John Adams, June 27, 1775: "I can't but hope you will make some suitable provision for our General Thomas. His merits in the military way have surprised us all. I can't describe to you the odds between the two camps. While one has been spiritless, sluggish, confused and dirty, I mean where General Putnam and our Friend Warren's influence have not had their effects; the other has been spirited, active, regular and clean."—*Warren-Adams Letters,* I, 68.

James Warren's charges do not lend themselves satisfactorily to critical dissection because of their sweeping generality and indefinite innuendo—lack of "military ability"; "I wish that was the worst of it," etc. They contain no specific point for analysis except the assertion that Ward "never left his house" on June 17, which is discussed on pages 142–143. They are also affected by consideration of the writer's career and character. James Warren was a man of marked ability in some lines (he succeeded Joseph Warren as President of the Provincial Congress; and Washington, later, wished him to accompany the army to New York as paymaster-general), but he never took any military

have pursued their object living and dead for several generations; have been fostered and nurtured and handed down even to this day. But, praise be, some measure of dramatic justice has also lain in wait, for he unintentionally left behind him high tribute to Ward's standing and influence among both the rank and file of the army and its officers, for, as I have noted in an earlier chapter,[11] it was *James Warren* who testified that *"we dare not superceed him here."*

To this testimony from the third president of the Provincial Congress, and Ward's enemy (writing *after* the Battle of Bunker Hill), following that of Joseph Warren, the second president of the Provincial Congress and Ward's friend, I may add the esteem with which he was regarded by both Samuel Adams[12] and John Adams—the latter testifying and recording that he had much to do to excuse himself, that many arguments were necessary to convince his friends that patriotism had demanded such a sacrifice "of all our

part in any Revolutionary, or any other, campaign; and never exhibited any military aptitude or knowledge. In personal disposition, furthermore, he was inclined to petulancy—and was querulously complainant under an adverse vote. On February 14, 1776 (to Samuel Adams, *Massachusetts Historical Society Proceedings,* XIV, 281), he complained that the Council had rejected his (assembly) election to the post of second major-general of the militia "in a manner as ungracious and indelicate as Bernard or Hutchinson would have done," adding, "I have serious thoughts of quitting my civil commission and become an independent man." And he was so great a stickler for a point of personal precedence that he resigned the post when it was later given to him because of a fancied indignity in a command assigned (page 245).

I have not come across the key to James Warren's animosity toward Ward; but prejudice, even if it were nowhere else shown, is portrayed by the manifest unfairness of his letter of June 27, 1775, to John Adams. It may have been easy to determine the zone of Putnam's influence if his reference to Putnam was intended to apply only to Putnam's own, or to Spencer's, Connecticut men, but there could have been no such zone to credit to Dr. Warren for he at no time exercised a military command (he was killed at Bunker Hill on the third day after his appointment as second Massachusetts major-general). James Warren's method was apparently to attribute the good spots to Dr. Warren and charge the bad ones to General Ward!

[11] See page 112.

[12] Samuel Adams promptly rebuked the criticisms (presumably including James Warren's attack on Ward) directed against "some of our Generals" following Bunker Hill. "My dear Sir," he wrote to James Warren, June 28, "take Care lest Suspicions be carried to a dangerous Length. Our Army have behavd valiantly. There may have been an Error; but that Error may have proceeded not from a Want of Spirit but a Want of Judgment."—*Warren-Adams Letters,* I, 69. And a few days later he was writing most cordially to Ward, wishing him "a still greater share of laurels" than the successful conduct of the siege had already brought him.—July 6, 1775, original letter owned (1921) by Agnes Ward White, Parkersburg, W. Va.

feelings to the union of the colonies" as the placing of Washington above Ward—for Ward was a "commander-in-chief universally esteemed, beloved, and confided in by his army and country." [13]

Why, in the face of such overwhelming evidence, should it have been considered necessary to belittle a man who labored so faithfully for his province and his country? Washington's fame did not require the contrast depicted—his figure is far too great to need a false background. It is consequently not easy to understand why Bancroft employed his talents as writer and historian to strip the hard-earned laurels from the brow of an earlier son of his own state. In so doing, he not only perpetuated the work of Artemas Ward's first and chief detractor—he also robbed Massachusetts of the finest, purest part of the honor that is due her for having placed the fate of all the colonies in Washington's hands.

Bancroft made a great point of his assertion that Massachusetts asked for Washington as commander-in-chief, but failed to see that the plain truth of the reason for, and the manner of, asking was in conception and purpose infinitely higher and stronger and nobler than his own specially-staged version. It is not a pretty picture that he conjures up—Massachusetts believing her commander-in-chief to be inefficient and yet afraid to remove him, asking the Continental Congress to please do so and take charge of her army for her! The *truth* is infinitely different: it discloses a divine blend of courage and patriotism worthy of the strong souls that led in the Old Bay State. It shows Massachusetts fully holding her own against an English army and proudly satisfied with the commander-in-chief born and bred on her own soil, but her spokesmen offering his abnegation—and their own—as they had already offered and risked all else, on the altar of patriotism.

[13] *Works of John Adams,* X, 166.

CHAPTER X

July 4, 1775–January 15, 1776: Age 47–48

The siege after Washington's arrival. Ward in command of the Right Wing. Incidents of the siege.

WASHINGTON held his first formal council of war on July 9. Present to confer with him were Major-Generals Ward, Charles Lee, and Putnam; Adjutant-General Gates; and Brigadier-Generals Thomas, Heath, and Greene. It probably galled Lee and Gates not a little that native officers now sat at the head of the table. It had been different in the old days of the French war—which they all remembered well, for both Lee and Gates had fought with Washington at Monongahela; and Lee, as we have seen, had fought also with Ward at Ticonderoga.

The council unanimously decided to maintain the posts taken under General Ward and also agreed not to attempt "to take possession of Dorchester Point[1] nor to oppose the enemy if they should attempt to possess it." It estimated that an army of "at least 22,000" was necessary to maintain the siege—5000 more than the existing total enrollment and 7500 more than the number of those returned as "fit for duty." It directed the commander-in-chief to apply to the Massachusetts Provincial Congress for temporary reinforcements, and ordered a campaign to stimulate recruiting. Weld's Hill, in the rear of the Roxbury positions, was chosen

[1] *I.e.,* Dorchester Neck. The title of Dorchester Point (or, briefly, "the Point"), later specifically applied to that part facing Castle Island, was then frequently employed to designate the entire peninsula.

as a rendezvous in the event of the army being dispersed by a British attack.

On the following day Washington reported to the Continental Congress, enclosing a record of the proceedings of the council. "Considering," he said, "the great Extent of Line, and the nature of the Ground, we are as well secured as could be expected in so short a Time and under the Disadvantages we labour." He further testified that one of the principal reasons for the decision to maintain the posts that had been "form'd with so much labor" was the "Uncertainty of finding a Place in all Respects so capable of making a stand."[2]

To Richard Henry Lee he wrote on the same day, "I should not, I think, have made choice of the present posts, in the first instance," but he added, "I believe the communication between the town and country could not have been so well cut off without them." In this letter also he acknowledged that "much labor" had "been bestowed in throwing up lines, and making redoubts."[3]

Washington continued the three-divisions plan of the army. On July 22 he assigned the largest division, that of the right wing, to Ward; the left wing to Charles Lee; and the center, under his personal supervision, to Putnam.

Ward, three days later, rode over to Roxbury to assume his new command. The occasion was made one of ceremony. Five regiments were "marched towards Cambridge" to meet him and "waited upon" him into Roxbury.[4]

The right wing comprised the Roxbury positions and their "southern dependencies." Its northerly lines held the mainland base of Boston Neck. Its easterly lines stretched across the mainland base of the Dorchester peninsula and, by pickets, out on the Neck itself. By detachments and special

[2] Ford, *Writings of Washington,* III, 10.

[3] *Ibid.,* 23.

[4] Journal of Samuel Haws, *Military Journals of Two Private Soldiers,* 62; Diary of Ensign Nathaniel Morgan, *Connecticut Historical Society Collections,* VII, 103.

commands, it later extended to a number of points along the coast: easterly to Squantum, Hingham, and Cohasset; and, for a time, southerly to Plymouth. Its strongest posts were the "Lower" and "High" forts. The Lower Fort commanded the Roxbury, or Boston Neck, road. It extended about 400 feet north and south and averaged nearly 300 feet in width, following on three sides the natural lines of rock. High Fort, southerly of the Lower Fort, was a quadrangular work, about 200 feet square, with bastions at each angle.[5]

The division under the new alignment was manned by twelve regiments of Massachusetts and Connecticut men, in two brigades under Generals Thomas and Spencer.

Roxbury was at that time still "a suburban village, with a single narrow street, and dotted with farms, many of which were yet held by the descendants of the original proprietors. . . . The business of the town was concentrated in Roxbury Street, the sole thoroughfare to Boston, through which [in normal times] as through a tunnel, crowded all the surplus produce of the country."[6]

Ward's headquarters was in the mansion "built about the year 1723, by Col. Francis Brinley, upon the estate of eighty acres formerly Palsgrave Alcock's," and "styled by its owner, 'Datchet House,' having been modelled after the family seat of the Brinleys, at Datchet, England."[7] It was at the time known as the Brinley Place, or "Pierpont Castle," deriving its latter name from its purchase in 1773 by Robert Pierpont, a Boston merchant. There is much vivid description of it in a little volume entitled "Fannie St. John," by Emily Pierpont Delesdernier.

"It was situated," she wrote, "in the midst of a large domain of park and wooded hills, and presented a picture of grandeur and stateliness not common in the New World.

[5] High Fort Observatory, Highland Park, today stands guard on its site, and well repays a visit. The inscriptions on the rail of the Observation Balcony balustrade direct the eye to many points of historic interest.

[6] *Memorial History of Boston,* III, 571.

[7] Drake, *The Town of Roxbury,* 327.

There were colonnades, and a vestibule whose massive mahogany doors, studded with silver, opened into a wide hall, where tessellated floors sparkled under the light of a lofty dome of richly painted glass. Underneath the dome two cherubs carved in wood extended their wings, and so formed the center, from which an immense chandelier of cut glass depended. Upon the floor beneath the dome there stood a marble column, and around it ran a divan formed of cushions covered with satin of Damascus of gorgeous coloring. Large mirrors with ebony frames filled the spaces between the grand staircases at either side of the hall of entrance. All the paneling and woodwork consisted of elaborate carving done abroad, and made to fit every part of the mansion where such ornamentation was required. Exquisite combinations of painted birds and fruits and flowers abounded everywhere, in rich contrast with the delicate blue tint that prevailed upon the lofty walls. The state-rooms were covered with Persian carpets, and hung with tapestries of gold and silver, arranged after some graceful artistic foreign fashion."

The "wide hall," forty-four feet in length and twenty-two feet in width, occupied the entire ground floor of the center of the house and opened into two large wings to left and right. In the right was the reception room in which Ward and his staff held council.[8]

On August 3 Ward took part in the perturbed council of war which discussed the crisis threatened by the nearly empty powder magazines. The American generals had been continuously concerned because of the small amount of gunpowder (only about 300 barrels) reported on hand. Now, suddenly, the 300 barrels had shrunk to only ninety barrels—not more than nine rounds to a man! The powder had

[8] "Pierpont Castle" was, later, for many years known as the "Dearborn House," General Dearborn—who as a captain had fought under Stark at Bunker Hill—buying the property in 1809 and making it his home until his death. In 1869 the estate was purchased by the Redemptorist Fathers and has since continued uninterruptedly in their possession. In 1876 part of the house was destroyed by fire, but the remainder continued in use as a dwelling until 1902, when it was torn down to make way for the present handsome brick and stone rectory of the Mission Church, adjoining.

not been used, nor stolen, nor wasted to any considerable extent. The greater part of the reputed 300 barrels had been but a will-o'-the-wisp supply, non-existent save as a clerical error of the Committee of Supplies. Washington, wrote Sullivan, "was so struck, that he did not utter a word for half an hour."[9]

The council voted not only to apply to the neighboring provinces for powder, but also to send a party of 300 men to raid the royal magazine at Halifax. The latter project was, however, allowed to subside.

The discovery of the mistake was reported to General Gage, but the story was considered so improbable that it was discarded as a ruse to draw him out.

The English commander was also undoubtedly influenced by the remarkable change of viewpoint brought about by the cost of his Bunker Hill victory. Even prior to Bunker Hill he had felt the need of a larger force for use in and around Boston, but he had apparently no idea of giving up the town. After Bunker Hill, its abandonment was his uppermost thought. We find his letters to Lord Dartmouth first hinting for, and then virtually requesting, permission to give it up and to transfer the seat of war to New York. "I have made your Lordship acquainted with the disadvantageous situation of his Majesty's Forces in this place, and the more it is considered, the worse it is found to be," he declared in his Secret Letter of August 20. Bunker Hill had robbed him of all hope of a successful issue with the New England army which so closely besieged him.

On September 2 there called at Ward's headquarters a man who later passed through glory into perpetual infamy—Benedict Arnold, then bearing a commission as colonel and about to start on his expedition through the wilderness to Quebec. He came to Roxbury with a letter from Washington's headquarters requesting the "advice and assistance" of

[9] August 5, 1775, to the New Hampshire Committee of Safety, *New Hampshire Provincial Papers,* VII, 572.

Ward and his brigadiers "in promoting this important service."[10]

Arnold's detachment consisted of about 1000 rank and file. A small force—but chiefly of picked men; and these leavened with many of more than ordinary daring. Young Aaron Burr was of its number; and Daniel Morgan, later terrible to the English as the chief of "Morgan's Rangers," commanded the three companies drawn from the Virginia, Pennsylvania, and Maryland riflemen who had joined the army a few weeks earlier.

The men were "taken off the roll of duty" on September 8, and on that date and the ninth were encamped in separate quarters at Cambridge while preparations were completing for their departure the following week.

The shaping of this enterprise—one so attractive to Washington's temperament; a project plentifully beset with adventurous danger—aroused in the Virginian a restless impatience over the deadlock to which his own campaign seemed tending.

The opposing armies lay in sight of each other, yet there promised no opportunity of decisive action. The English strengthened their works on the Boston and Charlestown peninsulas, and the Americans strengthened, and contracted, their encircling lines without; but the English army was not strong enough to raise the siege, nor the American to attempt a general assault. Instead, were only occasional skirmishes and a succession of fruitless alarms.

The enforced inaction sorely tried Washington's soul. The eyes of two continents were upon him and he had not yet learned the caution which the calamitous campaign of the next summer instilled into him. With mounting recklessness he planned to hazard his army on a single stroke.

[10] The letter enjoined "profound secrecy" concerning the project, but, as on many similar occasions, the news leaked through to the camps. Jedediah Huntington, writing to his father, Jabez Huntington, on September 5, refers to the Arnold expedition as "Secret, thou' known to every Body."—Original letter, September 4–5, 1775, *General Jedediah Huntington Letters,* Connecticut Historical Society.

The average reader—also, many a historian—takes as his model for the Washington of the siege of Boston, the resourceful self-contained commander-in-chief of two or so years later. And thereby greatly errs, and spoils the picture which should most interest him—the forming of the character of the "father of his country," of the Washington of Yorktown and the presidency.

The Washington of the siege of Boston was he of the French war—a man of but scant military experience, unused to the command of large bodies of men; older but still untamed, distrustful of what the future might bring, and ready to stake everything on the dice of the present.

His plan, submitted in letters on September 8 and argued in council of war on September 11, was to attack Boston by rowboats.

Truly the Washington of the French war, whose reckless disregard of his enemy's far greater strength had compelled his capitulation on that other earlier occasion when fate had given him the chief command. Time had not dimmed his rashness, for now, with his troops only partly armed, and crippled by shortage of powder, he proposed to storm a fortified town in open boats—a town, by his own description, "surrounded in a manner by ships of war and floating batteries."[11] Before he could attempt his musket attack, he must carry his men in those boats for a mile or more with artillery playing full upon them.

Among the reasons he advanced for so wild a move were the expense of keeping his men warm through the winter and the fear that necessity might destroy the fences and orchards in the vicinity!

He doubted equally his ability to hold an army together and the ability, or willingness, of the country to meet the cost of its subsistence.

He was far from realizing the length of the fight ahead

[11] To Robert Carter Nicholas, October 5, 1775.—Ford, *Writings of Washington,* III, 171.

of him. His idea was, and had been, that he could speedily crush the English army and then disband the American.[12]

It was well that Ward and the other New Englanders whom Charles Lee sarcastically referred to as the "Big Wigs," helped to hold the hotheaded Virginian in leash and, by their decision against attempting the assault, prevented him from thus wrecking the careful work of the Massachusetts patriots who had for years maintained a stout front against British domination.

Washington felt keenly also his failure to impress professional military standards on his army. In his first Cambridge letter to the Continental Congress he had apologetically referred to the several days' delay in obtaining the regimental returns, explaining that he had been "unapprized of the imperfect Obedience which had been paid to those [orders] of the like Nature from General Ward." To Richard Henry Lee he made the point still more strongly: "Could I have conceived, that what ought, and, in a regular army, would have been done in an hour, would employ eight days . . ." And he had added (in his letter to Congress) that he flattered himself that the reasons "will no longer exist; and of Consequence more Regularity and exactness in future prevail."[13] But the fulfilment of that laudable expectation was to be long deferred. Months later, on the same point and in the same camps, there was just as long delay; and not until nearly three years after Washington had assumed the chief command—not until after Steuben had overhauled and systematized[14]—

[12] "The state of inactivity in which this army has lain for some time," he wrote to the Continental Congress, September 21, 1775, "by no means corresponds with my wishes by some decisive stroke to relieve my country from the heavy expense its subsistence must create . . . there is not a man in America, who more earnestly wishes such a termination of the campaign, as to make the army no longer necessary."—Ford, *Writings of Washington,* III, 145, 146.

[13] Ford, *Writings of Washington,* III, 11, 22.

[14] Steuben, in the spring of 1778, working with Washington's headquarters army—the heroic little band at Valley Forge—found "Nothing was so difficult, and often so impossible, as to get a correct list of the state or a return of any company, regiment, or corps." The army had come to be "looked upon as a nursery for servants," and some of the

could the American army be described as a disciplined military force.

Washington was slow to perceive that much of the petty insubordination and many of the unmilitary habits rife in the American camps were inherent to the conditions, and he had at first essayed to treat the men besieging Boston as though they were professional soldiers. On July 17 the Reverend William Emerson had written, "There is great overturning in the camp, as to order and regularity. New lords, new laws. The Generals Washington and Lee are upon the lines every day. New orders from his Excellency are read to the respective regiments every morning after prayers. The strictest government is taking place, and great distinction is made between officers and soldiers. Every one is made to know his place, and keep in it, or to be tied up and receive thirty or forty lashes, according to his crime."[15]

The "new lords" and "new laws" did produce a considerable improvement in discipline—variously attributable to Washington's personal efforts, to the military experience of Charles Lee and Gates, and to the greater measure of authority carried by commissions issued by a congress representing all the colonies. But it was very far from being a complete transformation; it was largely temporary; and it was followed by severe reaction. Harsh words, rigorous punishments, and class distinctions were unpleasant fare, and the camps soon again seethed with friction. Before three months had passed we find the New Englanders in such an irritated condition that a deduction from their allowance was sufficient to produce the greatest alarm in their commander—Washington was compelled to advise Congress on September 21 that "the greater part of the troops are in a state not far from mutiny."[16] In the same letter he confessed his inability to

irregularities were extraordinarily flagrant. Regiments carried on their rolls men who had been absent for a year or more.—Kapp, *Life of Frederick William Von Steuben*, 115–119.

[15] Sparks, *Writings of Washington*, III, 491.

[16] Ford, *Writings of Washington*, III, 147.

obtain the men's subscriptions to the new continental articles of war.

These months were marked also by the birth and growth of the estrangement between Washington and Ward. No light was ever shed upon its original cause by either man, but indirect evidence points to a mutual lack of cordiality as having existed from their first meeting. There are three probable explanations: first, James Warren; second, Charles Lee; and third, Washington's biting comments on both officers and privates of the Massachusetts troops.

James Warren had conceived and expressed the idea that the failure to hold Bunker Hill, the lack of discipline, and pretty nearly every other trouble, was Ward's fault. Washington had not anticipated the conditions he encountered in the American camps and he apparently adopted James Warren's line of thought and hastened to the conclusion that the disorder he found was due to laxity in Ward's methods.

Next on the list we have Charles Lee, still smarting from the two wounds to his pride—the twice passing of his name in the selection of those to command the Revolutionary army. Under the circumstances one would *not* expect "Boiling Water" (so the Indians had nicknamed Lee) to appreciate a provincial general who had little to say for himself, who was a judge by profession instead of a soldier, and who had established Cromwell's practice of the troops' daily attendance at prayers—"Deacon Ward," Lee styled him; and one *would* expect Lee, never sparing in criticism of people whom he disliked or who might be in his way, to pass many sneers to Washington concerning Ward. We also know that until the battle of Monmouth (June 28, 1778) Washington held a very high opinion of Lee's military judgment and ability.

The third surmise—Washington's harsh criticisms of New Englanders: his impugning of their personal habits, courage, intelligence, and morality—was probably a fertile cause of the continuance and growth of the ill feeling, for General

Ward strongly resented disparagement of Massachusetts by Southerners.

Though no action of moment broke the period from Bunker Hill to Dorchester Heights, no commander lacked duties or troubles.

The defenses of the right wing grew steadily more formidable, and their construction and maintenance kept Ward's division fully occupied. The council of war of July 9 had debarred any attempt on Dorchester Neck, but the Boston Neck lines were pushed forward to within musket-shot of the enemy's advance-works, being there supported by a strong redoubt at Lamb's Dam.

Constant watchfulness was required to see that the works were at all times sufficiently manned, that ammunition was not wasted, and that the troops did no damage to private houses in Roxbury, nor wantonly to the fields of the surrounding country.

Also to guard against the weakening of the land blockade of Boston. Some cattle having been allowed to wander so close to the English lines that they had fallen prey to the enemy, to their nourishment and rejoicing, Ward issued notice to the owners of live stock that they would be deemed "enemies to their country" if their stock were found grazing beyond the advance-works on Boston Neck, and ordered sentries to fire on any cattle permitted so to stray.

A few weeks later he dispatched orders to the commanding officer at Hingham to strip Nantasket because of the suspicion that "an unjustifiable intercourse has been kept up between some of the inhabitants . . . and our unnatural enemies belonging to the Men of War." Its inhabitants and all "moveable necessaries of life"—live stock, hay, corn, etc., —were ordered taken off.

Unauthorized liquor selling was another evil to be guarded against, and pay-day generally spelled trouble.[17]

[17] "Peace with our Enemy, but disturbance enough with rum, for our men got money yesterday."—Revolutionary Journal of Aaron Wright, October 7, 1775, *Historical Magazine,* VI, 210.

Grievances, both real and imaginary; regimental gossip and scandal; stories of attacks projected by both armies, and all manner of other reports—from authentic news to the vaguest rumors—gave the men plenty to talk, think, and grumble about. One diary epitomizes the condition in the terse entry: "very much camp news, but nothing serious."

The long-distance cannonading (long, that is, for those days, and chiefly by the British guns) early became an old story. The men soon lost their first fear of cannon shot and contended for the balls as they ricochetted along the ground. The successful captor would take the ball to the general of his brigade and receive his reward in a gallon or two of rum with which to stand treat to his company. The sport was at first encouraged by officers as tending to offset the moral effect of the enemy's bombardment, but later it became necessary to discourage and suppress it, as a number of men were laid up from tackling the balls before they were sufficiently spent.

Even the bursting of shells in the camp became an occasion for glee instead of fear.

A Connecticut lieutenant describes an artillery duel between the American guns at Roxbury and those of the Boston forts, during the course of which "the dogs hove a ball right over our incampment, which made as bad a noise as a flock of wild geese." He adds, "I find that the exchanging these few shot has done more to exhilarate the spirits of our people than 200 gallons of New England rum." The shells "had scarcely time to break before they would surround them to pick up the pieces of them as so many curiosities!"[18]

Occasionally a shot or shell would strike unpleasantly close.

One of the Maryland riflemen attached to the Roxbury division tells of a 32-pound cannon shot which "rushed through the room and dashed one side out of the chimney, broke 2 partitions and filled our dishes with plastering, ceiling and

[18] Diary of Jabez Fitch, Jr., August 15, 1775, *Massachusetts Historical Society Proceedings,* 2d, IX, 45.

bricks." He and three others were breakfasting at the time. He adds that he couldn't speak for what his companions thought, but "I went down two pair of stairs, three strides without a fall, and as soon as I was out of doors ran to the Brestwork in great haste, which is our place of safety, without the least concern about my breakfast, to James McCancie's amazement!"[19]

Again, one of Ward's chaplains records in his diary: "Nothing special to day except we had one cannon ball shot, which threw so much dust into a man's bason of bread and milk as spoiled his breakfast."[20]

There was always intense interest in news from Boston—obtained from deserters from the English army, from occasional captives, and from letters written by residents of the town and sent into and through the American camps under the military arrangements made for the exchange of private communications.

The strict discipline and poor fare of the English army resulted in a number of its men deserting and slipping through to the American lines. They were welcomed with generous potations of rum as pay for the stories they told, until that practice was sternly forbidden in general orders. The deserters generally tuned their tales to whatever key they thought would gain the best welcome: sometimes giving solemn warnings of assaults projected; at other times attempting to ingratiate themselves by pictures of the great weakness of the enemy's camp. One man told with circumstantial detail of the low state of the English army—that there were not nine hundred rank and file fit for duty!

Some of these erstwhile redcoats were passed into the country, where they were joyfully set at the farm work which the besiegers had perforce left undone.

Traveling with the Boston news and gossip were many

[19] Daniel McCurtin's Journal, August 18, 1775, *Papers relating chiefly to the Maryland Line,* 13.

[20] Diary of the Reverend Benjamin Boardman, September 14, 1775, *Massachusetts Historical Society Proceedings,* 2d, VII, 406.

stories, true and otherwise, of happenings in England: the actions of the ministry, and of various prominent men aligned both for and against the government's American course; accounts of an "accommodation arranged"; numerous tales of large reinforcements coming or to be sent, and of great disturbances in England: "of the Parliament House in London being pulled down, and of Lord North and Governor Hutchinson flying to France"; that "the people in England were in great tumult, and that Lord North had been wounded."[21]

A rumor early drifted through the lines that the English ministry had ordered the abandonment of Boston; and Howe's failure to make any move to raise the siege gave it weight in Washington's estimation. The rumor was baseless —no such order arrived until several weeks later—but it accurately mirrored the desires of the English commander!

The (inevitable) transgressions in the American camps were met with penalties which—though mild compared with the English code—would seriously offend modern sensibilities.

Whipping has been referred to in an earlier page as a common measure. Its severity depended largely upon the disposition of those who carried out the sentence. Other punishments were "riding the wooden horse"—a barbarous torture—and the pillory. One man who was condemned to the pillory for an hour "for being concerned in writing an infamous letter" against his colonel, fainted before his time was up and gave "the doctors much ado to bring him to."[22]

The letter-writer had his satisfaction a few weeks later, for that particular colonel faced a court-martial for employing members of his regiment to work on his farm, and was dismissed from the service. *"Amen to that,"* rejoiced another private at the news.[23]

[21] Diary of Ezekiel Price, August 16, 20, 1775, *Massachusetts Historical Society Proceedings*, VII, 204, 205.

[22] *Paul Lunt's Diary,* September 20, 1775.

[23] Samuel Bixby's Diary, October 23, 1775, *Massachusetts Historical Society Proceedings*, XIV, 295.

It perchance happened that a culprit was popular, and then his punishment stirred the troops to mutiny. On September 10 there was "Great commotion on Prospect Hill among the riflemen, occasioned by the unreasonable confinement of a sergeant by the adjutant of Thompson's regiment; and before it was over, 34 men were confined and two of them put in irons at headquarters in Cambridge."[24]

On another occasion "their was a Rifle man whipt 39 stripes for Stealing and afterwards he was Drummed out of camp. If the infernal regions had been opened . . . there could not have been a biger uproar."[25]

These riflemen from the South had at first been the object of the greatest curiosity, admiration, and gratitude. Their marksmanship continuously commanded respect, but otherwise the rank and file speedily outwore their welcome. Ward, writing to John Adams, remarked, October 30, 1775, "They do not boast so much of the Riflemen as heretofore. Genl Washington has said he wished they had never come; Genl. Lee has damned them and wished them all in Boston; Genl Gates has said, if any capital movement was about to be made, the Riflemen must be moved from this camp."[26]

Charles Lee, as might be expected, reiterated his opinion freely and caustically. To Benjamin Rush he wrote, "I once was of opinion, that some Battalions from the Southward wou'd be necessary—but I have alter'd my opinion. I am now perswaded you have not to the Southward so good materials for common soldiers. Your Riflemen have a good deal open'd our eyes upon the subject, tho' to do justice to their

[24] Revolutionary Journal of Aaron Wright, *Historical Magazine*, VI, 209. So serious appeared the possibilities of this outbreak that Generals Washington, Charles Lee, and Greene in person took part in quelling it.—Jesse Lukens' original letter, September 15, 1775, sold by Henkels, Philadelphia, December 5, 1898.

[25] Samuel Haws, October 9, 1775, *Military Journals of Two Private Soldiers*, 76. McCurtin (October 9, 1775, *Papers relating chiefly to the Maryland Line*, 21) also recorded that occasion, stating that fifty-two drummers and as many fifers took part in the proceedings and that he could not even hear the man next him.

[26] Original letter, *Adams Collection*, Massachusetts Historical Society.

officers They are unexceptionable; their Privates are in general damn'd riff raff—dirty, mutinous, and disaffected."[27]

On September 27 came the arrest of Benjamin Church as a traitor, an intercepted cipher letter suddenly rending the high confidence that had been reposed in him. A few days later (October 3) a council of war was called to consider the charge against him. It resulted in a second meeting on the following morning, with the former head of the Committee of Safety present for examination. Church tried to explain away his clandestine epistle, but the assembled generals could see no merit in his defense and they unanimously found him guilty. Furthermore, the punishment prescribed by the army regulations seemed to them "very inadequate" for the offense—and they referred the matter to the Continental Congress "for their special direction," meantime isolating Church under strict guard.[28]

On the following Sunday (October 8) Ward took part in a council of war to decide upon the number of men needed to continue the siege; the length of service for which they should be enlisted; their pay, rations, clothing, regimental organization, etc.

It was unanimously agreed that the grand total of the army ought not to be less than 20,372 men; that enlistments should be until December 1, 1776; and that both pay and rations should be the same as for the "eight months' army" whose term was nearing an end. The council was divided on

[27] October 10, 1775, *Lee Papers,* I, 211.

[28] The Continental Congress ordered Church to be taken into Connecticut and held in close confinement there. On May 14 (1776), acting on his pleas of ill health, it authorized his return to Massachusetts and his release on bail. Reports followed that he was to be exchanged for an American officer held prisoner by the English. Ward protested against the move as "impolitick," and suggested that "for several reasons" well known to American councils it would be "highly proper to procrastinate the Exchange" as "I think no one can doubt that Doctr Church is fully acquainted with the state of our Publick Affairs, and can communicate to the Enemy Intelligence which may be greatly detrimental to the United States at this Juncture" (July 5, 1777, *Artemas Ward MSS.*). The plan was temporarily abandoned, but it was reopened in October of the same year by the offer of Joshua Loring, British commissary of prisoners, to exchange Dr. M'Henry of Philadelphia for him. The Congress negatived the proposal. Church was later permitted to embark in a vessel bound for Martinique. The ship was lost at sea.

the method of payment: Washington with four others (Lee, Heath, Sullivan, Greene) declared for monthly payments; and Ward with four others (Putnam, Thomas, Spencer, Gates) for a pay-day every three months.

A little later the camp was abuzz with the visit of Benjamin Franklin and his associates of a Continental Congress committee; and shortly after there spread a rumor, which became general toward the end of the month, that the French were willing to join and aid the Revolutionary cause if "we would trade with them."[29]

On October 17, under the new Massachusetts government, Ward was appointed chief justice of the Court of Common Pleas for Worcester County.[30] Just a month later the English commander-in-chief made Timothy Ruggles, the former chief justice, Commandant of the "Loyal American Associaters," one of Boston's volunteer loyalist organizations.

On October 18 Washington again submitted to a council of war the question of assaulting Boston. Resolutions of the Continental Congress had favored an attack. But again the project was voted down.

Contemporary observers chronicle the changes that the siege wrought on the country surrounding the capital.

The Reverend Emerson had early noted various results which were "a little melancholy" . . . "all the lands, fields, orchards laid common, horses and cattle feeding in the choicest mowing land, whole fields of corn eaten down to the ground, and large parks of well-regulated locusts cut down for firewood and other public uses,"[31] and each succeeding month multiplied the evidences of war's rough usage.

[29] Journal of Samuel Haws, October 24, 1775, *Military Journals of Two Private Soldiers,* 78.

[30] The original joint commission of Ward and the other three judges is owned by the American Antiquarian Society (*Massachusetts Papers,* 99). The first sitting of the court (the first since its closure—Ward participating—fifteen months before) was held in Worcester, December 5, 1775. Ward's military responsibilities prevented him from attending.

[31] Sparks, *Writings of Washington,* III, 492.

"All around the Encampment is one Scene of Desolation," wrote Moses Brown, the Quaker, visiting the province with contributions for the poor and distressed in and around Boston.[32] And Jeremy Belknap, the famous divine and historian, declared that nothing struck him with more horror than the condition of Roxbury—"that once busy, crowded street is now occupied only by a picquet guard. The houses are deserted, the windows taken out, and many shot-holes visible; some have been burnt, and others pulled down, to make room for the fortifications."

"After dining with General Ward," continued Dr. Belknap, "I returned to Cambridge; in the evening, visited and conversed with General Putnam. Ward appears to be a calm, cool, thoughtful man; Putnam, a rough, fiery genius."

Independence had by this time "become a favorite point in the army." Hope for an "accommodation" had lost its relish. The troops had brushed aside the distinction between the Crown and Parliament—"it was offensive to pray for the king."[33]

The army, as also many civilians in New England, were, however, on that point politically in advance of the majority of the inhabitants of the other American colonies. Outside of New England the general hope was for an alleviation of grievances and a resumption of the old relations.

Disturbing the minds of many, and checking their support, was the spectre, not yet laid to rest, of a victorious New England thrusting its domination on the other provinces—by force of arms if need be.[34]

The approach of winter again focussed attention on Dorchester Neck. The peninsula now stood bare of human life, save for Ward's sentries and outposts. Its former inhabitants had deserted it, as too exposed, during the summer and early fall.

[32] *Pennsylvania Magazine of History and Biography*, 1877, 171.

[33] *Life of Jeremy Belknap*, 92, 93.

[34] General Greene's letter of October 16, 1775, to Governor Ward of Rhode Island deprecates this fear.—Johnson, *Sketches of the Life of Nathanael Greene*, I, 39.

In council of war, November 2, the possibility of fortifying its hills was considered afresh. As "the situation of American Affairs with respect to Great Britain" might "be such as to render it indispensibly necessary, to attempt to Destroy the Ministerial Troops in the Town of Boston" before they could be reinforced in the spring, "even if it should be by Bombarding, & Firing the Town," the question was put whether it was "advisable to erect any kind of Works upon Dorchester Point, before Frost setts in; & what kind."[35]

Ensuing events prove that a negative decision was again reached, but the record disappeared long ago—the manuscript ends abruptly at the fourth page, leaving its interrogations unanswered.

The dearth of ammunition is thrown into high relief by one of the last questions:

"In our present Scarcity of Powder, had not our morning Gun better be discontinued?"

The meeting devoted much thought to officering the army of '76. Its report contains tentative lists of colonels, lieutenant-colonels, and majors for the new establishment. The lists are valuable as recording the general officers' approval of the field-officers named.

At English headquarters a few days later, Howe, who had replaced Gage as commander-in-chief, received Lord Dartmouth's letter of September 5 with word that he had been "commanded by the King" to say that it seemed "not only advisable, but necessary to abandon Boston before the winter."[36]

Here was the permission to quit Boston that Gage, first, and Howe, succeeding him, had hoped for. But now that it had reached him after a two months' voyage across the Atlantic, Howe was "with great reluctance" obliged to acknowledge that it could not safely be acted on. There were not enough ships in the harbor to complete the evacuation in

[35] *American Archives*, 4th, III, 1335.

[36] This is the advice, or order, quoted also on page 137.

one move, and the English officers considered it dangerous to divide their forces, especially "at a season when the navigation on this coast, from the violence of northerly winds, is so very precarious." Deflection of transports by gales might extend the separation into months.

The week marked in Boston by the arrival of Lord Dartmouth's letter declaring for the immediate abandonment of the capital of Massachusetts, saw across the ocean his resignation as Secretary of State for the American Department, and the installation of Lord Germain.

Germain's views differed from those of his predecessor and he was strongly against a precipitate desertion of Boston, but the wintry Atlantic permitted neither his letters, nor even the news of his appointment, to reach the besieged town. Not until after he had abandoned Boston did Howe receive any inkling of a possible change of the government's decision to surrender it.

The two last months of 1775 and the first of 1776 constituted a nerve-racking period for the American commanders. "Our situation is truly alarming," declared Washington on November 28.[37] The curse of the short-term enlistment set its blight upon the camp. The old enrolment terms expired and only a few men had joined the new establishment. The majority, dissatisfied with their treatment and conditions generally, scattered to their neglected homes. Many of them, after a short absence, did reënlist, but for a full two months the weakness of the American lines was very real and might have proved disastrous.

The first great defection was among the Connecticut men. Their sentiment was so clearly displayed toward the latter part of November that Washington arranged a conference (November 30) with a General Court committee to devise measures for meeting the dangers of the situation; Ward, Thomas, and Spencer of the right wing taking part in it at his request.

[37] To the Continental Congress.—Ford, *Writings of Washington,* III, 243–244.

It was decided to call in 5000 Massachusetts and New Hampshire militia to bridge the crisis. They came with an alacrity which brought high praise from Washington;[38] and Ward, also, observed "with great satisfaction and pleasure" the "peace and quiet" in the camp that followed their arrival.[39] But the "peace and quiet" were not enduring. Disorder approaching demoralization pervaded the ranks as December closed and the New Year opened.

The American generals kept anxious eyes on every movement in Boston. Washington wrote, "Not an officer but what looks for an attack."

Washington could not bring himself to a satisfactory estimate of either Howe's activity or his lack of it. When there was any unusual stir in the English camps, he was of two minds as to whether Howe was planning to attack, or preparing to abandon, the port.[40] When the English had permitted the precarious period to pass without an attempt to take advantage of it, he declared that Howe must either have been "very ignorant" of the American conditions ("which I do not believe"), or have received orders to take no risks until his reinforcements arrived ("which I think is natural to conclude").[41]

Tales of the weakness of Washington's force were current in Boston, but the British again feared that the reports had been designed to draw them out. To Boston eyes the American camps presented a formidable appearance, and the militiamen coming in from the country had given the impression of great numbers.

[38] Washington to the Continental Congress, December 11, 1775.—Ford, *Writings of Washington,* III, 271.

[39] *Ward's Order Book,* December 13, 1775.

[40] On December 11, 1775, part of the English troops on Bunker Hill moved into winter quarters in Boston. This was quickly magnified by American observers, and on the same evening Washington dispatched an express to Ward warning him that he had "this moment" received a report "that the enemy have Transported almost their whole Force from Bunkers Hill, to Boston; this semes as if their intention was, either to make some considerable Effort, or remove from their present Quarters."—Original letter owned (1921) by Agnes Ward White, Parkersburg, W. Va.

[41] To Joseph Reed, February 10, 1776.—Ford, *Writings of Washington,* III, 413.

The English felt severely the hardships occasioned by the American leaguer. Food at times ran dangerously low. Bounteous stores—cattle and provender, clothing and coal—were collected in England and shipped outward, but only a small part reached General Howe. Ill management delayed the sailing of the ships; and heavy storms held them, and scattered them, and ruined much of their cargoes. And, finally, the American "armed vessels"—fishing craft and merchantmen with cannon mounted on them—exacted a heavy toll of those ships which did successfully cross the ocean and essayed to beat their way into Boston Harbor. The "armed vessels" were chiefly privateers. Howe, writing to England, declared that they "infested the bay."

The miseries of Boston were multiplied by the curse of smallpox falling upon it. The horror of the pestilence reached through to the American camps, and every precaution was taken to prevent their infection.[42]

The proximity of the two armies and, especially, the weakness of the American, impelled unremitting vigilance, but it was difficult to impress the American privates, particularly new recruits, with the vital importance of outpost and sentry details. When both sides had been inactive for some time, and especially when the weather was severe, the farmer-soldier was tempted to shirk, and to get under cover for a spell of rest and a greater measure of comfort than is ordinarily found on sentry duty. This habit was the cause of inexpressible anxiety among commanding officers.

The week preceding Christmas was marked by several

[42] There are not many Americans of the twentieth century who realize the fear which smallpox excited in those days, but Revolutionary records are replete with evidence of it. Washington wrote to the Continental Congress, December 14, 1775, that he believed that the English held its prevalence in the capital as "a weapon of defence they are using against us."—Ford, *Writings of Washington,* III, 276. In the following year, after the evacuation, Ward warned the commanding officers at Dorchester and Castle Island not to permit any men to go into Boston who had not already had the disease, that it would be very dangerous to have those posts infected, "for in case of an attack by the enemy the Country people would not come to their assistance."—*Ward's Order Book,* July 4, 1776. At about the same time Governor Trumbull was writing to Washington that the Connecticut men had "a greater dread" of smallpox than of the British army.—Ford, *Writings of Washington,* IV, 218, note.

days of extreme cold[43] and on the night of December 22 a number of Colonel Learned's guards and sentries on Dorchester Neck deserted their posts. Ward's stern reprimand to the delinquents drew a graphic picture of the high responsibility assigned to them, and the disaster to the American cause that might follow neglect, and carried an earnest appeal to the more experienced officers "to use their utmost endeavors to teach others their Duty."

To these trials of the general officers was added the shortage of fuel. On November 2 Washington had emphasized the necessity of obtaining a sufficient supply of firewood by notifying the Massachusetts General Court that "different Regiments were upon the point of cutting each others' throats for a few standing locusts near their encampments," and by December 31 Greene was writing: "We have suffered prodigiously for want of wood. Many regiments have been obliged to eat their provisions raw for want of fuel to cook it."[44]

The same difficulty troubled the enemy in Boston. "In defiance of Repeated Orders," the soldiers so persistently helped themselves to firewood by pulling down fences and houses that Howe directed "the Provost to go his rounds attended by the Executioner, with orders to hang up upon the spot the first man he shall detect in the act, without waiting for further proof by trial."[45]

The American fuel supply was later eked out by the cutting of marsh turf.

Impatient criticism was now making itself heard through-

[43] "[December] 20, 21, 22 [1775]. Those two days past and this day are pronounced to be the coldest three days that ever happened, to the knowledge of many of the inhabitants here, . . . they certainly are remarkable in my eyes. The bay was frozed up in two nights."

"23. Very cold and frosty."

"24. Last night it rained and snowed heavy, and continued the whole day. I went in company with another young man about three miles out of our camp this day, and never felt such cold in my living days."—Daniel McCurtin's Journal, *Papers relating chiefly to the Maryland Line,* 29–30.

[44] Johnson, *Sketches of the Life of Nathanael Greene,* I, 48.

[45] *Howe's Orderly Book,* December 5, 1775.

out the country. To anxious patriots, ignorant of his difficulties, Washington seemed strangely inactive. The heralded "continental generals" had been in charge since early summer, and yet, despite the political advantage of the union of the colonies, there was little more to show than an extension of the work of Ward and the New England militia. It was freely stated that an attack on Boston was withheld out of regard not only for its inhabitants but also for its many fine private properties; and there were not wanting those who accused Washington of prolonging the siege in order to prolong his importance as commander-in-chief.[46]

Further perturbing the public mind was the undercurrent of suspicion that had been started by the arrest of Benjamin Church. Many sinister rumors ran a startling course: one, shortly after, that Knox, who had succeeded Gridley as artillery colonel—and who in later years was Secretary of War under President Washington—had been arrested and "discovered to be active in exposing our works to the enemy."[47] The rumor carried weight because Knox's wife was Lucy Flucker, daughter of the tory Secretary and mandamus councilor.

Another tale, of later date, was that John Adams and Hancock had deserted the cause and sailed for England on a British man-of-war. When the report reached Braintree, John Adams' home town, "such high disputes took place in the public house . . ., that some men were collared and dragged out of the shop with great threats, for reporting such scandalous lies."[48]

And while Washington sat outside the capital, longing for an opportunity to fight and chafing at the thought that he had submitted to the restraint of the other general officers,[49] the

[46] Marshall, *Life of George Washington*, First American edition, II, 272 (different page numbers in other editions); Ramsay, *History of the American Revolution*, I, 261.

[47] Diary of the Reverend Benjamin Boardman, October 31, 1775, *Massachusetts Historical Society Proceedings*, 2d, VII, 412.

[48] Abigail Adams to John Adams, March 2, 1776, *Letters of Mrs. Adams*, I.

[49] On January 14, 1776, Washington wrote to Joseph Reed, "Could I have foreseen the difficulties, which have come upon us; could I have known that such a backwardness

military fame of Charles Lee grew so great that it threatened to obscure all others.

Every month raised higher his name and further inflated his praise. He had come to Cambridge with a well defined halo, and his activity, his practical experience, and his eccentric personality had caused his reputation to grow apace. Public attention closely followed him at the siege; in Rhode Island; at New York. Wherever danger threatened, the first thought was for "General Lee."

The opinion seems to have been well-nigh unanimous.

An interesting reflection of the growth of reliance upon Lee, even among those not at first predisposed toward him, is in the letters of Abigail Adams. She who, on Washington's arrival, had quoted Dryden in order to depict the enthusiasm which he inspired in her, learned to look past him for salvation in Charles Lee, writing thus to John Adams in Philadelphia: "I feel sorry, that General Lee has left us, but his Presence at New York was no doubt of great importance. . . . But how can you spare him from here? Can you make his place good? Can you supply it with a man equally qualified to save us?"[50]

would have been discovered in the old soldiers to the service, all the generals upon earth should not have convinced me of the propriety of delaying an attack upon Boston till this time."—Ford, *Writings of Washington,* III, 344.

[50] *Letters of Mrs. Adams,* I, March 7, 1776.

CHAPTER XI

January 16, 1776–March 27, 1776: Age 48

The fortification of Dorchester Heights by Ward's division. The evacuation of Boston.

ON January 16 a council of war, attended by John Adams, discussed the problems of the siege in the light of the Continental Congress resolution of December 22, which authorized any offensive action that promised success —"notwithstanding the town and the property in it may thereby be destroyed."

The council decided that "a vigorous attempt" ought to be made on "the Ministerial army in Boston" as soon as practicable, and with that intent advised the calling in of thirteen militia regiments to serve during February and March.

Two days later, the number of regiments was reduced to ten. The other three must go to the aid of the American army in Canada, for the night of January 17 had brought word of the reverses before Quebec; of the death of Montgomery, and the wounding of Arnold.

As the new army gradually filled up and the reinforcing militia regiments began to come in, many in the American camps again turned inquiring and covetous eyes on the Dorchester hills.

Ward had, it will be remembered, thrice planned to occupy them in the early days of the siege prior to Washington's coming, and he tenaciously adhered to the project. The time for its consummation had not yet arrived, but his belief was shared by other American officers, and so it happened that, despite winter's grasp upon the camps, preparation had been set afoot.

To fortify the heights would call for extensive earthworks; and to raise these in winter, with the ground frozen deep, required the use of every available means to lessen the labor of digging. So fatigue parties had been set at work in Ward's division cutting swamp brush and converting it into fascines and gabions:[1] the former being bundles of sticks several feet in length tied together, to be staked down and then covered with earth; and the latter, bottomless hollow cylinders for filling with earth, made of wattled twigs and resembling very high bottomless baskets.

To accomplish the possession of the peninsula would mean much of the story of Bunker Hill over again: a stealthy "going on" at night—then a giant's labor at intrenching to be ready to defend the seizure when the dawn should break! But now, unlike Bunker Hill, Ward had time for preparation—and a supply of fascines and gabions would double the possibilities of the night's work, whenever that night should come.

Much thought had been expended also on the exposed condition of the approach to Dorchester Neck. A single causeway traversed the marshy ground of the low-lying isthmus (the "Little Neck") which connected the peninsula with the mainland, and it was commanded by the English artillery on Boston Neck. Among the plans discussed was a covered way to be built of turf, but this was rejected because of the difficulty of securing so large a quantity during the winter season. The next suggestion was a barricade of timber, stone, and earth, but that also was discarded.

Washington took part in a survey of the causeway "and the necessary ground there for erecting works"[2] on February 11, coming over to the Roxbury headquarters with General

[1] Gordon, *History of the Rise, Progress, and Establishment of the Independence of the United States of America,* First edition, London, II, 189–190 (different page numbers in other editions); Botta, *History of the American War,* I, 315.

[2] Washington (by Harrison) to Ward, February 11, 1776.—Original letter in the possession (1921) of Ward Dix Kerlin, Camden, N. J.

Putnam and Colonels Gridley and Knox, and there being joined by Generals Ward, Thomas, and Spencer, and Lieutenant-Colonel Rufus Putnam.

A reconnoitering visit to the Dorchester hills themselves by the same officers on the day following was responsible for an incident which at first alarmed onlookers but which fortunately developed nothing more serious than a good story for camp-talk.

The party had ridden across the causeway which they had so carefully inspected the day previous, and had then continued out upon the peninsula. As they were "on the Point, and within call of the enemy" they observed two English officers "on full speed on Horses from the Old to the New [English] lines and concluded they were about to order the Artillery levelled at them." Just at that moment also, they observed a man deserting from the American to the English lines. "This set em all a running & Scampering for life except the lame Col. Gridley, & Putnam who never runs & tarried to wait on Gridley. They had left their Horses ½ a mile back & feard the Enemy might attempt to encompass them."[3]

The visit to the hills was countered on the early morning of the fourteenth by the "British raid on Dorchester Neck." Howe's report of this to Lord Dartmouth says that "having intelligence that the enemy intended to possess themselves of Dorchester-Neck," he "ordered a detachment from Castle-William . . . under the command of Lieutenant-Colonel Leslie, and one composed of Grenadiers and Light Infantry from Boston, commanded by Major Musgrave, to pass over the ice, with directions to destroy the houses, and every kind of cover whatever upon that peninsula; which was executed, and six of the enemy's guard made prisoners."[4]

The English experienced much relief because they did not find "any Fascines or Gabions, as a preparation for building

[3] Letter of Captain Chester, *Magazine of American History,* VIII, 127.

[4] *American Archives,* 4th, V, 458.

a Battery on Fosters Hill [Nook Hill] as we had been given to understand was intended."[5] The relief was ill-founded, for the fascines and gabions had increased in number daily—stored, though, well behind the American lines awaiting the time for their use—but the conclusion which fathered it was very pleasing to Howe, for he was, in an orderly manner, getting ready to abandon the town in the spring,[6] and an American occupation of Dorchester Neck—or any other important military move—might disrupt his plans and perhaps also bring with it another large and unprofitable casualty bill.

It is not easy to explain why Howe had not in all these months essayed to occupy Dorchester Neck. He may have minimized the importance of its position, or he may have been afraid to further divide his forces—or he may merely have procrastinated. That he only awaited shipping to abandon the town undoubtedly influenced him, but it is not, alone, a satisfactory reason, for (as he should have seen, if he did not; and as events proved) upon the identity of the force, if any, that should occupy Dorchester Neck, depended the manner and time possible for evacuation. He professed not to feel the "least apprehension of any attack . . . from the Rebels,"[7] but his Bunker Hill experience must have given him some qualms at leaving open a similar potential battle site.

Curiously enough, Washington was imbued with similar lukewarmness. He found little comfort in preparing for the occupation of Dorchester Neck. His inspections of the peninsula had apparently confirmed his doubts of the practicability and value of the project, and he dwelt with impatient apprehensive alarm on the thought that the British might overwhelm him when their reinforcements arrived. So, after preparatory discussions and consultations which spread from major-generals to brigadier-generals and from brigadiers to

[5] Lieutenant-Colonel Kemble's Journal, February 13, 1776, *Kemble Papers,* I, 69.

[6] Howe to Lord Dartmouth, January 16, 1776: "that no time may be lost in transporting the army from hence to New York, I shall continue to take up all proper vessels that can be got."—*American Archives,* 4th, IV, 701.

[7] November 26, 1775, to Lord Dartmouth, *American Archives,* 4th, III, 1672.

field-officers, and thence to captains and subalterns, he in council of war on February 16 proposed to take advantage of the ice-locked harbor and make a musket attack on Boston.

The plan was not quite so reckless as the rowboat assault he had urged in September, but it was excessively rash for an army with powder magazines so low that little use could be made of artillery[8] and with 2000 of its men destitute even of firearms, against a well-garrisoned town—a town that was "almost impregnable—every avenue fortified"—Washington's own description of it a month later after he had viewed the English defenses from the inside.[9] It offered slight hope of success; and weighing against it were the disastrous results to the American cause which would surely follow a repulse.

"Gen. Ward opposed the idea, saying 'the attack must be made with a view of bringing on an engagement, or of driving the enemy out of Boston, and either end will be answered much better by possessing Dorchester heights.' Gen. Gates was also against it."[10]

The general officers upheld Ward and decided against an assault.

Washington then required their opinions "whether it would be advisable to begin a Cannonade & Bombardment with the present stock of powder?"

[8] The American army was again—or still—desperately short of powder. On February 3, Ward had written to Hancock: "We are in great want of the needful, Pray God to send us a supply. Accounts respecting that dwindle to almost nothing—If you have it I begg you will Impart to us that want."—Original letter, Library of Congress. Washington also wrote urgently, but also to little effect.

[9] To Joseph Reed, March 19, 1776.—Reed, *Life and Correspondence of Joseph Reed,* I, 177.

[10] Gordon's *History of the Rise, Progress, and Establishment of the Independence of the United States of America,* First edition, London, II, 189 (different page number in other editions). Gordon's history has been convicted of plagiarism of the *Annual Register* and Ramsay's *History of the Revolution in South Carolina,* but it holds value for the period of the siege of Boston as the only important contemporary history by a resident in and around the camps surrounding Boston who was also in close association with the American leaders. It is in describing military operations in other zones that Gordon's literary thefts become flagrant: his "use of borrowed material varying in amount according to the distance from Boston."—Colby, *American Historical Association Annual Report,* 1899, I, 376. Gordon's credit to Ward as the chief opponent of the assault and the chief advocate of the fortification of Dorchester Heights, carries special weight because (as in his account of, and references to, Bunker Hill) he was not by any means prejudiced in Ward's favor.

Their replies advised a cannonade and bombardment "as soon as there shall be a proper supply of Powder" but "not before."

The council of war followed this second refusal to accept Washington's views by resolving instead that "preparations should be made to take possession of Dorchester Hill, with a view of drawing out the enemy, and of Noddle's Island, also, if the situation of the water and other circumstances will admit of it." And this resolution, as it applied to Dorchester Neck, was approved for action.

To Ward thus finally came a full unanimous decision for the accomplishment of his long cherished plan.

Then commenced a very busy time in the Roxbury division. A large quantity of fascines and gabions had been collected, but there was still much to be done. A Massachusetts lieutenant who had come in early in February records "great preparations . . . for some new Enterprize, such as Fashienes, Gaboreenes, Barracks ready Framed, & boards cut. All imagined that Dorchester Hill was the Object of our Attention."[11]

The deep frozen ground continued, however, to worry the American commanders and engineers. Even with the use of fascines and gabions, it was considered doubtful if substantial works could be built within the brief space of a single night. The problem was solved by the construction of chandeliers, a device new to the experience of the besiegers.[12] They consisted of stout wooden frames in which the fascines could be set, held in place by picketing, and covered with soil.

The plan determined upon for the fulfilment of the council of war resolution was the fortification of the two main hills, "the Heights," overnight.

[11] *Journal of Lieutenant Isaac Bangs*, 9.

[12] By Rufus Putnam's testimony (Buell, *Memoirs of Rufus Putnam*, 58) neither he nor any one else in the American councils had thought of chandeliers as a solution of the difficulty until he happened upon a description of them in Muller's *Field Engineer*—and he did not even know the military meaning of the word "chandelier" when he first saw it.

Nook Hill,[13] one of the lower hills of the peninsula, bore more directly on the English positions—both on the Boston Neck lines and the town itself—but it was not tenable unless the higher points were first possessed; and it could not be occupied simultaneously with them without prematurely disclosing the American objective.

It was decided to screen the causeway with a great barricade of bundles of twisted hay—hay "screwed into large bundles of seven or eight hundred weight"[14]—the barricade to be raised on the same night that the peninsula should be occupied. The hay bundles could serve also for filling the chandeliers.

On February 21 Ward issued orders forbidding all intercourse between the English and American lines.[15] There was to be no more exchanging of letters or messages.

So great were the preparations necessary that the Dorchester Heights project was not the "secret" move indicated by more than one historian. On the contrary, it was of common report in the camp,[16] for there remained only one unfortified position of sufficient importance to serve as an explanation.

The secrecy essential was not of the intention, which could not be concealed, but of the time to be set for the attempt—lest word should be passed through to the English commander, and the Americans should be forestalled or should

[13] Also called "Foster's Hill," as in Lieutenant-Colonel Kemble's Journal, quoted on page 193.

[14] *Thacher's Military Journal,* March 4, 1776.

[15] Gates' letter of February 21, 1776, to Ward, says that Washington "intirely approves" of Ward's stopping all intercourse. The original is (1921) owned by Agnes Ward White, Parkersburg, W. Va.

[16] Lieutenant Isaac Bangs I have quoted on page 195. As February closed we find the occupation of the peninsula confidently predicted in contemporary diaries and letters: "Great talk of our army taking possession of Dorchester Hill in a few days."—Diary of Ezekiel Price, February 29, 1776, *Massachusetts Historical Society Proceedings,* VII, 239; "Great preparations making for our going on Dorchester Hill, which we believe will very soon happen."—Daniel McCurtin's Journal, March 1, 1776, *Papers relating chiefly to the Maryland Line,* 32; "I think we shall undoubtedly go on Dorchester next week."—Jedediah Huntington to Jabez Huntington, March 1, 1776, original letter, February 29–March 1, 1776, *General Jedediah Huntington Letters,* Connecticut Historical Society.

be caught at a disadvantage when at work on the heights. Hence, Ward's stoppage of all communication with Boston.

The confidence of the American rank and file in the success of so considerable an enterprise had been enhanced by Knox bringing into the lines a number of the cannon, mortars, and howitzers that had fallen into the hands of Ethan Allen, Benedict Arnold, and Seth Warner when they captured Ticonderoga and Crown Point during the first month of the war. The effect upon the general officers was less marked because of their knowledge of the scantiness of the gunpowder supply.

While Ward's division labored, the English commander-in-chief continued to plan his removal, looking forward to that spring day when he hoped to find himself so well supplied with ships that the army and its supplies, and the Boston tories and their belongings, could safely be slipped away from sight and sound and vengeance of that peculiarly constituted gathering of rebellious New Englanders which held him besieged. In anticipation, he dismounted a number of his heavy cannon and placed them on board his ships.[17]

By February 26 Ward's preparations were so far advanced that Washington advised both the Continental Congress and the Massachusetts Council of the determination to occupy the peninsula, and he asked the Council to direct the militia of the towns "most contiguous to Dorchester and Roxbury to repair to the lines at those places, with their arms, ammunition and accoutrements, instantly upon a signal given," as to weaken his center by detaching men for the Dorchester lines before the English had disclosed their point of attack might "neither be consistent with prudence nor good policy."

[17] This and other similar acts were noted by American observers, and Washington, February 26, sent word of them to Charles Lee in New York to warn him that the enemy's Boston fleet and army might soon be headed for New York—"They have removed the two mortars from Bunker's Hill and carried them with a great part of their heavy brass cannon on board their ships." To Hancock he sent a similar account, adding that "a Mr. Ides who came out yesterday says that the inhabitants of the town generally believe that they are about to remove either to New York or Virginia."—Ford, *Writings of Washington,* III, 436, 433–434.

Thomas, as was his due, had been selected to head the occupying detachment.

Washington was, however, still far from being satisfied. He did not yet realize the importance of the fortification of the Dorchester hills. He continued to nurse his disappointment that his musket assault plan had not been accepted, though still at this date a considerable number of his men were without arms.[18] His letter of February 26 to Joseph Reed dwells on his rejected project. "This [the formation of "some pretty strong ice from Dorchester to Boston Neck, and from Roxbury to the Common"] I thought . . . a favorable opportunity to make an assault upon the troops in town. I proposed it in council; but, behold! though we had been waiting all the year for this favourable event, the enterprise was thought too dangerous! . . . it is now at an end, and I am preparing to take post on Dorchester, to try if the enemy will be so kind as to come out to us."[19]

But the very day on which Washington had thus written, one of Ward's outposts notified him of new British activities —of loaded boats passing between Boston and Castle William; of a boat, with swivel-guns aboard, apparently viewing conditions around "the point."[20] And on the morrow (February 27) came a report that the British were landing men on Dorchester Neck, "upon which an alarm was beat, expresses galloping to Cambridge, the whole army in Roxbury in arms, and the soldiers quartered in the neighborhood all marching to join the main body and everything had the appearance of a sudden battle."[21]

It proved a false alarm, but it shocked Washington into a full sense of the importance of the work under way, and of the danger that Howe might forestall him in seizing the penin-

[18] Washington to Schuyler, February 25, 1776.—Ford, *Writings of Washington,* III, 430, note.

[19] Reed, *Life and Correspondence of Joseph Reed,* I, 166.

[20] Colonel Joseph Read to General Ward, February 26, 1776.—Original letter, *Knox MSS.,* II, 37, Massachusetts Historical Society.

[21] Diary of Ezekiel Price, *Massachusetts Historical Society Proceedings,* VII, 238.

sula. His mind dwelt upon and magnified the possibility that the enemy's apparent preparations to abandon the town might cloak some other design, and from that date he was very nervous lest Howe should overreach him.[22]

On Saturday, March 2, a council of war decided him to name the night of Monday, March 4, as the time to "go on" Dorchester Neck.[23]

Ward was ready for the call. And Washington, at headquarters, supervised preparations to storm Boston if Howe should move any considerable force against the positions to be acquired by the Americans on the Dorchester hills. Four thousand men under Putnam to make the assault: in two detachments, under Brigadiers Sullivan and Greene. One to land by the Powder House and gain possession of the enemy's work on Beacon Hill; and the other to land near Barton's Point and secure the post on Copp's Hill; then, uniting, to force their way through the town to the rear of the enemy's lines on Boston Neck.

Plans for the assault had been first formulated by Sullivan and Greene.[24] They had then been amended and submitted to Washington in a joint letter signed by Putnam, Sullivan, Greene, and Gates;[25] and accepted by him without change.

Thus was revived Washington's project of attacking Boston by a rowboat army. Still unwisely hazardous but improved to the extent that it was not to be essayed unless the enemy should divert a large part of his strength.[26]

[22] "Should the enemy get possession of those Hills before us they would render it a difficult task to dispossess them."—Washington to Ward, February 27, 1776 (Original letter owned, 1921, by Agnes Ward White, Parkersburg, W. Va.); "Considering the hazard of having the Posts on Dorchester Neck taken by the enemy and the evil consequences which would result from it"—Washington to Ward, March 2, 1776 (Copy in *Artemas Ward MSS.*); " . . . to discover whether they have any designs of Taking possession of Dorchester Heights as he [Washington] would by no means have them accomplish it."—R. H. Harrison to Ward, March 3, 1776 (Original letter owned, 1921, by Roxa Dix Southard, Groton, Mass.).

[23] Washington to Ward, March 2, 1776.—Copy in *Artemas Ward MSS.*

[24] The original of the Sullivan-Greene plan is (1921) owned by Agnes Ward White, Parkersburg, W. Va.

[25] Original letter, *Library of Congress.*

[26] Commenting on this plan to assault Boston, a curious error slipped into Sir George

To carry out this double operation—the occupation of Dorchester Neck and an assault upon Boston—every man was needed and every musket must be made to count. All working parties were ordered back to their regiments and the brigadiers were instructed to see that the firearms were "disposed of to the best advantage, placing them only in the hands of such as are fit for duty."[27] Spears were to be held in readiness and to be distributed as needed among those for whom no firearms were available.

Ward called upon the patriotism of his troops, demanding that "all officers be vigilant in seeing that their men are well equipt & prepared for action—and that every man be immediately prepared to meet the Enemies of his Country."

"It is expected," he continued, "that every man in every station & department will now exert all his powers for the salvation of America. Freedom & glory, shame & slavery, are set before us—let us act like men, like Christians, like heroes, & form a character for the admiration of posterity."[28]

There was one possibility of delay over which Ward had no control: that the east wind which was blowing on Sunday

Trevelyan's highly valued *American Revolution*. Trevelyan represents Washington as *disapproving* the project (1917 edition, I, 369–370). Continuing, he says (pages 370–371): "The prudence of Washington [in opposing the assault on Boston], so General Heath declared, was applauded by military men of several nations, after they had made an inspection of the land and water which was to have been the scene of action. And the veteran was mindful to direct his gratitude higher still, and to aver that Providence, kind not for the first time, must have interposed to save his countrymen when they were bent on self-destruction."

"Heath's Memoirs" is given as authority (foot-note, I, 371) both for the statement that Washington opposed the storming of Boston and for the lines concerning "The prudence of Washington."

The sentiments quoted are, it is true, to be found in Heath's *Memoirs,* and on the dates given in the foot-note (February 15 and March 5, 1776), but they are *Heath's* sentiments, *not* Washington's.

The mistake is attributable to Heath's peculiar habit of referring to *himself* as "Our Captain" and "Our General."

Another error, less easily explained, is Trevelyan's reference (I, 370; III, 50) to Heath as the commander-in-chief whom Washington succeeded. Heath was in charge at Cambridge for only the few hours of April 20 which preceded Ward's arrival on the afternoon of that day.

[27] General orders, March 3, 1776, *Ward's Order Book.*

[28] March 3, 1776, *Ward's Order Book.*

evening might raise the tide so high as to flood the causeway over the Little Neck and thus render the task impossible.

This danger was foreseen and discussed,[29] but the wind died down, and the next morning (Monday, March 4) Ward issued his orders for the fortification of the heights.[30]

Some historians speak of the occupation of the Dorchester hills as of Washington's careful detailed planning. This

[29] Washington to Ward, March 3, 1776.—Original letter owned (1921) by Roxa Dix Southard, Groton, Mass.

[30] Ward's order to Thomas is reproduced opposite page 202. It was supplemented by the following detailed instructions for the conduct, relief, and support of the detachment.

Genl. Ward Orders Roxbury 4th March 1776

That 2100 Men viz 1 Brigadier Genl. 3 Coll. 3 Lieut Coll. 3 Majors 23 Capts 71 Subs. 100 Sergts. 3 Drums 1916 Rank & file 3 Surgeons 3 Mates are to be Paraded this Eveng at Six oclock precisely, at Dorchester, completely Armd & accoutred, with one days Provision ready cook'd. Before the men are marchd from the regimental Parades, they are to be handsomely drawn up two deep. Their arms, Amunition & Accoutraments strictly examin'd, the commission'd & non-commission'd Officers properly posted. The Officers will give particular Attention to their own Divisions, whether they are employ'd in the work, or as a covering Party, & not shift from one part of the Battallion to another. This will give an Opportunity for ye free Circulation to the Orders of the Commanding Officer, & enable him to conduct any movement with less Danger of Confusion, & greater Probability of Success. The Officers will mark well the Behavior of their men; that ye Bravery & Resolution of the good Soldier may not pass unrewarded; & Meanness & Cowardice meet with just Contempt. At 3 Oclock Tomorrow morn'g, will be paraded for the Relief of the above Party, at ye same Place, 3000 Men viz 1 Brigadier Genl. 5 Coll 5 Lieut. Coll 5 Majors 30 Capts 92 Subs 118 Sergts 5 Drums 2342 Rank & File 5 Surgeons 5 Mates, Accoutred & posted as above with one Days Provision ready cook'd. The 5 Companies of Rifle men equipt as above are to parade at the same Place & time. At which time the Remainder of all ye Regts are to be turn'd out & take their respective Alarm Posts. The Party that is reliev'd from Dorchester is not to be dismiss'd as soon as reliev'd; but to join their respective Regts at their Alarm posts, & wait for further Orders. The Genl. expects that in case of an attack, the Officers exert themselves to prevent their men from throwing away their Fire before the Enemy are within Reach, & recommends that no Soldier fire at any time without a particular Object in View; single Guns well aim'd and briskly fir'd, have a greater Tendency to disconcert & do more Damage to an Enemy, than firing by Plattoons. The Surgeons and Mates are to be equip'd with every thing necessary for their department. It is ordered that the whole Camp keep by them one Days Provision ready cook'd; & that no Officer or Soldier strole from their Quarters. 2500 Men Are to parade every Morng equip'd, at ye same hour & Place.

4th March

Capt. Hugh Stevenson is to take the command of the three Companies of Rifle men in this Incampment, & also the two Companies which are ordered here from Cambridge; & at three Oclock tomorrow Morning proceed to Dorchester Point, there to obey such orders as he shall receive from Brigadier Genl. Thomas, or the Commanding Officer on that Point. By order of Majr Genl. Ward.

J W Adc

—*Ward's Order Book.*

is inaccurate, for we have Washington's letter to Ward on March 3, only twenty-four hours before the fortification commenced, saying that his suggestions were only tentative. "You will," he wrote, "settle matters with the Officers with you, as what I have here said is intended rather to convey my Ideas generally, than wishing them to be adhered to strictly."[31]

The months of preparation crowd to an issue.

"A very large party of teams" make their appearance in camp (teams of oxen, be it understood). An atmosphere of general expectation is everywhere present. "Going on to Dorchester Neck tonight" is the general toast and salutation.[32]

The Roxbury positions are held in greater force than ever before: their lines generously reinforced by militiamen from the surrounding towns, present for a special three days' service. Attracted by the reports of an impending action, the men have been coming in all Saturday and Sunday without awaiting the formal call.

"A little before sunset" the several units of Thomas's detachment marched to their juncture at the Dorchester lines. A short wait there, and then the signal was given and the American guns at the Lamb's Dam redoubt opened fire on the enemy. The English cannon responded smartly. Other American batteries took up the tune. And thus commenced the fiercest artillery duel that Boston ever experienced.[33]

It was a matter of supreme importance to keep the English so fully occupied that they should divine nothing of what Thomas and his men were to do that night—so the American cannon coughed and roared as they had never been permitted before—loudest of all from the Roxbury forts—for once

[31] Original letter, *Artemas Ward MSS.*

[32] Diary, *Historical Magazine,* VIII, 328.

[33] On the two preceding nights also (Saturday and Sunday, March 2 and 3) there had been brisk artillery exchanges. They form part of the conventional story of the siege but had little or no bearing on its outcome.

Camp at Roxbury 4 March 1776

Brigadier General Thomas is to take the
Command of 2100 Men which are to be paraded at
Dorchester at six o'Clock this Evening,
with which he is to proceed to Dorchester Point, and there throw up such
works on the two commanding Emi-
nences, as he with the advice of the
Engineer, shall think most proper for
the defence of the ground & annoyance
of the Enemy, and defend the same.

By order of Major Genl Ward.

Joseph Ward
Aid de Camp

From the original (6½ × 8½), owned by the Massachusetts Historical Society

WARD'S ORDER FOR THE FORTIFICATION OF DORCHESTER HEIGHTS

reckless of the consumption of powder![34] And for every Yankee shot or shell, the English returned threefold or fourfold, until it seemed to the terror-stricken inhabitants of Boston "as if heaven and earth were engaged."[35]

To this deafening accompaniment Thomas starts his men forward. In front, is the covering party of eight hundred. Closely following, are the carts with the intrenching tools. Then comes the working party of twelve hundred, Thomas riding with it. Behind, stretches a "mighty train" of 360 carts[36] loaded with the bundles of screwed hay, the chandeliers, the fascines, and the gabions. And thus "we went over the marsh in fine order and good spirits."[37]

The "Little Neck" traversed, the covering party divides: half quietly make their way to Nook Hill point to keep watch on Boston; half proceed to the point facing Castle Island. A line of sentries connects the two posts and extends also along the south shore.

The working detachment and the carts with the intrenching tools press steadily on to the "twin hills"—the famous Dorchester Heights of history.

The carts with the hay bundles drop them along the causeway and then turn back for new loads; those with the fascines, etc., continue out on the peninsula and slowly and laboriously trail the working detachment to the two summits.

The fatigue men set to the task, Gridley and Rufus Putnam directing. An hour's labor[38] is sufficient to enclose a fort by

[34] The free American bombardment has led numerous authorities to state that powder had become plentiful in the camp. They overlook Washington's "if we had powder" on March 7, 1776, to Joseph Reed.—Ford, *Writings of Washington*, III, 462.

[35] Newell's Journal, March 4, 1776, *Massachusetts Historical Society Collections*, 4th, I, 272. Within the American lines, a soldier in the Roxbury division wrote: "It's impossible, I could describe the situation of this town and all about it. This night you could see shells, sometimes 7 at a time in the air, and as to cannon, the continual shaking of the earth by cannonading dried up our wells."—Daniel McCurtin, March 4, 1776, *Papers relating chiefly to the Maryland Line*, 33. Washington described the cannonading as a "continued roar."

[36] *Thomas Papers*, 1774–1776, 67, Massachusetts Historical Society.

[37] *Asa Waters MS. Account,* Stoughton (Mass.) Historical Society.

[38] Diary, *Historical Magazine*, VIII, 328.

the use of the chandeliers, fascines, and gabions; then all hands that can be used are put to digging to complete the job. The mildness of the night and its clear moon favor the work.

Some histories place Washington on the heights riding the lines all night. He was not there at all. He was where he should have been, at his central headquarters, ready to strike at the enemy from left or center; or to receive them at either point; or to reinforce his right: according to circumstances or as his opponent might move.[39]

The relief—3000 men (2342 rank and file)—came on between three and four o'clock in the morning. They found "two forts in considerable forwardness and sufficient for a defence against small arms and grape shot."[40]

With them came the five companies of riflemen. "[We] went and lay in ambush close by the water side expecting every moment that the Butchers belonging to the Tyrant of Great Britain would be out among us."[41] But the artillery duel held the English attention. Howe had no inkling of the works rapidly taking shape.

"The carts were still in motion with materials; some of them have made three or four trips."[42] Their later trips brought several pieces of artillery.

Before daybreak the two main forts had been supplemented by four smaller auxiliary positions. "A very great work for one Night."[43]

For a finishing touch, the bristling points of the abattis[44]—war's rough usage of neighboring orchards—are faced with barrels of sand and stones. "They presented only the appearance of strengthening the works; but the real design was, in case the enemy made an attack, to have rolled them down

[39] His letter to Ward, on the night of March 4, asks "how the works goe on."—*Artemas Ward MSS.*

[40] *Thacher's Military Journal,* March 5, 1776.

[41] Daniel McCurtin's Journal, March 4, 1776, *Papers relating chiefly to the Maryland Line,* 33.

[42] *Thacher's Military Journal,* March 5, 1776.

[43] *Revolutionary Journal of Col. Jeduthan Baldwin,* March 4, 1776.

[44] Howe's report, *American Archives,* 4th, IV, 458.

the hills." As "the hills on which they were erected were steep, and clear of trees and bushes . . . They would have descended with such increasing velocity, as must have thrown the assailants into the utmost confusion and have killed and wounded great numbers."[45]

Thus the night passed, its every hour filled with unceasing activity.

Then came the dawn—and through its haze the forts loomed before the enemy with a menace that none could mistake.

The English generals gazed, astounded, at the threatening lines which had thus magically crowned the heights.[46] The size and strength of the works amazed them. They "must have been the employment of at least twelve thousand men," declared the English commander.[47]

There was an immediate convening of a British council of war. The fortification of the twin hills had been planned only as a first step in the possession of Dorchester Neck—but its possibilities were manifest—the English officers did not have to await the full gestation of the project! Unless the

[45] Heath's *Memoirs,* March 4, 1776. The credit for this use of barrels of sand and stones is given by General Heath to William Davis, a Boston merchant. Stedman, the contemporary English historian who is still quoted with respect by modern military critics, considered the plan most effectively practical: "To dislodge the Provincials from their new works . . . was impossible," he wrote, "for the British troops must have ascended an almost perpendicular eminence, on the top of which the Americans had prepared hogsheads chained together in great numbers, and filled with stones, to roll down upon them as they marched up: a curious provision, by which whole columns would have been swept off at once. . . . This would effectually have destroyed all order, and have broken the ranks."—*History of the American War,* I, 187–188. In these barrels one finds the genesis of a curious story of later years that at the time of the fortification of Dorchester Heights, barrels were filled with sand and headed up to deceive the American troops into the belief that this time they had an unlimited supply of powder with them! (Reference to this story was made by Wm. H. Sumner, *New England Historical and Genealogical Register,* XII, 229.) But their real purpose was necessarily known to many, as any delay in their use would have nullified the expected advantage. They are also perhaps the foundation of similar fanciful stories, told of earlier months of the siege, preserved in Elkanah Watson's *Men and Times of the Revolution* and Hale's *Memories of a Hundred Years,* I, 147.

[46] The forts had been raised, testified an English officer, "with an expedition equal to that of the genii belonging to Aladin's wonderful lamp."—Almon's *Remembrancer,* III, 106.

[47] To Lord Dartmouth, *American Archives,* 4th, V, 458–459.

Americans could be ousted, Boston was no longer a safe berth for either His Majesty's navy or army.

Howe still held Lord Dartmouth's instructions to abandon the town, but he was in not much better position to carry them out than he had been four months earlier. His recent preparations availed him little, for he was still short of shipping. A divided removal (which, four months earlier, he had declared to be dangerous) was now impossible with the Americans intrenched on Dorchester Neck. An undivided removal meant, at best, leaving behind great quantities of military and other supplies. And, then, the disgrace! Instead of a voluntary evacuation of the town, a flight from it enforced by the muzzles of colonial cannon.

Howe's decision was to fight, and the Americans cheerfully made ready to receive him. Washington rode up the hills to view the works, and reminded the men that it was the anniversary of the "Boston Massacre." And Putnam's division assembled along the Charles River, awaiting the word to man the boats for a spectacular raid upon the town.

The English essayed the effect of artillery on the American intrenchments:

"They endeavored to Elevate their Cannon so as to reach our works, by sinking the Hinder wheels of the Cannon into the Earth, but after an unsuccessful Fire of about two Hours, they grew weary of it & Desisted."[48]

The Americans intently watch also the other and more threatening English moves—the gathering of the boats, the marching of the companies to the wharves, the emptying of the boats into the transports. It looks as if Howe intends to duplicate Gage's methods at Breed's Hill, and the Americans laugh and pray that the "Philistines" will give them another such opportunity.

As Washington turned his eyes from the Boston shore to scan the American works, built with an expedition that had

[48] John Sullivan to John Adams, March 15, 1776, *Massachusetts Historical Society Proceedings,* XIV, 283.

staggered the trained soldiers of Great Britain and manned with those same indomitable New Englanders who had made history at "Lexington and Concord" and again at Bunker Hill—anxious now only that their enemy should "come on": he himself said, "I never saw spirits higher, or more ardor prevailing . . . our officers and men appeared impatient for the appeal"—he probably felt compunction for the harsh epithets he had applied to the New England troops. The project, the preparation, the command, the engineers, and the work (and the Bunker Hill lesson back of them) were all of New England's sons; and their result was to mean much glory for the Virginian who had aspersed them.

The neighboring hills—as also the housetops and wharves of Boston—are crowded with spectators awaiting taut-nerved the commencement of a drama that bids fair to be bloodier even than the carnival of death on Breed's Hill. But Howe remembers too vividly the price to be paid for storming American intrenchments with daylight sighting American muskets. The five regiments filling the transports are to go first to Castle Island. From there, during the night, to be landed on the easterly point of Dorchester Neck; while other regiments, direct from Boston, disembark "on the side next the town." Then, from the two directions, a simultaneous assault upon the works: no pausing to fire this time—but a quick short march and a rapid clambering of the hills—hoping that in the uncertain moonlight the rush of English bayonets may offset American marksmanship.[49]

But this is unknown to the American commanders and they watch with disappointment the ebbing of the tide which they had thought would bring the foe to them.

What is the British intention? That is the question in every one's mind as the afternoon wanes. The redcoats had

[49] *Howe's Orderly Book,* 225; Howe to Lord Dartmouth, *American Archives,* 4th, V, 459; Diary of a British Officer, *Atlantic Monthly,* XXXIX, 553; Lieutenant-Colonel Kemble's Journal, *Kemble Papers,* I, 71.

not been filled into the transports for nothing. Where is the blow to be struck?

There are several possibilities in addition to that of a direct attack upon Dorchester Heights. As one, the enemy may land at some nearby point to the south and attempt to break through the American right from the rear.

Washington returned to Cambridge early in the afternoon and from there he wrote to Ward requesting him to send "orders to Braintree, Hingham & that way, that a good lookout be kept there, and if any discoveries respecting 'em can be made, that instant notice thereof be brought to Head-Quarters." He did not "much suspect their going to or landing at those places," but he believed that "the utmost vigilance & care" were necessary, "as their embarkation certainly is to answer some purpose."

Because of the unreliability of night signals, he also requested Ward to keep "Two Expresses with Horses in constant readiness" to communicate any motions of the enemy which he deemed in any way important, and "the same will be done here."[50]

The English transports went down the bay in the evening, a floating battery towed along to cover their landing; but a March tempest was brewing and it came up with such fury that three of the vessels were driven ashore on Governor's Island. The proposed assault became impossible. "[No] boat cou'd possibly land."[51]

In Boston that night the people again cowered in their homes as the wind rocked their walls, broke their windows, and blew down their sheds and fences.[52] "A wind more violent than any thing I ever heard," an English officer wrote

[50] Washington (by Harrison) to Ward, March 5, 1776.—Original letter owned (1921) by Roxa Dix Southard, Groton, Mass.

[51] Diary of a British Officer, *Atlantic Monthly,* XXXIX, 553.

[52] *Letters and Diary of John Rowe,* 300. "A hurrycane, or terrible sudden storm."—Newell's Journal, *Massachusetts Historical Society Collections,* 4th, I, 272. "In the night was as violent a storm as was ever known."—Dr. John Warren's Journal, John C. Warren's *Genealogy of Warren,* 94.

home. "A violent storm," wrote Washington. "Almost a hurricane," says Heath.

The cannonading, too, started afresh, giving promise of war on the morrow.

The alarmed residents of Boston were, nevertheless, vastly more comfortable than the Americans upon the Dorchester hills! There had been no time to set up the barracks which a few days later ameliorated conditions. There was nothing to protect the men from the weather save a few apple trees —"a miserable shelter from storms and March winds." "I never before felt such cold and distress, as I did this night"; "[we were] drenched by the copious rain, exhausted by severe exertion": such are the comments that have come down to us in the diaries and reminiscences of officers and privates.[53]

The wind and sea still ran high in the morning, and the transports were ordered back to Boston. The English had lost what little appetite they had at first felt for assailing the American position. They decided to give up the town, and Halifax was selected as the immediate destination of both the troops and the civilian tories.[54]

Despite the earlier rumors that Howe planned to abandon the capital, the crisis which thus confronted them—definite this time, an inexorable fact—came as a crushing blow to the loyalists cooped within it. But the patriots of the beleaguered town rejoiced in great relief. "Blessed be God our redemption draws nigh," cried Deacon Newell.

The wind and sea continued rough all Wednesday, but the

[53] *Journal of Lieutenant Isaac Bangs*, 12, 16; Daniel McCurtin's Journal, *Papers relating chiefly to the Maryland Line*, 33; *Diary of Samuel Richards*, 26–27.

[54] The decision was not formally reached until Thursday, March 7 (Howe to Lord Dartmouth, *American Archives*, 4th, V, 458), and Howe in Wednesday's general orders had explained that he desired "the Troops may know that the intended expedition last Night was unavoidably put off by the badness of the weather"—but the intention to evacuate the town was of general knowledge on Wednesday, among both army men and civilians.—Newell's Journal, *Massachusetts Historical Society Collections*, 4th, I, 272; *Letters and Diary of John Rowe;* Diary of a British Officer, *Atlantic Monthly*, XXXIX, 553; letter in Almon's *Remembrancer*, III, 106; letter of Major-General Hugh, Earl Percy, who was to have commanded the English assault, *Letters of Hugh, Earl Percy*, 66.

weather was not severe enough to hinder Thomas in his work. The American fortifications were strengthened, and several additional guns were hauled over the causeway and up the hills—the performance being closely observed by the English officers.

On Thursday, the seventh, the three days' emergency militia returned to their homes, and the responsibility of maintaining both the Roxbury lines and the new positions on Dorchester Neck rested almost entirely on Ward's original Roxbury division. Two regiments from the center had joined him early on the fifth, but it was considered unwise to detach any more men from the center or any at all from the left. This double labor involved heavy demands on his men's energy and willingness—many "were obliged to be on Duty two Days & Nights successively"[55]—but they stood the test well.

On March 9 a battery was planted to the north of the east point of the peninsula as a special menace to the British shipping. Two[56] attempts were made to fortify Nook Hill also, but they were both frustrated by artillery fire.

There was no swerving from the English decision to leave Boston. On the eighth, the very day that a committee of Boston civilians informed Washington of the intended evacuation and of Howe's promise not to harm the town if his troops were not harassed in departing, Howe attempted to stimulate the military spirit of his men by requiring in general orders "The Commanding Officers of Corps to give the strictest Attention to the regularity and Discipline of their respective Corps . . . as the Troops may be hourly called upon to

[55] Lieutenant Bangs (*Journal*, 15, 16) wrote feelingly of the "Fatiegues & Hardships that were underwent by that part of the Army which were Stationed at Roxbury from the time of our first building upon the Hill." . . . Because of the lack, at first, of barracks, no regiment could be stationed there as a permanent garrison, and the "25 Hundred Men or thereabouts" which "it was absolutely necessary to keep constantly upon the Hills . . . must be drawn from those at Roxbury. This Party together with the Guards at Roxbury kept half of our Men on duty constantly, & many being taken ill about that time, some with what we termed The Hill Fever & others with real Sickness, many Men were obliged to be on Duty two Days & Nights successively."

[56] *Revolutionary Journal of Col. Jeduthan Baldwin*, March 9 and 12, 1776.

Attack the Enemy in case a proper Opening should offer where the Rebels Least Expect it"; but, excepting that, his orders, commencing with March 7, were all directed to getting away from Boston as speedily as possible and to attempts to maintain discipline amid the hurry and its concomitant disorder.[57]

The English officers were, however, overwhelmed by the multitude of details thrust upon them in the sudden necessity of quickly setting the army and its supplies, and the loyalists and their families and effects, upon the voyage; and their preparations consumed so much time that Washington feared that the delay held some sinister motive—perhaps that Howe "has some design of having a brush before his departure and is only waiting in hopes of find'g us off our Guard"[58] or of "attempting by some bold stroke in some measure to wipe off the ignominy" of his retreat;[59] perhaps the expectation of reinforcements sufficiently large to shift the advantage won by the Americans.

Howe suffered from similar nervousness concerning the American plans. His "preparations to be gone" were, it is

[57] Extracts from *Howe's Orderly Book:*

March 7.—"The Regts are to bring immediately all the Barrack furniture, but such as are Judg'd necessary for the Voyage to the Store in Kings Street, . . . Every Regt is to take care of the Hand Carts they have; the Wheels are to be fastened in the Quarters of the several Transports, these being very necessary for a future service, and not easily replaced."

"Each Regt to receive 18 Butts of Porter at Cowper's Meeting House, to morrow Morning at 10 O'Clock, to be put on board their respective Transports, & issued to the Troops after they embark."

March 10.—"The Commanding Officers of Corps to be responsible to have all their Sick, Convalescents, & Women, on board their respective Transports before Six O'Clock this Evening . . ."

March 11.—"The Troops to have all their Baggage on board Ship by five O'Clock this Afternoon, if any is found on the Wharfs after six, it will be thrown into the Sea."

March 14.—"The Officers & Soldiers on board Ship not to come on Shore on any Account without the General's express Permission."

"The Commander in Chief finding notwithstanding the Orders that have been given to forbid Plundering, Houses have been forced open & robbed, he is therefore under a Necessity of declaring to the Troops, that the first Soldier who is caught plundering, will be hanged on the Spot."

[58] March 10, 1776, Washington (by Harrison) to Ward.—Original letter, *Artemas Ward MSS.*

[59] March 12, 1776, Washington (by Palfrey) to Ward.—Original in the possession (1921) of Ward Dix Kerlin, Camden, N. J.

said, "much accelerated by an accidental fire" in the Prospect Hill barracks "which Howe supposed was an alarm to the inhabitants" of the surrounding towns to come in to storm Boston.[60]

On March 13 Washington wrote to Ward that he wished to consult with him, Thomas, and Spencer "upon many matters," and as he did "not think it prudent at this time" that they "should be so far as Cambridge" from their posts, he would come over to Roxbury to meet them.[61]

At this council, held in Ward's headquarters the same morning and attended also by Putnam, Heath, Sullivan, Greene, and Gates, it was decided to fortify Nook Hill "at all events" if the English army should not remove on the morrow; and also to dispatch five regiments and the rifle battalion to New York because of the probability that Howe would make that town his next point of attack.

On Saturday night (March 16) the Nook Hill resolution was successfully put into effect and the American officers felt confident that the new array of cannon thus planted at point-blank range would compel Howe's immediate removal.

Fortunately for the English commander and his forces—and for the town of Boston—it was not necessary to demonstrate its effectiveness. Howe had completed his arrangements. His ships were loaded to their capacity and he had on Saturday morning (7:30 A.M. and later) issued orders for the final embarkation—"the whole Garrison to be under Arms at 4 O'Clock" Sunday morning "to be in readiness to embark when ordered."[62]

During the night some of the English cannon not taken on board barked noisily at the Americans laboring on Nook

[60] Edmund Quincy to John Hancock, March 25, 1776, *Massachusetts Historical Society Proceedings,* IV, 27–28.

[61] Washington (by Moylan) to Ward, March 13, 1776.—Original in the possession (1921) of Ward Dix Kerlin, Camden, N. J.

[62] Numerous histories aver that it was the fortification of Nook Hill on the night of March 16 that decided Howe to leave Boston early in the morning of March 17. He had, though, as noted above, given his orders for the abandonment of the town a number of hours before the detachment of the party which planted the Nook Hill batteries.

Hill, but they were chiefly old iron guns destined to be spiked, and their seeming ferocity was only a temporary precaution, for by daybreak the abandonment of the capital was well on toward fulfilment—a fleet of boats carrying redcoats and tories out to the waiting vessels.

All the early hours of that memorable Sunday morning the final scenes of the evacuation continued without interruption, and about nine o'clock the last boats shoved off from the wharves.

Quickly thereafter[63] Ward entered the town over Boston Neck, riding at the head of five hundred troops under the immediate command of Colonel Learned.

At about the same time a detachment of Putnam's men debarked on the west side of the peninsula.

The capital of Massachusetts after eleven months' siege thus returned to the control and possession of the provincial patriots.

A strangely silent town, though, it appeared to its armed redeemers tramping through its narrow streets. "The enemy had, very properly, forbid the inhabitants to leave their houses during the embarkation, and from this cause or their ignorance of his movements, or the timidity produced by their long residence with him, and the fear of reproach from their countrymen, the houses . . . continued shut up, and the town presented a frightful solitude in the bosom of a numerous population."[64]

After a short stay in the delivered capital Ward returned to his headquarters in Roxbury, Putnam being installed in command of the town. A few days later he was succeeded by Greene.

Washington did not yet feel sure that the English were

[63] "It was almost 11 o'clock before the Gates were opened": Jedediah Huntington to Captain Joshua Huntington, March 17, 1776.—Original letter, *General Jedediah Huntington Letters,* Connecticut Historical Society. "Our men . . . about noon . . . took possession of Boston": Reverend David Avery, March 17, 1776 (one of two entries, in different volumes, of that date).—Original diary, Connecticut Historical Society.

[64] James Wilkinson, *Memoirs of My Own Times,* I, 33.

reconciled to a submissive bloodless abandonment of Boston. The enemy's ships remained in the harbor and gave him "a strong violent presumption" that something was "meditating" and made him "extremely apprehensive" that General Howe had "some scheme in view & designs of taking advantage of the hurry, bustle and confusion among our troops which he may immagine his departure to have occasioned."[65]

Again, on March 21, he wrote to Governor Trumbull of Connecticut, "For my own part, I cannot but suspect they are waiting for some opportunity to give us a stroke at a moment when they conceive us to be off our guard, in order to retrieve the honor they have lost."[66]

Washington's disquiet was very generally shared. "The enemy have not yet come under sail," wrote Abigail Adams, on Sunday noon, March 17. "I cannot help suspecting some design, which we do not yet comprehend. To what quarter of the world they are bound is wholly unknown; but 'tis generally thought to New York, . . . From Penn's Hill we have a view of the largest fleet ever seen in America. You may count upwards of a hundred and seventy sail. They look like a forest."[67]

The delay concealed no plan of retaliation. The English continued in the roads because some of their ships needed repairing. But the Americans did not know this, and on March 25 Washington wrote to Joseph Reed that he was "under more apprehension from them now than ever," and that they might be awaiting the dispersal of the militia at the end of the month as a favorable opportunity "to make a push . . . upon the back of our lines at Roxbury."[68]

None of these things happened, and on March 27 the greater part of the fleet set sail for Halifax.

The first chapter of the Revolution thus came to a victor-

[65] March 17, 1776, to Ward.—Original letter (by Harrison) in possession (1921) of Francis D. Fisher.

[66] Ford, *Writings of Washington,* III, 485–486.

[67] *Familiar Letters of John Adams and his Wife,* 142.

[68] Ford, *Writings of Washington,* III, 494.

ious climax. England's plans for the subjugation of Massachusetts had utterly failed. The rebellious province had shaken itself free.

But what if Washington had had his way, instead of Ward? A boat attack, or a musket assault across the ice, on a town "almost impregnable—every avenue fortified." Quebec on a larger scale! Suppose the Americans had lost, as at Quebec? Then—a broken army, accomplishing a miracle if it could even hold the enemy within the town. A great moral loss, also, which might have obliterated the effect of Bunker Hill. Instead—the enemy driven out of the province, and the American forces, strength unimpaired, free to march to New York.

The evacuation gave great impetus to the theory of independence. It bred converts even in the middle colonies, where —eleven months after Lexington and Concord, and nine months after Bunker Hill—the word "independence," so fraught with decisive finality, was still horrifying to many minds—was still to them much too closely allied with the ogres of treason and rebellion.

CHAPTER XII

March 18, 1776–March 20, 1777: Age 48–49

Ward assumes the continental command in Boston. Because of ill health, he tenders his resignation. The Continental Congress accepts his resignation, but both Washington and the Congress request him to remain in command. He continues until relieved by Heath on March 20, 1777.

GENERAL WARD'S health had declined to a somewhat alarming extent during the first months of 1776.[1] He had made no complaint while the outcome of the siege of Boston remained in doubt, but after the successful occupation of Dorchester Heights he felt compelled to retire from army life. Dorchester Heights had shifted the principal site of the struggle. The next step was to be a fight to hold New York against the enemy, and he was physically unequal to the responsibilities of his position in a province and under conditions alike unfamiliar to him.

He waited until the enemy had evacuated the capital and then he wrote to Washington tendering his resignation, for "to eat the Continental bread & not do the duty is what I am much averse to."[2]

He accompanied his letter to the commander-in-chief by one in similar strain to Hancock as President of the Continental Congress.[3]

On Washington's comments on Ward's resignation rest the

[1] "Genl Ward's health being so precarious."—Joseph Ward to John Adams, March 14, 1776, *Massachusetts Historical Society Proceedings,* XIV, 282.

[2] March 22, 1776.—Original letter, *Library of Congress.*

[3] *American Archives,* 4th, V, 467.

conventional stories of the ill feeling between the two men.[4]

[4] WASHINGTON'S COMMENTS ON WARD'S RESIGNATION.

To Joseph Reed, April 1, 1776: "Nothing of importance has occurred in these parts, since my last, unless it be the resignations of Generals Ward and Fry, and the re-assumption of the former, or retraction, on account as he says, of its being disagreeable to some of the officers. Who those officers are, I have not heard. I have not inquired. When the application to Congress and notice of it to me came to hand, I was disarmed of interposition, because it was put upon the footing of duty or conscience, the General being persuaded that his health would not allow him to take that share of duty that his office required. The officers to whom the resignation is disagreeable, have been able, no doubt, to convince him of his mistake, and that his *health* will admit him to be *alert* and *active*. I shall leave him till he can determine yea or nay, to command in this quarter."—Reed, *Life and Correspondence of Joseph Reed,* I, 179.

To Charles Lee, May 9, 1776: "General Ward, upon the evacuation of Boston, and finding that there was a probability of his removing from the smoke of his own chimney, applied to me, and wrote to Congress for leave to resign. A few days afterward, some of the officers, as he says, getting *uneasy* at the prospect of his leaving them, he applied for his letter of resignation, which had been committed to my care; but, behold! it had been carefully forwarded to Congress, and as I have since learnt, judged so reasonable (want of health being the plea) that it was instantly complied with." [This statement is inaccurate, for the letter of resignation referred to—that of March 22—was never accepted by Congress. It was not until Ward repeated his request for permission to retire that Congress, a month later, took action.]—*Lee Papers,* II, 13–14.

WARD CONFRONTED WASHINGTON WITH ONE OF THE ABOVE LETTERS?

Following are the two chief forms of the story (unauthenticated—and, as it applies to Ward, entirely uncharacteristic—but nevertheless persistently handed down by tradition) that Ward confronted Washington with a letter in which the Virginian had aspersed him: perhaps one of the two quoted above; perhaps a third which I have not come upon.

"It is well known that Washington spoke of the resignation of General Ward, after the evacuation of Boston, in a manner approaching contempt. His observations, then confidentially made, about some of the other generals, were not calculated to flatter their *amour propre* or that of their descendants. It is said that General Ward, learning long afterwards of the remark that had been applied to him, accompanied by a friend, waited on his old chief at New York, and asked him if it was true that he had used such language. The President replied that he did not know, but that he kept copies of his letters, and would take an early opportunity of examining them. Accordingly, at the next session of Congress (of which General Ward was a member), he again called with his friend, and was informed by the President that he had really written as alleged. Ward then said *'Sir, you are no gentleman,'* and turning on his heel quitted the room." —S. A. Drake, *Historic Fields and Mansions of Middlesex,* 260 (also, same page number, in the same work later published as *Old Landmarks and Historic Fields of Middlesex* and *Historic Mansions and Highways around Boston*).

"Of his [Ward's] bravery there is no question, although Washington accused him of cowardice in leaving the service before Boston. Benjamin Stone, the first preceptor of Leicester Academy, gave me the following account of Ward's misunderstanding with Washington. Soon after the establishment of the Government at New York, Ward, then a member of Congress, came into possession of a letter written by Washington, in which the offensive charge was made. He immediately proceeded to the President's house, placed the paper before him, and asked him if he was the author of it. Washington looked at the letter and made no reply. Ward said, 'I should think that the man who was base enough to write that, would be base enough to deny it,' and abruptly took his leave." [As a minor correction, note that Congress sat in *Philadelphia* during both of Ward's terms.]—*Reminiscences of the Reverend George Allen of Worcester,* 42.

A LEGEND OF WASHINGTON'S DESIRE TO MAKE AMENDS.

The Massachusetts Historical Society possesses a letter from C. Gore to General

Washington was apparently glad to receive Ward's resignation as first major-general—its acceptance by the Continental Congress would leave only Washington himself as superior in rank to Charles Lee—but he requested him (March 29) to take the command in Boston and, following, the general continental command in Massachusetts after the main army's departure for New York. High and peculiar responsibility would attach to the post, but it did not involve the rigors of a marching campaign, and Ward accepted the charge until some other general could be spared to take it over—continuing to place the public service above all personal consideration.

It will be noted that neither Washington nor Ward permitted his personal sentiments to affect his sense of duty. Washington did not hesitate to ask, nor Ward to give.

Regiment after regiment from the American camps around Boston was now marching toward New York, and on April 4 Washington himself set out.

On the same day Ward formally assumed the command in Massachusetts of both the land forces and the heterogeneous little fleet in the continental pay.

The fleet consisted of a few armed schooners, armed whaleboats, and floating batteries, etc. It had no vessels capable of coping with the larger British warships, but its schooners—both alone and in coöperation with privateers—were efficient in cutting out enemy supply ships—and, occasionally, transports also.

The New England fishermen—their customary livelihood wiped out by war—took with increasing zest to the occupa-

Ward's son, Judge Artemas Ward, dated January 22, 1819. It gives a conversation with Samuel Dexter as authority for the statement that Washington, on his retirement from public life, wrote to Ward denying that he had written "a letter published in the early part of the Revolutionary war, which contained Remarks injurious to the Reputation of General Ward," and expressing "in unequivocal Terms, the highest Regard for the character and Conduct of General Ward, in all the Departments of public Duty in which he had acted."—*Massachusetts Historical Society Proceedings,* XII, 125.

I have found neither contradiction nor affirmation of such a letter from Washington.

It will be noted that Gore's letter gives a much earlier date for the disclosure of the contents of the Washington letter than do the traditional accounts.

tion of privateering. Once essayed—and a prize or two secured—they found its hazards and irregularities much more to their taste than the regulations of army life.[5]

The land forces remaining for the protection of the harbor consisted of only four very lean regiments. Two were stationed in Boston, one on the Charlestown peninsula, and one on Dorchester Neck. A fifth regiment had been left behind by Washington, but this also was weak in numbers—it had fewer than 300 men fit for duty—and was posted at Beverly to guard the prize vessels and their cargoes.

Furthermore, southward with Washington had gone the bulk of military stores of every description, and practically all available teams. And the scant military stores that had been left behind lay scattered from Medford to Dorchester.

It was thus with but the ill-equipped remnants of an army, garrisoned in a pest-ridden town, that Ward assumed the dangerous responsibility of holding the main seaport of New England against the possible return of the enemy's fleet.

It was to be supposed that the English commanders would welcome an opportunity to efface the humiliation of having surrendered Boston—and several English ships, including one of fifty guns, remained in the vicinity of Nantasket in the lower harbor. Admiral Shuldham had stationed them there to warn incoming English vessels, but no one in the American councils could divine their orders, nor whether or not they

[5] In succeeding years, the rich possibilities of a lucky cruise constituted a fruitful cause of desertion from the army. On June 9, 1779, Paul Revere complains to the Council that several of his men "have deserted, and gone in Privateers, and are now upon a Cruise, that one of them has sent in a Valuable Prize. That your [word omitted] has forbid the Agent paying any part of their share to them or Order. He therefore prays that the Honorable Court would take the matter into consideration, and pass such an Act as will hinder them from recovering their Wages or Prize Money. That they may have no inducement to Desert."—Goss, *Paul Revere*, II, 325.

Only four days later, Colonel Shepard wrote: "Desertions have become so frequent as to be really alarming, and threatens the Ruin of the Brigade . . . about Forty Men have deserted from it within a few Months; eight of whom went off last Night from one Regiment. . . . The Men seem to be chiefly induced to desertion by the Prospect of Gain in the Business of Privateering, and I have great Reason to think that, if they are not encouraged to desert by Commanders of Vessels, they are at least secreted by some of them after shipping themselves for a Voyage."—Original letter, *Massachusetts Archives*, CCI, 113.

would be, or expected to be, reinforced. If the English *had* returned, the American forces would have been hard put to it to prevent their retaking the town.

Both military and civilian authorities realized the danger, and Washington refers to it in several letters.[6]

The streets of Boston still presented a desolate appearance. The anniversary of Lexington and Concord came around and passed; yet, except for the men engaged on the defenses, there seemed scant life in the once busy little capital. The shutters continued up on most of the shops. Open to attack by the enemy, and infected with smallpox, the town offered few inducements for the return of its former inhabitants.[7]

The conditions to be faced were enough to discourage the strongest. For a sick man, they constituted a cruel burden. Ward's disorder had taken a strong hold on him, but no one of sufficient experience and ability was available to relieve him and he manfully stood it out, although, as he later remarked, he had "everything to do & nothing to do with."[8]

There was truly "everything to do." The forts raised by the English army in Boston had been designed against an enemy attacking from the mainland. The protection that Boston needed now was chiefly of forts to defend her from an enemy coming in by the sea.

Ward immediately set about preparations for defense.

His Order Book shows the close attention he gave the work and his earnest efforts to recover order and safety, meantime in patriotic terms exhorting both officers and men to their highest efforts. He made the most of his small command and by May 4 he could report that "the Forts on Fort Hill

[6] April 29, 1776, to Ward, *American Archives,* 4th, V, 1124, etc.

[7] "The town yet looks melancholy; but few of the inhabitants being removed back into it, occasioned by its not being sufficiently fortified and garrisoned against any further attempt of the enemy, to which it now lies much exposed. The shops in general remain shut up."—April 19, 1776, Diary of Ezekiel Price, *Massachusetts Historical Society Proceedings,* VII, 272.

[8] To the Continental Congress, September 20, 1776.—Copy in *Artemas Ward MSS.*

in Boston, Charlestown Point, and Castle Point, are almost compleated, with a number of heavy cannon mounted in each; a work is in good forwardness on Noddles Island, and a Detachment of the Army is at work at Castle Island repairing the Batteries there."[9]

There were many rumors of British armadas on their way to devour the province.

One, apparently well confirmed, was brought by a captain arriving from Europe on May 2.[10] It told of the coming of a "fleet of 60 sail of transports" with instructions, if peace could not be arranged, "to risque every thing to Penetrate into the country," and, failing in this, "to burn and Destroy all in their power."

Ward urged his men to still greater efforts. He set aside every detail of garrison duty that consumed the time of an able-bodied man and put his entire force—officers and privates alike—to work on the defenses.[11] Sundays and weekdays the work went on unceasingly.

Following closely after the report of a fleet from England, was another that the fleet and troops from Halifax were to return "and that they intended to land their Troops below and march to Boston by land while the Men of War made an attack by Water." This news came from a man "who appears to be an honest American" and who had got it from an officer of the big English warship still in the lower harbor. "The same account was given by another man who made his escape from the same Man of War the night before last."[12]

[9] To Washington, *American Archives,* 4th, V, 1194.

[10] Captain John Lee, arriving at Newbury, May 2, 1776.—Original letter, Richard Derby, Jr., to Ward, *Artemas Ward MSS.*

[11] *Ward's Order Book,* May 3, 1776—"every officer, non-commissioned officer and private off duty is to turn out to fatigue until further orders."

[12] Ward to James Warren, May 6, 1776.—Original letter, *Massachusetts Archives,* CXCIV, 376.

Following is the Ezekiel Price diary entry of the incident, crediting the information to a deserter: "Monday May 6,—Went to Boston. Examined papers at the custom-house. Reports of the day,—that a deserter came from the man-of-war below, who says that it was the talk among the officers of the ship that the troops and navy which fled from Boston were ordered back to Boston."—*Massachusetts Historical Society Proceedings,* VII, 254.

Both the threats proved to be phantoms—the new enemy fleet came not, and the old enemy fleet remained at its Halifax moorings for another month—and then sailed direct for New York; but the danger was real and called for constant vigilance.

Not only Boston felt the menace of the English fleets. The inhabitants of other coast positions also earnestly solicited Ward for ordnance and ammunition to protect themselves against British attacks.

Busy pens and busy tongues endeavored to widen the estrangement between Ward and Washington. More work had, probably, never been done in the same space of time by so comparatively small a force than on Boston's defenses during that April of 1776, yet there were found people to complain because a few hundred men had not been able to throw up fortifications as fast as six or seven thousand had done when the entire American army was encamped around the city!

Their stories inspired Washington to write to Ward, April 29, complaining that he heard that defense works "go on exceedingly slow." His informants were prejudiced, for on May 13 Washington characterized as "very agreeable" Ward's account (May 4) of what had actually been accomplished.

Again, May 2, Washington had written that he had "heard that the regiments stationed on Dorchester Heights and Bunker Hill are not employed in carrying on the works for the defence of Boston"; which Ward indignantly denied (May 9) —and requested the name of the author of the statement. We find a much more conciliatory communication from Washington on May 16.[13]

The Continental Congress had not acted on Ward's resignation, so he wrote again on April 12. He referred to his first letter, which had asked permission to give up his command because of his poor health, and continued: "I must re-

[13] The six letters of this correspondence are in *American Archives,* 4th, V, 1124; VI, 436; V, 1194, 1174; VI, 401, 478.

new my request for the same reason. I cannot be content to continue in office when I am conscious I am not able to do the duties."[14]

Congress heeded this second request and on April 23 accepted his resignation.

Hancock, as President, notified Ward in a very cordial letter, declaring that "The Motives which first induced the Congress to appoint you a Major-general in the Continental Service would naturally make them regret your retiring from the Army. But when it is considered that in the course of your duty in that high rank you have acquitted yourself with Honor and Reputation, I am persuaded, the Reluctance they feel at your retiring is much increased."[15]

Hancock's letter reached Ward on May 4 and he immediately wrote to Washington, saying that "The sooner I am relieved the more agreeable it will be to me, as my health has declined much this Spring."[16]

The acceptance of his resignation availed Ward nothing, however. No competent general officer could be spared to take his place, and Washington perforce requested him, despite his sufferings and general ill-health, to continue in command.

The end of May marked a noteworthy advancement of the harbor defenses. A new provincial regiment (Whitney's) and Crafts' artillery battalion, together with local volunteers and detachments from nearby towns, had added their labor to such good result that on June 8 Ward felt justified in announcing a Sunday of general rest, "and that the officers lead their men without arms or musick to places of public worship."[17]

Of the routine difficulties of Ward's position, the most

[14] *American Archives*, 4th, V, 872.

[15] *Ibid.*, 1048, dated April 24. The original letter, owned by the Massachusetts Historical Society, is dated April *26*.

[16] *Ibid.*, 1194.

[17] *Ward's Order Book.*

vexing was the low state of the continental treasury. Numerous letters show the difficulty of obtaining money, both for the troops and for the crews of the continental privateers.[18]

In pleasurable contrast was the consideration of the prizes made by the privateers. Several were brought in during May and June despite the waiting English ships.

The choicest of the prizes was, May 17, that of the *Hope* from Cork, captured by the schooner *Franklin,* James Mugford, Master, with a cargo of gunpowder and other military stores. Despite increasing domestic production, gunpowder was still a scarce article in the American army and such a cargo was worth its weight in gold. Five hundred barrels were quickly on their way to Norwich, Conn., to be forwarded to Washington at New York, together with two tons of musket balls, five hundred carbines, a thousand spades, etc.

Three days later Ward had to write of Mugford's death in a desperate fight with the enemy. "He was run through with a lance while he was cutting off the hands of the Pirates as they were attempting to board" his ship, "and it is said that with his own hands he cut off five pair of theirs."[19] The English were beaten off; several of their boats were sunk, and a number of their men killed.

In a later dispatch Ward gives high credit to the crew, only seven in all, of the little *Lady Washington* which came to Mugford's aid. "She was attacked by five boats which were supposed to contain near or quite an hundred men, but after repeated efforts to board her they were beaten off by the intrepidity and exertions of the little Company who gloriously

[18] On April 11 Ward wrote to Washington for instructions concerning the pay of the men on board the continental privateers.—Original letter, Library of Congress. Washington replied, April 18, that their wages ought to be paid out of the sales of the prizes taken, which should give "cash . . . much more than sufficient to answer the demands upon them."—*American Archives,* 4th, V, 977–978. This decision was reported to Captain Bartlett, agent for the privateers at Beverly, but he retorted, April 26, that though he was "well satisfied that there will be a Sufficiency when the Prizes are Sold, that does not Satisfy the Hungry belly at Present."—Original letter, *Artemas Ward MSS.*

[19] To Washington, May 20, 1776, *American Archives,* 4th, VI, 532.

defended the Lady against the brutal Ravishers of Liberty."[20]

On May 30 Ward was again elected to the Council, but the General Court continued to sit at Watertown through the summer and the greater part of the following autumn, and he seldom found it possible to attend the Board there.

In June the town and harbor forces were strengthened by the gradual filling up both of Whitney's provincial regiment, already referred to, and a second provincial regiment (Marshall's), the raising of which had been authorized early in May.

These troops, enlisted to December 1, did not come within Ward's command. As provincial regiments on a provincial establishment, they served under the direction of the General Court committee of fortification until August 2 when by Council appointment, Benjamin Lincoln became their general officer. (The committee of fortification had the supervision of the work on the harbor defenses whether done under the continental or provincial command.)

The English ships lying in the channels remained, though, a prolific source of anxiety—adding to the general uneasiness which their presence excited, the direct annoyance that they rendered very risky both the ingress and egress of American coasters. A sudden attack was planned to drive them away.

It was completely successful. A detachment of five hundred men, under Colonel Asa Whitcomb, duplicated on a small scale the methods of Breed's Hill and Dorchester Heights. An evening trip to Long Island, June 13, landing at about 11 P.M.; a busy night, intrenching and mounting their cannon and a solitary 13-inch mortar; then, in the early morning of June 14, an abrupt cannonading of the startled enemy.

The attack was so unexpected that the Englishmen, without waiting to investigate the strength of their assailants, slipped their cables and quitted the harbor with all possible

[20] May 27, 1776, to Washington, *American Archives,* 4th, VI, 602.

speed; the provincial regiments posted on Pettick's (Peddock's) Island and Nantasket Head (Hull) giving them a few parting shots as they passed out.

Opposite is a facsimile of Colonel Whitcomb's report to Ward.

After the departure of the English ships many in Boston experienced an unwonted feeling of security, and the town began to display some of its old-time activity. The shops opened, and there was much bustle along the docks.

June was marked also by the American privateers' success in capturing several transports with Scotch Highlanders sailing to reinforce Howe: one transport was taken on the night of the seventh, two on the sixteenth, and one on the eighteenth.

"Great numbers of spectators were in the streets" when Lieutenant-Colonel Campbell and the other officers of the second capture "passed up King Street, in their way to General Ward's."[21] It was a grateful sight to Boston eyes, a most welcome manifestation both of the activity of Massachusetts' sailors, and of Massachusetts' full possession of Boston harbor.

The week of the twenty-second raised hopes of a still bigger haul, for several privateer captains sent word that they had sighted eleven transports convoyed by a frigate.

Ward improvised a squadron of the privateers in the harbor and at nearby points. It was not large enough to attempt an ocean capture of so many sail, but he laid plans to make reasonably sure of the taking of the entire fleet if it should enter the roads.

[21] Diary of Ezekiel Price, June 17, 1776, *Massachusetts Historical Society Proceedings,* VII, 258. A little less than a year later, Lieutenant-Colonel Campbell was exchanged for Ethan Allen, who had been taken prisoner by the English in September, 1775. The exchange, as also that of other prisoners, was effected by correspondence between General Ward and the English Major-General Eyre Massey.—Massey to Howe, January 12, 1778, *Report on American Manuscripts in the Royal Institution of Great Britain,* I, 178. Ward and Massey had thus as opposing generals renewed an acquaintance formed when they had together fought the French at Ticonderoga in 1758: Massey as a major of the British regulars, and Ward as lieutenant-colonel in the provincial forces.

Boston June 15th 1776

To General Ward — Sir

I Recd. your Orders with great pleasure to go to Long-Island with Five Hundred Men, & Two Days Provision, with proper implements to throw up Works to anoy the Enemies Ships near that Island. And it is with equal pleasure, That I am able in this my Return, to acquaint your Honour with our Success. Through the Divine Goodness, we have prosecuted your Plan in such a Manner, That our Enemies were obliged to leave the Harbour with their Men of War & Transports, with a large Number of Ministerial Troops, & tho' in a manner honorary to the Continental Troops, yet in a manner shameful to them, their Strength and Numbers being vastly superior to ours. and as an Evidence of their Cowardice, & final remove, they destroyed ye Light House, which was in their hands. And what is more extraordinary than any thing

is, That the whole was effected with out a man Killed, or wounded. So that the Port of Boston is now open which has been shut two Years to a Day.

Asa Whitcomb Coll

From the original (6¼ inches in width), owned by Roxa Dix Southard, Groton, Mass.

COLONEL WHITCOMB'S LETTER TELLING OF THE EXPULSION OF THE ENGLISH SHIPS FROM BOSTON HARBOR

The ships hovered around for a week, and then set out to sea again without coming close enough for Ward's preparations to endanger them—much to every one's disgust and disappointment!

Abigail Adams wrote that they "kept us all with our mouths open, ready to catch them, but after staying near a week, and making what observations they could, set sail and went off, to our great mortification, who were [ready] for them in every respect."[22]

On June 30 Ward received an express from New Hampshire with an urgent prayer for gunpowder to replace the fifty-two barrels that she had lent the continental forces during the summer of 1775. Reports from Canada had warned her of a projected invasion by the enemy and his Indian allies.

"The time necessary to obtain an order from General Washington to deliver us the powder lent," wrote Meshech Weare, President of the New Hampshire Council, "may decide the fate of our Frontiers & leave open the lower Settlements of your & our Colonies to the Devastations of Canadians and Savages—Therefore we entreat you (in this time of eminent danger) so far to dispense with the common method or rule in such cases, as to order the delivery of fifty-two barrels of gunpowder to the Bearer, Mr. Champney, to be forwarded by him to us; and we will without delay send to General Washington for his order to you for that purpose; which we are sensible will greatly recover the almost despairing spirits of our Brethren in the Frontiers, and be esteemed a Favor to the common cause and this colony in particular."[23]

Ward promptly cut the red tape of military regulations and endorsed Weare's letter with an immediate "order to ye Commissary for fifty two barrels of powder."

Smallpox continued to infest Boston, and Ward, early in July, arranged for the inoculation of the two regiments (Whitcomb's and Phinney's) stationed in the town.

[22] *Familiar Letters of John Adams and his Wife,* 201.

[23] June 29, 1776, *New Hampshire Provincial, State, and Town Papers,* VIII, 178.

A few days later came the news from Philadelphia that the Continental Congress had declared the colonies independent! Ward marked the occasion by giving "America" as parole, and "Independence" as countersign, and on the following morning (July 17) the immortal Declaration was read at the head of the regiments.

Simultaneously with, and closely following, the Continental Congress letter which enclosed the Declaration, Ward received orders from Washington, based on accompanying resolutions by the Continental Congress,[24] that all of his five continental regiments march to join the northern and New York armies: the three "fullest regiments" to go to Ticonderoga to strengthen the slim garrison there against the expected English attempt to recover its possession; the other two regiments to serve under Washington's personal standard in New York.

All the regiments were to march to Norwich, Conn., to sail from there down Long Island Sound to New York; the troops destined for Ticonderoga going thence up the Hudson, it being "the opinion of all the officers, that it will be better for the whole, as well the three intended for the northward as those to reinforce the troops here, to take this route in preference to any other."[25]

An English fleet swung in New York's lower harbor, and Howe's Boston army, with other troops, was encamped on Staten Island; but Washington and his council felt that the Hudson was safely held by the hulks blockading, and the guns

[24] *Journals of the Continental Congress:*

July 5, 1776—"*Resolved,* That General Washington be empowered, if he shall judge it adviseable, to order three of the fullest regiments, stationed in Massachusetts bay, to be immediately marched to Ticonderoga; and that an equal number of the militia of that state, be taken into pay, and embodied for its defence, if the government of Massachusetts bay judge it necessary."

July 8, 1776—"*Resolved,* That General Washington be vested with discretionary power to call to his assistance, at New York, such of the continental regiments in the Massachusetts bay, as have not already received orders to march to Ticonderoga; and that the general court of that province be requested to supply their places with militia, if they think it expedient."

[25] July 11, 1776; received in Boston July 15.—*American Archives,* 5th, I, 194.

sweeping, the approaches to both the East and North rivers. It was thought by all "that there remained scarcely a possibility that the passage could be forced, by vessels exposed to such a tornado of shot and shell as would be hurled upon them in the attempt."[26]

Ward quickly had three regiments equipped and ready for marching. Hutchinson's and Sargent's set out on July 18, and Glover's on July 20. Whitcomb's and Phinney's regiments were perforce held over to recover from their smallpox inoculation.[27]

The same week (on July 18) "Independency" was formally declared "from the Balcony of the Council Chamber,"[28] with simple impressive ceremonies which Ward had assisted in arranging as both continental commander and a member of the Council committee.

The smallpox had prevented the people of nearby towns from coming in, as was their general custom when any affair of importance was held in the capital, but "all the inhabitants assembled" and stood in absorbed attention as the proclamation was read; breathing in every word of that document of political freedom which had grown from the seed planted and chiefly nurtured by the bold spirits of their own province.

"When in the course of human events," began the orator, *"it becomes necessary for one people to dissolve the political bands which have connected them with another. . . ."*

And so the reading proceeded: clearly, deliberately, and resolutely to the concluding pledge, made *"with a firm reliance on the protection of Divine Providence,"* of *"our Lives, our Fortunes, and our Sacred Honor."*

[26] Field, *Battle of Long Island,* Memoirs of the Long Island Historical Society, II, 125.

[27] This was before the days of cowpox vaccination. Inoculation then meant the introduction of human smallpox virus into the system. It was often very severe, and sometimes disastrous, in its effect because of the numerous impurities of the virus. The patient, unless isolated, also became a fruitful source of infection. The men's recovery after inoculation was followed by thorough "cleansing" as an essential precaution against carrying the disease into the other American armies. "Cleansing" consisted in the liberal use of sulphur, pitch (or tar or rosin), vinegar, and soap.

[28] *Letters and Diary of John Rowe,* 313.

As the reading ended, a cry went up, "God save our American States," and then "three cheers which rent the air. The bells rang, the privateers fired, . . . the cannon were discharged . . . and every face appeared joyful." "Thus ends royal authority in this State. And all the people shall say Amen."[29]

Brave words and high thoughts, nobly expressed! But speedily to be subjected to the test of severe trials and cruel discouragement.

As a foretaste of disaster, came a new message from Washington[30] changing the orders for the two remaining regiments getting ready to march. They must go overland to Ticonderoga, instead of by way of Norwich, New York, and the Hudson River. The three regiments that had set out for Ticonderoga by the latter route must remain with the New York army, for two English warships had made their way into and up the Hudson—neither checked by the great preparations made to thwart just such an attempt nor seriously damaged by the furious cannonade poured at them by the American batteries—and they cut off all communication with the north by its waters.

The news of the easy forcing of the Hudson bred a great host of misgivings through the country. Patriot eyes anxiously followed all reports and rumors from the new seat of war. "Great is our Solicitude for you and the Army under your Command at New York," wrote Ward to Washington, August 19. "We are in constant expectation of the Enemy's making a violent attack. May the God of Armies give you Success!"[31]

Whitcomb's regiment set out for Ticonderoga on August 8, and Phinney's on the ninth. Their departure left only the two state regiments (Whitney's and Marshall's) and the train (Crafts') in the vicinity of Boston—not enough men to

[29] Abigail Adams, July 21, 1776, *Familiar Letters of John Adams and his Wife,* 204.

[30] July 19, 1776, *American Archives,* 5th, I, 451.

[31] *American Archives,* 5th, I, 1075.

make anything beyond a pretence of garrisoning the town and harbor fortifications. To reinforce them, the Council issued a call for every twenty-fifth man in the training-band and alarm lists of every town in east and central Massachusetts (excepting only Dukes and Nantucket counties) and in two of the three counties which then comprised the present state of Maine, to serve until December 1 under the continental (Ward's) command.

As the men came in they were formed into two regiments under Colonels Dike and Francis.

Ward during these several months had continued in the command: always about to be relieved, but the relief always failing; his resignation officially accepted, but the duties and responsibilities still adhering to him; retaining his post at Washington's repeated requests, despite a serious turn to his sickness which for a time confined him closely to his room, but refusing to draw any salary because he held no official status.

There were many objections—both public and personal—to this irregular tenure, and as there was still no one else both competent and available for the post, Congress clarified the situation by a special request, August 21, to Ward that he remain;[32] and an order, entered November 7, defining his rank as that of a "major-general commanding in a separate department."

President Hancock's letter (August 26) accompanying and emphasizing the request, concluded with the assertion that Ward's readiness to comply with the wishes of his country gave him the "strongest reason" to believe that he would not resist "its application at this juncture."[33]

It is a high tribute to Ward that, in spite of his ill health, the embarrassing division of military authority in Boston, and

[32] *Journals of the Continental Congress,* August 21, 1776—"*Resolved,* . . . That Major General Ward be authorized & requested if his Health will permit to continue in the Command of the Forces in the Service of the United States, in the Eastern Department, until further orders."

[33] *American Archives,* 5th, I, 1157.

the animosity of the James Warren clique, his patriotism was relied upon to hold him in the continental command of the most important port under American control and a military position which at any time might have developed into one of paramount importance.

On September 16 Ward reviewed the "new-raised Company of Independents," making "their first Appearance in their Uniforms (black, turned up with red). They performed the Exercise, various Manoeuvers and Firings, to the Universal Acceptance of the numerous Spectators."[34]

This item has local interest even today after a lapse of nearly a century and a half, because the First Corps of Cadets, Massachusetts National Guard, is the direct legitimate descendant of those Boston "Independents" of 1776.

The division of the port's military authority had worked passably well while Lincoln acted as chairman of the committee of fortification and general of the state troops, but after Lincoln's appointment, September 16, to command instead the militia ordered to be raised to reinforce the army at New York, its evil possibilities very quickly became apparent.

The fortification committee removed the cannon from Dorchester Heights to mount them elsewhere, and Ward protested vigorously. "They are important posts and ought not to be destitute of proper ordnance and ordnance stores one day," he declared.[35]

The Council immediately instructed the committee "without delay" to equip the forts with ordnance of the same size as that removed, and followed this by an order transferring all the state troops to Ward's command. Notifying Ward of this action, the Council express the hope that it "will be agreeable to your Honor & that you for the service of the Common

[34] *Independent Chronicle,* September 19, 1776. The Company of Independents was a revival of the Governor's Company of Cadets, created in 1741 by Governor Shirley. It had disbanded in 1774 because of the dismissal of its colonel, John Hancock, by Governor Gage.

[35] September 30, 1776, *American Archives,* 5th, II, 624.

Cause will take these Troops under your Command & directions."[36]

Southward, American fortunes under Washington grew steadily blacker.

High hopes and rejoicing had followed the evacuation of Boston. So pleasing indeed had the prospect appeared to England's European rivals, that France and Spain had stimulated and encouraged the surreptitious shipment of money and arms to the new "United States," and there was hope that they would openly enter the conflict.

All this had been changed by the defeat at Long Island and the abandonment of New York: the American forces routed and driven back.

Men of all classes again turned their faces toward and longed for "General Lee."[37] Wherever Lee had been, he had won new laurels—or at least additional encomiums. It had lately been Lee in Virginia, Lee in the Carolinas, Lee in Georgia. We of today know that much of the credit for his successes belonged by right to others; but in the eyes of the revolutionists of 1776 he was the greatest of martial heroes.

Congress hurried Lee to New York, and he found Washington on Harlem Heights with the enemy manœuvering to trap him and his army. In the days following, Lee confirmed and added to the army's high opinion of his ability by his inspiring and successful command of the rear-guard which covered the American retreat.[38]

[36] October 4, 1776, *American Archives,* 5th, II, 886.

[37] "If General Lee should be at Philadelphia, pray hasten his departure—he is much wanted in New York": John Jay, Fishkill, N. Y., to Edward Rutledge, October 11, 1776.—Johnston, *Correspondence and Public Papers of John Jay,* I, 93. And, shortly before, Colonel Malcolm had written to John McKesson, "General Lee is hourly expected, as if from heaven, with a legion of flaming swordsmen."—Moore, *The Treason of Charles Lee,* 37.

[38] Joseph Reed to Charles Lee, November 21, 1776: "I do not mean to flatter, nor praise you at the Expence of any other; but I confess I do think that it is entirely owing to you that this Army and the Liberties of America so far as they are dependant on it are not totally cut off. You have Decision, a Quality often wanting in Minds otherwise valuable; and I ascribe to this our Escape from York Island, from Kingsbridge and the Plains. . . . Nor am I singular in my Opinion; Every Gentleman of the Family, the Officers and soldiers generally, have a Confidence in you—the Enemy con-

Ward's difficulties in fulfilling his responsibilities, both to the Continental Congress and to the state, increased with the coming of winter. The immunity which Boston had enjoyed since the evacuation, had rendered the Massachusetts Council as apathetic concerning defense as it had before been eagerly anxious. The enlistment terms of the regiments guarding the port expired December 1, but up to November 26 no action had been taken either to hold them over or to raise others in their place.

Ward expressed himself strongly on the subject in a letter to Samuel Adams. "At present," he wrote, "it appears to me that after the last day of this instant, there will be no troops in and about Boston, excepting the train. All the others were raised for no longer time than the last of the month; and I cant find that there is any measures taken to raise others in their room, or even to desire them to continue longer in the service, although I have repeatedly mentioned it at the Board, and told them the consequence that would follow upon such delay, and also that I thought it my duty to inform some of the members of Congress of this neglect. Should that be the case it will not do for me to continue in command in this department, and have none to command but the train, neither will it be expedient for me to leave the command, without directions from Congress, as it was at their request that I consented to continue in Service.

"It is disagreeable to me to mention anything to the disadvantage of the State to which I Belong; but in Justice to myself I have done it to you, in confidence."[39]

On November 26 Ward again laid a formal application before the Council[40] and this time his warning was in some degree heeded. Reënlistments were opened for two regi-

stantly inquire where you are, and seem to be less confident when you are present."—*Lee Papers,* II, 293.

[39] November 17, 1776.—Original letter, *Samuel Adams Papers,* New York Public Library.

[40] Original letter, *Massachusetts Archives,* CCXI, 205.

ments for the local defense. A small garrison, but better than none.

The decision was only a few days old when reports reached Boston that the English commanders intended to profit by the defenseless condition of the capital and were directing their forces—land and naval—for a sudden, overwhelming assault upon it.

Apprehensions were wrought to the point of real alarm by news of the English seizure of Newport. Word was momentarily expected that an enemy army was marching on Boston.

Several hundred militia were called in for the defense of the harbor, and between three and four thousand, quickly gathering, set out toward Rhode Island to help hold the redcoats in check.

So serious was the perturbation of the state authorities that, December 7, on the excitement of the early reports of the movements of the English fleet, a committee from the House of Representatives waited on Ward with an offer to assist him in the removal of his military stores.[41]

Ward did not accept the suggestion—instead, instructing Colonel Crafts, his artillery officer, to see that all was "in order for action in case the enemy should attempt anything this way."[42]

The English commander (General Clinton) held, however, no instructions to essay a winter campaign in New England, or even to push any considerable distance beyond his lines in the vicinity of Newport. He was content to await developments in the spring. Then, as the first of the "operations of the next campaign," Howe had proposed to Secretary Germain "an offensive army of ten thousand rank and file" to take possession of Providence and thence to penetrate "into

[41] This step had shortly before been suggested by Charles Lee in a letter to James Bowdoin, as president of the Massachusetts Council.—November 25, 1776, *Lee Papers,* II, 312.

[42] *Ward's Order Book,* December 9, 1776.

the country toward Boston, and, if possible, to reduce that town."[43]

Nor, on their part, could the Americans make any immediate attempt to oust Clinton. Even if the season had been propitious, there was no available force of sufficient strength. So, to the chagrin of the people of Rhode Island and of the continent generally, the English troops settled down in undisputed possession.

The winter had brought with it improvement in Ward's health, and (the General Court having returned to Boston on November 12) he took an increasingly important part in the Council deliberations and activities. So diversified soon became the calls upon his time and judgment in the military affairs of both the state and the continent, that Knox, visiting Boston a few weeks later, remarked that "whether he acts as a councilor of the Massachusetts or a continental general is difficult to say."[44]

Northward, the situation had temporarily improved. Carleton, the English commander-in-chief in Canada, had come down to, and occupied, Crown Point, destroying Benedict Arnold's gallant little fleet in his stride; but the fame of Arnold's preparations had delayed his start and, with the winter upon him, he gave up for the moment the design to recover Ticonderoga for the King. Instead, abandoning Crown Point, he turned back to Canada and winter quarters.

To the south, though, the American cause has grown sinister. We have had the loss of Fort Washington and the surrender of its garrison; and we see Washington with the remnants of his army fleeing through New Jersey into Pennsylvania. And Charles Lee holding aloof with the larger force under his command—all but ignoring Washington's

[43] November 30, 1776, *American Archives,* 5th, III, 926. Three weeks later, Howe inclined to the postponement of "the offensive plan towards Boston" until the arrival of reinforcements from Europe—not because he had discarded the project but because the growth of tory sentiment in Pennsylvania favored the first spring movement being made in that quarter.—December 20, 1776, *American Archives,* 5th, III, 1317–1318.

[44] Drake, *Henry Knox,* 41; Brooks, *Henry Knox,* 87.

need of reinforcements and his orders to join him, and planning an independent attack on the British which should further enhance his personal distinction and further detract from Washington's.

It was supremely fortunate for the United States that, in the midst of his dreams of supremacy, Lee was, on December 13, captured by Harcourt at Basking Ridge. Let us call it a direct dispensation of Providence. To merely pass it by, saying that Lee was careless in placing himself in so exposed a position, is not sufficient. Washington, near Elkton, in the following August (the twenty-sixth) was equally imprudent,[45] but, happily for America, Lee was taken prisoner, whereas Washington was not.

It is not improbable that a successful stroke by Lee at this juncture—viewed in the halo which he had gained, partly by his own efforts and partly by good fortune—would have sufficed to depose Washington. Lee then would undoubtedly have been given the chief command. Many possible results present themselves—and most of them evil.

When Lee was returned in May of 1778 no such danger existed. Times and conditions had changed.

But that metamorphosis of times and conditions was of the future. At the moment, his capture seemed another cruel blow to a reeling cause.[46] The day before, the Continental Congress had fled from panic-stricken Philadelphia. "If every nerve is not strained to recruit the new army with all possible expedition I think the game is pretty near up," Washington admitted to his favorite brother, John Augustine.[47]

[45] *Memoirs du Général Lafayette,* First Paris edition, I, 21–22 (different page numbers in some other editions); F. V. Greene, *Life of Nathanael Greene,* 79–80; G. W. Greene, *Life of Nathanael Greene,* I, 443–444.

[46] "Our cause has received a severe blow in the captivity of General Lee."—Washington to Lund Washington, December 17, 1776. "I feel much for the loss of my Country in his Captivity."—Washington to the Continental Congress, December 15, 1776. Ford, *Writings of Washington,* V, 79, 100.

[47] December 18, 1776.—Ford, *Writings of Washington,* V, 111. "My situation and that of our cause is critical, and truly alarming," Washington wrote to Heath on December 21, 1776.—Ford, *Writings of Washington,* V, 125.

But Washington's courage of spirit was inexhaustible. The short span of one week later he smashed the Hessians at Trenton, suddenly and with overwhelming success; and then struck again at Princeton: and the American cause, responding instantly to the magic of reviving hope, throbbed with new life. True, the flame in the torch of its independence burned low, but the torch was in the resolute hands of a chief who through trials and defeats and adversity was becoming one of the select company of the world's great men.

The dramatic forcefulness of Washington's success halted the dangerous swing of public opinion into the tory camp and held patriot criticism in check for many months. On the enemy, and in other foreign circles, it reacted still more strongly. It compelled a radical change in the disposition of the English troops in New Jersey; and its narration, reverberating through the courts and politics of Europe, created much the same effect as had been wrought by Bunker Hill.

As the year 1777 opened, great anxiety was bred in Boston by reports that the English planned a winter attack upon Ticonderoga, hoping to profit by the weakness of the American garrison there.

Ward (January 9) directed the colonels of four regiments recruiting—including Francis'—to march their men northward "in small detachments" as quickly as they could be enlisted. He also wrote to Meshech Weare of New Hampshire urging the dispatch of two regiments "with all possible expedition"—to march them "by companies or half companies as fast as they can be raised."[48]

On January 28 Ward renewed his request to the Continental Congress to appoint some other officer in his place.[49]

Among the reasons prompting him was the very low ebb of his garrison in Boston as the result of the necessities of Ticonderoga. Despite Congress's desire that he continue in

[48] *New Hampshire Provincial, State, and Town Papers,* VIII, 462.

[49] MS. draft, *Ward's Order Book.*

the post, he felt uneasy at drawing the salary of a major-general in a separate department while commanding so slender a force. "I conceive," he wrote, "it will be an unnecessary expense to the public for me to continue."

More weighty and more impelling was a new danger engaging his attention—the breeding of a tory party in the hitherto strongly patriot counties of central and western Massachusetts. He wished to be freed from the routine of a garrison command, feeling that as a member of the Council without the continental appointment he could render wider and more useful service.

On February 7 the General Court determined to probe the reports of seditious activity within the state. Declaring that it had been informed "that divers ill minded persons inimical to the Rights, Liberties and Happiness of the United States have concerted and are endeavoring to carry into execution Plans highly injurious to them," it passed a "Resolve for discovering Secret Plans" and appointed a committee with an appropriation "to be applied in the most secret Manner, according to their Discretion, for the Discovery thereof."

James Warren, Aaron Wood, and Samuel Freeman constituted the committee, but Ward was intimately connected with its work and on the following day he rode to Worcester and, with Judge Levi Lincoln, set James Case of Leicester to work in the county to ferret out the underground plans taking shape.[50]

Tory sentiment was also showing in considerable strength in the north. It was wide-spread in the colony "without a government"—the southern part of the present state of Vermont, which had rejected the jurisdiction of New York and had not yet developed its own government or institutions. Its unsettled condition offered a fertile, and comparatively safe, field for tory activities; and patriot committees sent earnest requests to General Ward for advice and assistance. One

[50] James Case's statement.—*Worcester, Original Papers,* I, 101, American Antiquarian Society.

of March 4, from a committee of the town of Guilford, declared that "we that live in ye New Hampshire grants not being in any state labor under greater difficulties than any state by reson of having a grate many enemies to ye glorious cause of America." They had imprisoned two prominent and active tories in the Westminster jail, but they added, "We have so many Tories we fear they will soon be let out of jail . . . We should be very glad if your Excellency would take them under your Custody and judge them according to ye marshal law . . . Pray send us sum directions what we shall do with them."[51]

These conjoined circumstances made very welcome the news that Heath had been appointed in his place, and on March 20 Ward gladly turned the garrison over to its new general.

[51] Original letter, *Heath Papers,* III, 267, Massachusetts Historical Society. Another letter, fifteen days later, from a committee representing a number of Vermont towns, asserted that "the greatest part of the people, viz., on these New Hampshire grants are true friends for the grand cause of America," but that "too many Enemies to the cause afor'sd being found and convicted as such, and at present being in such state of anarchy, having no place of Confinement for just offenders to the cause afors'd, [we] are utterly at a loss what to do. Therefore as in Duty bound for our own safety and the safety of the cause afores'd we humbly crave your Excellency's Counsel in Directing us to such Measures, as your Wisdom shall think proper."—Original letter, *Heath Papers,* III, 307, Massachusetts Historical Society.

CHAPTER XIII

1777–1783: Age 49–55

The Secret Committee to offset tory intrigues. The Rhode Island expeditions. General Ward a delegate to the Continental Congress. The danger that a part of Massachusetts might return to British allegiance; and the Hampshire County Committee. Ward's opinion of Hancock. The conclusion of peace and the full recognition of the independence of the United States.

RELIEVED of the continental command, Ward was able to devote full attention to the duties and responsibilities of the Council.

With few exceptions he was present at every meeting of the Board during the next three years, and during much of that time acted as president of the Council—that is to say, as the executive head of the state, for there was no governor in Massachusetts during the War of the Revolution until after the election of September, 1780, under the new constitution.

In the Massachusetts Archives are scores of letters in Ward's handwriting: copies carefully made by him of letters that he had still more carefully written to other state governments; to continental generals on divers military matters; to officers concerning enlistments; to town officials regarding prisoners, the property of loyalists, etc.

On May 1 (1777) General Ward, for the Council, and Generals Palmer and Preble of the House, were appointed "a Secret Committee to repair forthwith to Providence to advise with the Governor of that State and the Commanding officer of the Continental Troops there" concerning a proposed expedition against the enemy on Rhode Island.

The committee at once set out in a coach and four, arriving in Providence the next day.

There, crowded into seventy-two hours, were consultations on the total number of troops needed for such an enterprise; the proportion that the state of Rhode Island could raise; the aid that Connecticut could send; the questions of ordnance, provisions, etc.

The committee left Providence on their homeward journey about noon on Monday, May 5, reaching Boston the day following in time for Ward to take his place in the Council.

Consideration of his report resulted in the plan being dropped for a time, the General Court deciding that it was impracticable with the forces available because of the domination of both bay and river by the English fleet.

The protraction of the struggle and the precarious condition of the American cause emboldened the tories and they became "Exceeding busy." Reports of internal sedition multiplied and the General Court on May 3 appointed a new "Committee of Secresy."

Only two weeks later Heath advised the Council that he had received information that May 20 was to be made "the hottest Day that ever America saw, for on that Day the Tories would Rise and show themselves."

He added that he believed "from several other concuring circumstances uncommon vigilence and Exertion are necessary. Distrust is the Mother of security. It is said that a Rendezvous of the Paricides is to be somewhere in the County of Worcester. Are there not in that County a considerable number of Highland Soldiers? Should there be an insurrection, can there be any doubt, that they will not instantly join? and as to their getting of Armes they can easily effect it." [1]

May 20 passed innocuously, but dangerous disorder still threatened. The preparations to meet the projected uprising had caused its fomenters to delay the attempt, but did not

[1] Original letter, *Massachusetts Archives,* CXCVII, 56.

cure their mutinous spirit. They continued "visiting & journeying from place to place . . . ploting measures to oppose public exertions, and assist the enimy should a favorable opportunity present."[2]

Ward's home county being especially affected, he left Boston to return to Shrewsbury for the secret committee—which was equipped with a wide range of power and held authority to direct "Warrants to any Persons Inhabitants of this State for the Purpose of arresting and convening any Persons who are liable by Law to be arrested for transgressing . . . the Act against Treason and Offences less than Treason and any Acts for punishing Persons inimical to the American States."

Ward also took advantage of his return to Worcester County to preside at the session of the Court of Common Pleas which opened June 10—one of the only three occasions on which his other duties permitted him to attend the court during the first six years of the war.

He was back in the capital on June 20, to find the ominous rumors of tory plots supplemented by reports that the British fleet at Newport was about to set out for Boston.

Soon after, overshadowing all, came Burgoyne's descent from Canada with his lavishly equipped army of redcoats, Hessians, Canadians, and Indians. Ticonderoga and its valuable stores fell to him on July 6.

Following the news from Ticonderoga came an urgent call (July 21) from Governor Cooke of Rhode Island stating that "a fleet of about 40 square rigged vessells were . . . coming through the Sound standing Eastward, so that it is past doubt that they are bound into Newport. We request that you immediately send all the assistance in your power. . . . We imagine that the Enemy intend to possess themselves of this town [Providence] & then penetrate the Country so far as your Capital. We are directing all our Militia

[2] Levi Lincoln to Ward.—*Worcester, Original Papers,* I, 102, American Antiquarian Society.

& alarm men to march into this place & to such other places as we expect it probable they mean to land."[3]

The dispatch reached Boston about ten o'clock of the same night. Ward and other members of the Council "immediately met and sat until after two in the morning."[4]

No time could be spared to test the accuracy of Cooke's surmise. Instant action was needed to forestall the danger threatened, and Ward hurried expresses out into the night with orders for the draft of a large body of militia to march immediately to Providence: the men to be "well equipped with arms and ammunition" and furnished with six days' provisions, and the selectmen of their towns to arrange for additional supplies to follow them.

Early on the following morning Ward hurried an express to Meshech Weare of New Hampshire, sending him a copy of Governor Cooke's letter, telling him of the forces that Massachusetts was collecting, and warning him to be on the lookout.

Two-thirds of the New Hampshire regiments had been weakened a few days earlier by detachments for the famous little army with which Stark was planning to check and harass Burgoyne, but the New Hampshire Committee of Safety immediately issued orders to draft one-half of the remaining full regiments.

In these urgent preparations James Warren made a sorry spectacle of himself. He was appointed to the command of the Massachusetts militia being raised, and instructed to join the continental forces in Rhode Island under General Spencer. He refused to go on the plea that he felt it beneath his dignity as a major-general of the Massachusetts militia (though he had never been, and never was, in any action) to serve under Major-General Spencer of the continental army, because his commission (June 19, 1776) as militia major-general antedated Spencer's commission (August 9,

[3] *New Hampshire State, Provincial, and Town Papers,* VIII, 645.

[4] Preble's Diary, Monday, July 21, 1777.—*First Three Generations of Prebles,* 81.

1776) as continental major-general (by less than two months), though Spencer had been in active command from the early days of the siege of Boston, and continental brigadier-general (of the first appointments) until his promotion to major-general.

James Warren's contention—made in a time of stress and emergency—appears the more unnecessary when it is noted that under similar conditions a few months later the command was not considered an indignity by John Hancock, *first* major-general of the militia and for years president of the Continental Congress—and, furthermore, a man who was never accused of self-depreciation!

A few days later (August 7) Warren submitted his resignation—and that was the end of his brief career in a military capacity.

Close upon the heels of Governor Cooke's cry of alarm, came later dispatches which threw doubt on Providence as the enemy's objective, and marching orders were countermanded, the militia being instead instructed to hold "themselves in Constant readiness to march on the shortest notice."

Then followed several days of anxious watching. The manœuvres of the English fleet apparently threatened Massachusetts.[5] "We have never, since the evacuation of Boston, been under apprehensions of an invasion equal to what we suffered last week," wrote Abigail Adams. "All Boston was in confusion, packing up and carting out of town household furniture, military stores, goods, etc. Not less than a thousand teams were employed on Friday and Saturday; and, to their shame be it told, not a small trunk would they carry under eight dollars, and many of them, I am told, asked a hundred dollars a load; for carting a hogshead of molasses eight miles, thirty dollars."[6]

[5] "No doubt an attack on this State is intended."—Massachusetts Council to Governor Trumbull of Connecticut, August 1, 1777, *Massachusetts Archives,* CXCVII, 379.

[6] August 5, 1777, *Familiar Letters of John Adams and his Wife,* 287.

But again the alarm died out and Massachusetts' attention returned to Burgoyne's invasion from the north.

There was much dissatisfaction with the management of the army opposing Burgoyne. Ward shared New England's dislike of General Schuyler—though he did not carry it to the same extent as many of his contemporaries, among whom were many who thought Schuyler traitorous and openly objected to serving with him. The loss of Ticonderoga had intensified such suspicions.

Schuyler accused Massachusetts as one of the states whose slowness in sending reinforcements he declared to be the cause of his retirement before the enemy.

Ward, for the Council, retorted, August 11: "You are pleased to say that your little Army is obliged to retire before the Enemy neglected and unsupported by those whose Duty as well as Interest it is to prevent the Enemy from taking possession of this State. At present we can't see how it is in the power of this State to send a reinforcement In Season sufficient to Stop the Enemy before you reach Albany, Provided you Continue your rapid Retreat & dispute no one Inch of Ground."[7]

In common with other New England leaders, Ward made the mistake of preferring Gates to Schuyler, and he welcomed the order transferring the northern command to Gates. He declared that it gave "general satisfaction."

The letter which records this sentiment, comments on Stark's decisive victory near Bennington (August 16) which destroyed two detachments of Burgoyne's hitherto victorious army—won, so it happened, because Stark had countermanded Schuyler's orders to march from Manchester on August 7, bidding Lincoln tell Schuyler "that he considered himself adequate to the command of his own men."[8]

It speaks also of Ward's third son, "Tommy" (Thomas Walter Ward, later in life to be known to every one in

[7] *Massachusetts Archives,* CXCVIII, 25.

[8] Foster and Streeter, *Stark's Independent Command at Bennington,* 47.

Worcester County as "the sheriff"), at Bennington as a volunteer, and of his second son, Captain Nahum Ward,[9] then at Fort Stanwix.

On September 17 the General Court decided in favor of the "Secret Expedition" by Massachusetts, Connecticut, and Rhode Island contingents against the English at Newport which had been set aside in the spring after Ward's committee report on the project.

The expedition, made in the following month, proved abortive and Ward journeyed again to Providence to sit as president of a court of inquiry composed of committees appointed by the three participating states.

The court's report exonerated General Spencer. It expressed the opinion that there had been a "fair opportunity" to make a descent on Rhode Island on the night of October 16 and that it was "highly probable that the attack would have been crowned with success" but that the opportunity had been lost by General Palmer's failure to embody his brigade and to seasonably distribute the boats needed by both his and the other brigades. As no other equally good occasion afterwards presented itself—because of bad weather, the expiration of enlistment periods, and new dispositions of the enemy's forces—the report justified the abandonment of the enterprise as "judicious and well founded."

The failure of the expedition had comparatively little effect on the public mind of Massachusetts, for, during the entire period of its short campaign, the attention of the state had been centered upon the absorbing development of Burgoyne's campaign.

The Council had toward the end of September distributed a House resolution, dated September 22, calling for militia to hurry to the reinforcement of General Gates. The army under Burgoyne, it said, "have far advanced from Water Carriage and by that means have rendered their retreat more

[9] Captain in Colonel James Wesson's regiment, Continental Army. He died in Boston of smallpox, March 6, 1778 (not March 7, as in family records).

Difficult,"—and if the army under Gates be "speedily and strongly reenforced, there is a great Prospect under the smiles of Divine Providence, of wholly destroying them."

The highest expectations were realized. Before the end of October came the news of Burgoyne's surrender. All New England rejoiced. It seemed a proper confirmation of its preference for Gates![10]

The success was a most substantial one. It meant not only the elimination of a formidable English army and the flattening out, for a time, of the tory conspiracies in western Massachusetts and the New Hampshire Grants—it was also speedily to show an equally important result in France's openly allying herself with America.

The following year (1778) was, nevertheless, one of many difficulties for Ward and the other members of the Council. No fear was felt of any new invasion from the north, but the continued English occupation of Newport and the nearby presence of a powerful enemy fleet compelled the state to be constantly in readiness for an attack either overland or from the sea—or both together. It was necessary to keep a substantial militia force constantly in service, in addition to raising a large body of men for the continental army and furnishing Massachusetts' quota for another attack on Newport—this year a continental undertaking with Major-General Sullivan in chief command.

The people of Rhode Island were increasingly nervous at the continued presence of an English army on their soil, and they were inclined to cast blame in every direction. On August 17 Governor William Greene complained that Massachusetts had not sent all the troops expected as her share of the Newport expedition. This drew from Ward a rather sharp

[10] Typical is a gathering, October 22, 1777, of the people of Springfield, Mass., and several neighboring towns to celebrate "the great and important success of the American Arms under the brave and immortal General Gates, whose name will ever with Gratitude be mentioned by every Tongue inspired with the Love of Virtue, to latest Posterity." A toast was drunk to "the generous British Gates, who bravely step'd forth in the Cause of Virtue and America, and captivated the Northern British Army."—*Continental Journal and Weekly Advertiser,* November 13, 1777.

retort. He declared that it was "with no small degree of surprise" that the Council read the charge that Massachusetts had disappointed General Sullivan. It would have been "more satisfactory" had Greene "made out" his assertion.

"This State," he continued, "has ever been ready, and ever will be, to do everything in its power, Consistent with reason, for the benefit of the United States, or any Sister State, but for any State to Expect that this State must bare the whole burden or at least the greatest part of it, & when they have Exerted Every Nerve to be thus Stigmatized with neglect of Duty is hard, & in our opinion is what doth not become any State to Charge us with.

"The Council previous to the receipt of your letter had given orders for the making up all deficiencies that had arisen by reason of any men having left the Army on account of their time for which they were drafted having Expired."[11]

Prospects seemed very bright for this new Rhode Island campaign. Sullivan's army of Continentals and militiamen was to be strengthened by 4000 French troops, and the French fleet was to bombard the enemy from the sea.

Lafayette and Nathanael Greene had joined Sullivan, and they commanded the two wings of the attacking divisions. The second line was commanded by Hancock, as Massachusetts major-general.

But a heavy gale damaged the French fleet and resulted in its withdrawal to Boston to refit. The French troops went with their fleet. This doomed the expedition. Its final phase was crowned by the "Battle of Rhode Island," in which Continentals, militiamen, and American negroes contended savagely with English regulars and Hessians, but the approach of English reinforcements compelled the abandonment of the effort. The enemy thenceforth remained undisturbed in Newport until their voluntary evacuation in October of the following year.

The coming of the French fleet into Boston Harbor to re-

[11] *Massachusetts Archives,* CXCVIII, 64.

pair the ships damaged by the storm which had driven it from Newport, led the Council to urge upon the Continental Congress the importance of the further fortification of the harbor.

Its letter (December 15), signed by Jeremiah Powell but prepared by Ward, expressed the conviction that it was indispensably necessary "for the Honorable Congress to take some effectual measures to have some Port within the United States Fortified and Secured, in such manner, as to make it a Safe Port, for any squadron this our Allie may see fit to send to our Protection or Assistance, to repair to, in case of Disaster or otherwise." It further declared that "It does not appear to the Council that any Port within these States has as yet been sufficiently fortifyed or Secured to answer the purpose beforementioned. And The Council are humbly of Opinion that there is not upon the Continent any Port Preferable by nature or Equal to the Port of Boston to answer this End. But this was by the Count D'Estaing found unsafe without throwing up Temporary works on the Main and on several Islands, and taking Cannon from his Ships & Planting them within those works, Which cannon he Carried off with him when he took his departure from hence as he had a Right so to do. If our Allies when they come to the Assistance of these States, have to fortify our Harbours to Secure themselves, will it not be discouraging to them, and Highly derogatory to the United American States?"[12]

It was on April 10 of this year that the "South Parish of Worcester" (a precinct formed five years earlier of land set off from Worcester, Sutton, Leicester, and Oxford) was incorporated as a separate township to be known as "Ward"—this name having been bestowed upon it by its inhabitants out of their affectionate admiration for General Ward.[13]

[12] *Massachusetts Archives,* CC, 260.

[13] As "Ward" the town flourished for more than half a century, but unfortunately the town of "Ware" had preceded it both in establishment and incorporation. The consequent confusion in addresses caused much trouble, and the title of "Auburn" was substituted for "Ward" on February 17, 1837.

On April 29 and 30 of the following year (1779) Ward acted as chairman of the General Court conferences on two bills—passed on the days following—for the confiscation of the estates of absentees.

A few weeks later, about June 20, word came from the north that an English squadron from Halifax had seized the Majorbagaduce peninsula (now "Castine"), Maine, which commands the mouth of the Penobscot River and dominates Penobscot Bay. The move aroused instant apprehension. It was not only a direct assault upon Massachusetts territory (for Maine was then politically a part of Massachusetts); it also greatly increased the potential menace of the English fleet. With Penobscot to the north and Newport to the south both occupied by the English, Boston and the entire coast line of Massachusetts proper lay within two enemy naval bases less than three hundred miles apart.

Massachusetts determined on immediate action in the hope of dislodging the enemy before he could strengthen his possession. So rapidly were plans conceived and carried out that, only twenty-odd days after the first reports of the English landing, a fleet of nineteen armed vessels and twenty-four transports had been organized, equipped, and provisioned, and was ready to sail. It was the largest American fleet that had ever been assembled.

Less satisfactory proved the size of the landing force, for the militia detachment totaled less than two-thirds of the 1500 men called for by the General Court order.

The fleet was under the command of Richard Saltonstall; the land force under Brigadier-General Solomon Lovell. Second under Lovell was Peleg Wadsworth, one of Ward's aides at the siege of Boston. Paul Revere (lieutenant-colonel since November, 1776) had charge of the artillery.

The expedition came, however, to a sorry fate.

It reached Penobscot on Sunday, July 25, and its first days were illuminated by a brilliant episode: the scaling of the steep southerly side of the peninsula in the face of withering musketry fire. The party lost a fourth of its men but won its objective and threw up a breastwork within point-blank shot of the enemy's main fortification.

An excellent start—and the American fleet looked menacingly formidable to the Englishmen entrusted with the defense of the position. But possible success was thrown away by lack of concerted initiative, by want of decision, and by continuous disagreements between the fleet and land commanders. A fortnight of varied dissensions and minor activities—then the end came quickly. On August 13 a reinforcing English squadron was sighted, turning the odds heavily against the Americans, and an immediate retreat was ordered.

The story of the siege and its disastrous termination has often been told—to recount it here would serve no purpose. The result was the loss of the entire American fleet (save only one vessel, the *Pallas,* which had previously been dispatched on a special detail) and the ignominious dispersal of the American force.

The utter collapse of the expedition raised a storm throughout the state, and the General Court on September 9 appointed a committee of investigation.

Ward served as president of the committee.

Its report (October 7) declared that "want of proper spirit and energy" on the part of Commodore Saltonstall was "the principal reason of the failure." It praised and exonerated General Lovell.

The report was accepted by the General Court[14] and by it forwarded to the Continental Congress.

Later sessions of the committee also found Lieutenant-Colonel Revere censurable for insubordination.[15]

The failure of the project was a grievous disappointment to General Ward. On September 8 he wrote to Joseph Ward:

"Was in hopes when I wrote you last, should have been

[14] *Massachusetts General Court Records,* October 8, 1779, XL, 65–67.

[15] *Massachusetts Archives,* CXLV, 375.

able the next time I wrote, to do it in the congratulatory stile, on account of our expedition to Penobscot. But alass, I am totally deprived of that pleasure and am under the disagreeable necessity of acquainting you that the siege was raised, and the whole fleet destroyed or taken, excepting the *Pallas*.

" . . . I have been told that it has been said by some one in the army, that we wanted advice in planning the expedition, and insinuating thereby that that was the reason why the enterprise failed. They had better spare their reflections, and re-examine their own conduct in all its parts. I think it was well done."[16]

Ward felt strongly the danger in leaving Penobscot in the possession of the enemy, but it was not possible to make a second attempt to recover it. English successes in the south followed so quickly that the general needs of the colonies forbade the diversion northward of any considerable part of the Massachusetts forces.

The following November (the eighteenth), the General Court elected Ward a delegate to the Continental Congress for the year 1780. Hancock, Samuel Adams, and Elbridge Gerry were among the others who completed the delegation of seven.

As the state's representatives they were "fully impowered, with the Delegates . . . from the other American States, to concert, direct and order such further measures as shall appear to them best calculated for the establishment of the Rights, Liberty and Independence of the United States of America upon a basis permanent and secure against the power and art of the British Nation; for prosecuting the present War, concluding peace, contracting alliances, establishing commerce, and guarding against any future encroachments and machinations of their enemies."

The General Court did not expect the continuous attendance in Philadelphia of all of its seven delegates. It sug-

[16] Printed in *Scribner's Monthly,* XI, 716. The original letter is (1921) in the possession of Joseph F. Ward, Evanston, Ill.

gested their serving "in rotation," though enjoining that "four at least . . . attend constantly upon the business of their delegation." Three instead of four was, however, the general Massachusetts representation during the years 1780 and 1781.

The prestige of members of the Continental Congress was so high and their opinions carried such weight that in Massachusetts politics they constituted a kind of upper chamber.

On May 16, 1780, Ward left Boston for Shrewsbury in order both to prepare for his journey to Philadelphia to attend the Congress, and to take part in his township's consideration of the proposed new state constitution drawn up and submitted by the Constitutional Convention.[17]

[17] Shrewsbury held four meetings to discuss the proposed constitution: May 1, May 25, May 29, and June 1.

At the first meeting the "form of Government was read and conversed upon," but no formal action was taken. The other three meetings discussed and voted upon both the "Bill of Rights" and the "Frame of Government," article by article, and suggested numerous changes.

At the second meeting, twenty-eight of the thirty articles of the Bill of Rights were approved by a nearly unanimous vote (92 of a possible 96). The exceptions were Articles III and XXIX. Article III established the principle of compulsory support of a religious establishment; Article XXIX made the terms of the judges of the Supreme Judicial Court for "as long as they behave themselves well." Neither of these received in Shrewsbury the two-thirds vote required to express approval.

At the third meeting, a proposed amendment to Article III, which received 44 votes in favor and only 15 against, left the legislature power to *authorize* towns and parishes "to make suitable provision . . . for the institution of the public worship of God," but struck out its authority to *require* them to do so. It also eliminated the paragraph authorizing the legislature to "enjoin" attendance upon church services, and declared that no one should be held by the action of local authorities or bodies for the support of "any sect or persuasion" if he "congregate elsewhere." (A number of other towns made similar objections to Article III, but it nevertheless became a part of the constitution. It stood for a little more than half a century, and was then annulled by the Tenth Article of Amendment.)

The fourth meeting voted 39 to 11 in favor of amending Article XXIX so that judges should be chosen for a term of five years only. It was feared that otherwise they might become too independent of the people and that the door might be opened to favoritism.

The Frame of Government was much less generally acceptable. Few of its provisions attained a two-thirds support and several of them failed to receive even a majority. Among the latter was Article II of Chapter I, Section I, which gave the governor veto power over the legislature.

A number of suggested amendments to the Frame of Government were introduced and some of them were highly approved. That applying to *Article IX, Section I, Chapter II,* gave the appointment of all judicial officers to the legislature, instead of to the governor and Council; to *Article X, Section I, Chapter II,* gave to the legislature the duty of nominating continental officers, instead of entrusting their appointment entirely to the governor and Council; to *Article XIII, Section I, Chapter II,* provided for annual

He set out from Shrewsbury on June 2, accompanied by Daniel Newton[18] as his personal attendant—both on horseback.

Eleven days were consumed on the road, but this included a stay of one and a half days in Suffield, Conn., half a day at Goshen, N. Y., and a half day in Bethlehem, N. J. They rode into Connecticut south of Springfield (Mass.), entered New York westerly of New Fairfield (Conn.), crossed the Hudson from Fishkill Creek to New Windsor, entered New Jersey westerly of the Wawayanda Mountains, and came into Pennsylvania during the forenoon of June 12, ferrying over the Delaware River at a point near the bridge now uniting Stockton, N. J., and Center Bridge, Pa. The following morning they arrived in Philadelphia.[19]

The next day (June 14) Ward took his place in the Congress sitting in Independence Hall.

It was not a large gathering which greeted him as a new member arrived to help it struggle with a multitude of problems. There were only twenty-seven delegates present

grants to the governor and higher justices instead of permanent salaries established by law; to *Article I, Chapter III,* required, instead of permitting, the governor and Council to remove judicial officers upon the address of both houses of the legislature; to the third paragraph of *Article II, Chapter VI,* added "settled ministers" and seamen to those excluded from holding a seat in either the Senate or the House of Representatives, and prohibited any individual from holding more than one civil or military commission at the same time; to *Article X, Chapter VI,* required the calling within five years (instead of in 1795) of a convention to consider the revision of the constitution.

The original report of the Shrewsbury discussion and vote is in the *Massachusetts Archives,* CCLXXVII, 108.

In *Massachusetts Historical Society Proceedings,* L, 353, is an interesting paper by S. E. Morison on "the Struggle over the Adoption of the Constitution of Massachusetts." Professor Morison raises the question whether the constitution was ever legally ratified, remarking that "the Convention's method of tabulating the popular vote raises the suspicion that the [necessary] two-thirds majority was manufactured."

[18] Daniel Newton "kept a diary [whereabouts now unknown] in which he recorded the texts of all the sermons he heard, some delivered by the most eminent preachers of that day: related the substance of conversations he had on the subject of religion with Major-General Ward, whose servant he was, and with Samuel Adams, then a member of Congress."—*1901–1902 Report of the Daughters of the American Revolution,* 297.

[19] Ward took rooms in the house of "Mary Dalley." He was shortly joined there by Samuel Adams, who reached the capital before the end of the month.

On October 13 they moved to the house of "Mrs. Miller," both of them remaining with her until their departure from Philadelphia in the following spring. "She is a well bred woman," wrote Samuel Adams to his wife, November 24, 1780, "and my situation is agreeable."—Cushing, *Writings of Samuel Adams,* IV, 227.

(including Ward), and during the entire twelve months thus commenced, the number never exceeded thirty-one—the attendance being indeed generally under twenty-five.

It was a precarious period and was destined to grow worse during the year. August was to see Gates routed at Camden. In September came Benedict Arnold's treason.

The energies of Congress were especially directed to efforts to obtain European recognition of the United States, to keep the army supplied, and to breathe health into the terribly demoralized public finances. Continental paper money had become almost worthless.

The reciprocal esteem of Ward and Samuel Adams continued as complete during their service in the continental legislature as it had been in the earlier and equally critical period which had preceded Lexington. There were three Massachusetts delegates present during Ward's attendance: Ward himself, Adams, and Lovell. In voting, Lovell sometimes divided against Ward, or Adams, or both; but Ward and Adams always voted alike—it was always "no" or "ay" from both.

Ward's first committee appointment was, June 19, on a plan for conducting the quartermaster's department. Four other members were named with him, one of them being General Philip Schuyler—the same Schuyler with whom he had exchanged sharp repartee during the Burgoyne campaign.

Four days later he was added to the Board of War.

He figured also, concurrently, on a succession of committees.

Among the earliest was one (June 27) to consider the report of the Treasury Board which declared that the Treasury was "totally exhausted" and that the Board "knew not which way to turn themselves to afford any relief to the daily pressing demands made on them from many quarters."

The committee's report, delivered June 29, resulted in expresses being dispatched with treasury warrants drawn on the treasurers of New Hampshire, Massachusetts, Rhode

Island, Connecticut, New York, New Jersey, Pennsylvania, Delaware, and Maryland, to the total of their unpaid assessments. With the warrants went letters to the state executives telling of the "urgent necessity" for funds to maintain and supply the army—if they were not furnished, it would "be impossible for the operations to proceed."

In a division, August 2, Ward voted "ay" for the removal of earlier resolutions which restricted Washington to operations within the United States.

On September 22 Massachusetts reëlected Ward to the Continental Congress for 1781—the General Court giving him the highest vote accorded to any delegate, only one other member equaling it. Among those named with him were again Samuel Adams and Gerry—but both of them with lower votes.

Ward during this fall was again severely attacked by his persistent malady. On December 19 Lovell wrote to Dr. Samuel Holten (another Massachusetts delegate, then in Boston): "Genl Ward is quite unwell, he has attended Congress & the Bd of War while he ought to have been in his Bed Room."[20]

Meantime, in Massachusetts had been held the first elections of executives under the new state constitution.

Ward's choice for governor (as also that of many other Massachusetts leaders) had been James Bowdoin, but Hancock's general popularity carried the day.

Ward's opinion of Hancock had suffered seriously from the latter's long and continuing delay in accounting for the funds of Harvard College, entrusted to him as treasurer from July, 1773, to July, 1777.[21]

[20] *Essex Institute Historical Collections,* XIII, 222.

[21] On October 20, 1778, after years of patient requests, waiting, and postponements, the Overseers of Harvard College had named Ward (an Overseer by virtue of his membership in the Council) on a new special committee to try to bring Hancock to a reckoning. Hancock again promised to submit his accounts, but again broke his word, and on December 9 Ward wrote to him saying that, in view of his promises, his failure was inexplicable. "I am," he continued, "constrained in behalf of the Committee to beg and beseech you as you regard your own Honor, and the interest of the College to cause

He also felt that Hancock devoted too much time to social functions and too little to affairs of state. On March 13, 1781, he wrote to Samuel Osgood:[22] "Measures ought to be taken by the States to inform Congress of everything they have done in consequence of their requisitions for men & money. Since Novr last the Governor gives no more information than if he was at the East Indies, notwithstanding it is his duty. If he don't know his duty I wish his Council would advise him; if they don't know it to be his duty, do let some body be appointed to teach them."[23]

The year 1781 has high historic importance, for it was marked by earnest efforts to achieve the stronger central authority which was increasingly recognized as the country's greatest need. Thus we find the endeavor to obtain for Congress the right to levy import duties to meet the pressing necessity for a more certain national revenue; the unfolding of plans for executive departments and a federal judiciary; and the establishment of a national bank.

The first day of March witnessed the final signatures to the Articles of Confederation. The United States had thus a fully authorized written constitution, but it was a document lacking the enforcement provisions essential to a competent national government, and on March 6 a committee was appointed "to prepare a plan to invest the United States in Congress assembled with full and explicit powers for effectually carrying into execution in the several states all acts or

your accounts aforesaid to be prepared for examination . . . without any further delay." But Hancock continued to delay and on May 20, 1779, Ward and the other two members of the committee asked "to be excused from any further concern" in the matter when the other overseers demonstrated that they lacked the courage to put Hancock's bond in suit to protect the college and enforce the payment of the much needed money due it (*MS. Records of Overseers,* III, 159). Hancock reached a "settlement" of his accounts in February, 1785, but the first payment on the balance due the college was not made until 1795—two years after his death (Quincy, *History of Harvard University,* II, 182–209).

[22] One of Ward's aides-de-camp during the siege of Boston (Chapter V, page 90)—at the date of this letter, a newly elected delegate to the Continental Congress; later, Commissioner of the Treasury and Postmaster-General.

[23] MS. draft in possession (1921) of Ward Dix Kerlin, Camden, N. J.

resolutions passed agreeably to the Articles of Confederation."

The committee recommended application to the states for an article granting Congress authority "to employ the force of the United States, as well by sea as by land," to compel any neglectful or refractory "State or States to fulfill their federal engagements."

The report was on May 2 referred to a "Grand Committee" of thirteen members—one from each state. Ward represented Massachusetts. The committee proved ineffective because of the departure soon after of Ward and several other members, and its business was later turned over to a new committee.

The completed Confederacy seemed headed for swift bankruptcy, but French money saved the day. On May 28 Congress heard the welcome news that King Louis had "resolved to grant the United States a subsidy of six million livres tournois and to enable Dr. [Benjamin] Franklin to borrow four million more." So the ship of state steadied itself and continued its long and difficult voyage over the uncharted political seas.

Despite the heavy laboring and threatening storms, the port of success was steadily nearing. England was weary of the protracted expensive struggle, which had embroiled her with all of continental Europe. Spain and Holland had followed France into the war with her, and Russia's League of Armed Neutrality supported the hands of all her enemies. English statesmen and English merchants alike longed for the termination of the conflict, and thus it came about that Ward's last votes were cast on June 14 for the election of Benjamin Franklin, Thomas Jefferson, and Henry Laurens (John Jay had been elected on June 13) to "be joined to the honorable John Adams in negotiating a treaty of peace with Great Britain."

On the preceding day Ward had received leave of absence and he set out on his homeward trip on the following Monday (June 18). He had been a full year in Philadelphia and he could leave with a clear conscience, for two other Massachusetts delegates had reached the capital to take his place and that of Samuel Adams (who had returned to Boston a few weeks earlier).

On June 22, while he was on his way back, Massachusetts reëlected him to Congress for the year 1782—the General Court giving him 104 out of 131 votes—but his "state of health" and the circumstances of his family[24] caused him to decline this third term.

Samuel Adams and Gerry were also reëlected, but both again by considerably fewer votes.

The General Court was now, under the new constitution, composed of representatives and senators, instead of representatives and councilors. The Council's duties had become exclusively executive, being confined to advising and assisting the governor. Its old share in lawmaking had passed to the Senate.

Ward spent the months of July and August in Shrewsbury, giving needed attention to his private affairs but devoting most of the time to rest and recuperation.

On September 4 he presided in the Worcester County Court of Common Pleas for the first time under the new constitution.[25] The *Massachusetts Spy* of September 6 notes that "He gave a charge to the jury, which it is hoped, will have a tendency to reform the morals of the people."

Adjuration was needed, for western Massachusetts was beginning to ferment with the unrest that culminated in Shays' Rebellion. The strain of the long war was telling on the poorer western counties, who plentifully supplied men for its armies but profited little by its commercial inflation.

In this month there occurred also an interesting tribute to the regard in which Ward was held by the Massachusetts

[24] Ward, December 20, 1781, to Samuel Adams.—Original letter, *Massachusetts Archives,* CCIV, 9.

[25] He had been confirmed as justice of the Court of Common Pleas of Worcester County on March 1 (1781).

House of Representatives—the House passing, September 20, a special vote that, though not a member, "a chair be assigned for the Hon. Genl. Ward to set in, to hear the Debates of the House when he sees fit."

The next month brought the glad news of the surrender of Cornwallis and his army to American-French forces under Washington's personal direction.

From a military standpoint the war had ended, with the new republic victorious, but two more years were to drag before the goal was fully won.

On May 29 (1782) Ward was again in Boston as a member of the Massachusetts House.

On the following day the General Court elected him Senator by a vote of 115 out of 126, but he declined to serve, preferring to retain instead his old-time familiar place in the House.

June 25, he received from Governor Hancock a commission as "Judge of Probate of Wills, etc., in the County of Worcester," but he refused this also, "as I am honored with a seat in the House of Representatives, & know it to be the wish of my Constituents to have me continue there through the year; and as holding both is incompatible by the Constitution."[26]

His return to the House was very popular among the Representatives. There were few days of the legislative year which did not place him on some committee.

Prominent among the appointments was that of June 4, on the committee of finance "To consider all money matters that concern this Commonwealth" and whatever "reform and alteration" seemed necessary in the conduct of the state treasury.

Another, October 22, was on the condition of the inhabitants of Nantucket Island; the fishermen there being much distraught by war's interference with their livelihood—and,

[26] June 26, 1782, to Hancock.—Original letter, *Massachusetts Archives*, CCVI, 161.

by their countrymen elsewhere, being not a little suspected of aiding the enemy.[27] The committee reported (October 29) that the people of Nantucket Island were justified in their complaints and that they were entitled to relief, but it advised referring their memorial to the Continental Congress, "as no adequate relief can be given them but by the United States." Both House and Senate concurred, and a copy of the memorial was sent to the Massachusetts delegates in the Continental Congress with the admonition that they "use their utmost endeavors to impress the minds of Congress with just ideas of the high Worth and Importance of the *Fisheries* to the United States in general and this State in particular."

A third committee appointment was, November 12, to repair to Berkshire County and "fix the places for holding the courts."

Yet others were: February 18, 1783, by the joint vote of the House and Senate, as one of three commissioners "to meet such as might be appointed on the part of [the] several states to treat upon the subject matter of Impost and Excise"; and, February 8, 1783, to bring in a bill relative to "Negros and Molattos," to be based on the principle that there never had been *legal* slaves in Massachusetts, and to provide both for indemnifying masters who had held slaves *in fact* and for any assistance to negroes and mulattos that the commissioners might find expedient.

The trouble in the western counties had by the early summer of 1782 grown to serious proportions. In April a Hampshire County mob led by Samuel Ely, an irregular preacher, had disturbed the sitting of the courts in Northampton. Ely was arrested, and imprisoned in Springfield, but his

[27] *New England Historical and Genealogical Register,* XXIX, 141–145. At an earlier date (the winter of 1779–1780) Ward had served as chairman of a committee to investigate charges of treason brought against several of Nantucket's prominent inhabitants. The charges came to nothing, the complainant retracting his accusations.—*Massachusetts Archives,* CXXXVII, 279–292. See also "Nantucket in the Revolution," *New England Historical and Genealogical Register,* XXIX, 48–53, 141–145; and, in the same periodical, "An Autobiographical Memoir of William Rotch," XXXI, 262, XXXII, 36–42, 151–155.

adherents broke into the jail and released him. The authorities retaliated by arresting three of the ringleaders among the rescuers, and committed them to jail in Northampton. A wave of excited protest swept the county, and a body of three hundred men so thoroughly overawed General Porter, despite the twelve hundred militiamen called out, that on a thirty-minute ultimatum he freed the prisoners on their personal paroles.

The farmers and mechanics of the western counties, especially the poorer class, were ripe for the arguments of malcontents and agitators.

The absence of so many men in the continental armies—and from time to time in the militia—had wrought its mark upon the farms and homes they left: crops not planted, or ill-cared for, cattle too often neglected, fences and buildings out of repair. All of these things, many times multiplied, changed plain living to poverty; and poverty in hundreds of instances reached to the borders of destitution. The fluctuation and depreciation of the continental currency—and, finally, its extinction—had also brought losses and hardships to many individuals. And the second year under the new constitution had seen the commencement of a great rush to the courts by creditors with claims held in abeyance by the unsettled conditions of the earlier years of the war.

These conditions lent special weight to the bitter complaints against the taxes levied. It was held that the legislature was wasteful of the public moneys; and it was charged that on the poorer counties was laid an unjust share of the expenses of the war, the while merchants and others well-to-do were fattening on it.

The agitation and discontent had passed beyond the hope of relief by either state or continental action. In Hampshire County, where it rose the highest, many planned a return to allegiance to Great Britain in the belief that they could thus lighten their burdens.

"We have had it huzza'd for George the third within 8

rods of our Court House," wrote Joseph Hawley, June 24, from Northampton. "You would be astonished," he declared, "to know with what amazing rapdity the spirit of the Insurgts propagates. Many are infected with it, of whom you never would have the least suspicion. We are not certain who, besides the Devil, sprang Ely at first. But we are not at loss who ventilates the flame, for the fire is now become such a flame as I cannot describe to you. The General Court have not had any affair of greater magnitude before them since the Revolution."[28]

A most critical condition was threatened. On March 4 the English House of Commons had extinguished even the most stubborn British hope of continuing the conflict, by its declaration that it would consider as enemies to His Majesty and the country, all those who should advise, or attempt, the further prosecution of offensive war on the Continent of North America; but domestic discord in the United States would assuredly lessen American prestige and might thus very unfavorably affect the terms of the agreement establishing peace.

So delicate a situation demanded both prompt and careful handling, and the General Court on July 3 appointed a joint committee to visit Hampshire County "to enquire into the grounds of dissatisfaction, to correct misinformations, to remove groundless jealousies." On this committee Ward and Nathaniel Gorham represented the House, and Samuel Adams represented the Senate.

On the same day the legislature checked the enforcement of execution sales for unsatisfied judgments by passing a "Tender Act" which made cattle and other specified articles legal tender at prices to be determined by impartial arbitrators. This served as an effective temporary safeguard for debtors, but its operation covered only twelve months and acceptance of "tender" was not compulsory on creditors who

[28] Joseph Hawley to Caleb Strong.—Original letter, *Hawley Papers,* New York Public Library. Printed in part in Trumbull's *History of Northampton, Mass.,* II, 465–466.

had previously commenced proceedings. If they refused it, they could not add new costs or interest to the amounts due them, but they could—and a great many did—hold their judgments over awaiting the expiration of the act. And a great many other creditors, who had not commenced proceedings before its passage, also held back their claims awaiting its expiration.

The General Court committee reached Northampton on July 27 and thence proceeded to Conway, Ely's home town, their intent being "to visit all those Towns where Discontent had in any great Degree prevail'd."

At Conway it was found that though the inhabitants, as individuals, "convers'd freely and publicly with the Committee upon Matters supposed by them to be just Grounds of Uneasiness," they were averse to going on record with a separate town memorial. A special meeting, July 29, called at the request of the committee, voted "that the Town had no Grievances destinct from the County." They preferred the greater strength of a united county protest.

The same sentiment was voiced by delegates attending from thirteen other towns, so it was decided to call a county convention, to be held at Hatfield commencing August 7.

Delegates from forty-five towns came together at Hatfield, and the convention proceedings quickly assumed the form of an interrogatory debate. The initiative was taken by the leaders of the insurgent element and they poured out their complaints against the government.

Replying to them, the members of the committee explained the reasons for the various acts and resolves passed by the legislature.

The story of the three principal days is succinctly told in a contemporary diary:[29]

"Thursday 8. The Mobb began to tell their Grievances and the [Committee] to answer and to give Information.

[29] Jonathan Judd's.—Trumbull, *History of Northampton, Mass.*, II, 468.

The Day was spent in this way. The Mobbists began to feel themselves more a ground than they expected. The Tories who are spectators in very great plenty do not hold their Heads so High as they have done of late:

"Fryday 9. Began where we left off. Afterwards chose a committee to state Grievances to us. Then the Mobb still continued to tell their Grievances but got upon the Shoals long before Night. Committee report near Night.

"Saturday 10. Began in the Morning upon the Report of the Com[ttee] which consisted of 8 Articles. 3 we passed and the rest we through out. Friends of the Mobb could not get things to their Mind. They [are] Disappointed and Chagrined. What they may produce is uncertain, but 'tis certain that they cannot answer the arguments of the Com[ttee], or gainsay the facts they asserted. The appearance is that there is more probability of their being still, if nothing more. Convention broke up about 6."

In the resolutions with which the convention concluded its sessions, the delegates held to their belief that the county was "burdened with more than its just proportion of taxes" and "that the grants of money by the General Court to particular persons and officers" were too large, and they expressed the opinion that "the common people" were "kept in unnecessary and unhappy ignorance of the state of the public debt and the appropriations of the public money"; but they promised support of the government "to the utmost of their power," and disclaimed the design to renounce the "Great American cause" and to "return into a state of subjection to Great Britain." They declared that the disturbances in the county had "in a great measure arisen from misrepresentations and mistakes."

They also resolved to return "sincere thanks to the honorable Gentlemen of the Committee . . . for the satisfactory information they have given this Convention concerning the state of public affairs; and for the patient, friendly, & generous Attention with which they have heard our various representations."

The result of the committee's visit was very gratifying to the legislature, and on October 2 it passed a formal resolution "highly approving" the proceedings of the committee and "their indefatigable and successful endeavours in so great a degree quieting the disturbances that had arisen."

The committee had indeed so efficiently discharged its mission that Massachusetts reassumed a united front of patriotic determination to reap the full profits of independence.

Thus again had Artemas Ward well served his country by employing in its behalf the influence he drew from his intimate knowledge of the life and thought and sentiments of the rural communities of his state. Samuel Adams' name added luster and high ability to the committee—one readily pictures the force of his addresses and arguments—but in the rural townships (as several House elections had proved) Ward's quiet imperturbability held the greater strength.

Meantime, through all that summer, and on through the autumn, continued the negotiations toward a preliminary treaty of peace. Many obstacles delayed agreement. Two of them vitally concerned the people of Massachusetts: the northeastern boundary line and the northern fisheries. England claimed a substantial part of the present state of Maine, and both England and France planned to withhold from the new nation its old fruitful participation in the fisheries.

During the winter, reports were circulated that England planned to emphasize her claim on the Maine territory by extending her lines westerly from Penobscot to the east bank of the Kennebec.[30] Public apprehension made itself strongly

[30] "The situation of the Eastern part of this Commonwealth is very Alarming. The late Movements of the Enemy plainly indicate that they Intend to Possess themselves of all that Country that lies between Kenebeck & Nova Scotia, a Country Contiguous to a British Province and from which Brittain may be supplied with Masts, Their West India Islands with Lumber, & the European States with fish."—Lieutenant-Governor Thomas Cushing to Samuel Holten, delegate to the federal congress, February 9, 1783 (Original letter, *Danforth Collection,* Henkels sale, Philadelphia, December 11, 1913).

felt, and the General Court on February 8, 1783,[31] wrote to Washington asking him to send northward a force sufficient to drive the English from Penobscot—"or at least such a number as will confine them to their present possessions," reminding him that for years Massachusetts had been "constantly throwing in forces and supplies" to the assistance of her brethren in the south, even when the "enemy ravaged within our own borders," and that at the present time, when "there is no particular object that seems to engage the attention of the army," it seemed only just that the other states should reciprocate.

The delivery of this request for assistance was entrusted to Major-General Benjamin Lincoln—he who had acted as general officer of the Massachusetts state troops during Ward's continental command in Boston—and Stephen Higginson, one of the Massachusetts delegates to the federal congress.

Washington could not comply with the request, whether or not he wished to, as Congress was considering an attempt to reduce New York if peace negotiations should fail,[32] and such an undertaking would require every available man in the American army; but Lincoln, from headquarters at Newburgh, sent a reassuring letter to Ward, saying "There cannot in my opinion be any doubt but that we shall receive all the succour we wish for unless the reduction of New York should be undertaken."[33]

Washington's own reply to the General Court was not so pleasingly worded. His conclusions, and the reasons for them, were respectfully accepted, but an apparently disparaging reference to the suggested campaign against Penobscot aroused some ill feeling, despite his complimentary reference

[31] *Massachusetts General Court Records,* XLIV, 304–305.

[32] The Provisional Articles of Peace had been signed by England and the United States on November 30, 1782, and toward the end of February, 1783, the newspapers published a report to that effect, but official advice of the signing did not reach the United States until March 12, 1783.

[33] February 18, 1783.—Original letter, *Artemas Ward MSS.*

to Massachusetts as a state "whose exertions have been so great and meritorious."[34] Ward, writing to Lincoln, remarked that Washington "gives credit to the Exertions of the States and informs he shall readily (when in his power) consent to any *Judicious Plan* for the removal of the Invaders of this State; Which I take to be a slap, for which I shall not be in a hurry to thank him. If peace takes place, we shall not I trust want his aid for that purpose."[35]

Massachusetts' impatience was heightened by the laxity of several of the other states; by their avoidance of their share of the support of the continental army.

"How is it," demanded Thomas Cushing of Samuel Holten, "that while we are exerting every nerve for furnishing our Quota of Men and Money, Virginia as well as some of the other States do little or nothing?[36] Will this be born with long! Will not our People be out of Patience? and will not such a Conduct, if long persisted in, tend to shake the Union?"[37]

It was indeed good news that reached Boston the following month of the arrival in Philadelphia, March 12, of authentic advice that Provisional Articles of Peace had been signed by the English and United States representatives, and that the firmness and ability of the American commissioners had inserted in them England's recognition of the United States' right to the Maine territory in dispute,[38] and also an agreement "that the people of the United States shall continue to enjoy unmolested the right to take fish of every kind on the Grand Bank and on all the other banks of Newfoundland;

[34] February 22, 1783.—Original letter, *Massachusetts Archives,* CCIV, 322–324.

[35] Original letter, April 23, 1783, *Fogg Collection,* Maine Historical Society.

[36] The same quotas had been assigned to Massachusetts and Virginia for 1783, but Virginia furnished only 629 men for the continental line, against 4370 from Massachusetts.—*American State Papers, Military Affairs,* I, 14.

[37] February 9, 1783—the same letter quoted on page 267, note 30.

[38] Later, there came controversies over the identification of the Saint Croix River agreed upon as the southerly part of the eastern border, and, in succeeding years, much wrangling over the intent to be drawn from words and phrases defining the northeastern boundary. But such troubles were of the future—they did not dim the satisfaction felt in Massachusetts that the line of British dominion was set well to the east of the Penobscot.

also in the Gulf of St. Lawrence, and at all other places in the sea where the inhabitants of both countries used at any time heretofore to fish. And . . . on such part of the coast of Newfoundland as British fishermen shall use . . . and also on the coasts, bays, and creeks of all other of his Britannic Majesty's dominions in America."

The Provisional Articles could not be transferred to a definitive treaty until the completion of a peace agreement by Great Britain and France, but they tended greatly to clear the political atmosphere and relieve the tension under which the country had been laboring. And they were soon followed by word that Great Britain and France (and Spain) had also signed preliminary articles.

It was with a well satisfied heart that Ward read the proclamation of Congress, April 12, announcing the cessation of hostilities.

Ward was not a candidate for the Massachusetts House of 1783–1784, but he was a much interested observer of the Hancock-Bowdoin contest for the governorship. "It is astonishing," he wrote to Lincoln, "to see the Arts that are made use of to keep the little man [Hancock] in the chair. . . . Low art and cunning never was more prevalent since my remembrance than at this day. He that espouseth the little one's cause is represented as a friend to America: but he that is in favor of Mr. Bowdoin is at once dub'd an Enemy and not to be trusted. . . . In some [towns] he has made but a very indifferent figure, howsoever I expect nothing but he will be chosen and the State suffer the Calamity one year more at least."[39]

The "calamity" happened as Ward expected, but he probably did not let it trouble him very long, for in the fall came official advice of the definitive treaty with England.[40]

It was during the autumn of 1782 and the early part of

[39] Original letter, April 23, 1783, *Fogg Collection,* Maine Historical Society.

[40] Signed September 3, 1783; received in the United States in November, 1783; ratified by Congress January 14, 1784; ratified by George IV April 9; ratifications exchanged May 12.

the year of definite peace, that Ward was frequently associated with Timothy Dwight, the famous divine, revolutionary chaplain, writer, and educator—then Representative from Northampton—who recorded his opinion of Shrewsbury's representative in the following terms:[41]

"I knew General Ward well: and having been often with him on Committees, charged with interesting business, necessarily developing the views, and principles of the several members, had a very fair opportunity to learn his character. He was possessed of an excellent understanding, directed chiefly to the practical interests of mankind; was of few words, and those always pointing to the purpose in hand; was frank, undisguised, of inflexible integrity, an unwarping public spirit, and a fixed adherence to what he thought right: a subject which he rarely mistook. His reverence for the Christian religion was entire; and his life adorned its precepts. I have known no person, to whom might be applied the 'Justum et tenacem propositi virum' of Horace with more propriety, or whose firm mind would be less shaken by the 'Civium ardor, prava jubentium,' or the 'Vultus instantis Tyranni.' "[42]

[41] Dwight, *Travels in New England and New York,* I, 370.

[42] The quotations—the "man just and steadfast in his purpose" . . . "the excited citizens demanding evil" . . . the "frowning face of the tyrant"—are from the opening lines of the famous Third Ode of Book III.

CHAPTER XIV

1784–1787: Age 56–59

The financial distress and discontent in Massachusetts. "Shays' Rebellion." The fear that England was fomenting the disturbances. General Ward harangues the rebels from the steps of the Worcester County court-house.

THE United States had won a place among the self-governing nations of the earth, but greater than ever was its need of the highest wisdom and the strongest leadership that it could muster.

The inevitable difficulties of reconstruction were multiplied by the lack both of an effective national government and of a national currency.

The Confederacy, dangerously weak even under war's driving necessity for unity of purpose, became after the conclusion of peace completely powerless to hold the states in harmony; and equally impotent to cope with the commercial and financial problems, international and domestic, which beset them. There was everywhere a great deal of dangerous unrest.

A stronger union was needed, a stronger central government—and a general accord of state governments—to foster commerce and to set running again the wheels of normal peacetime life and occupations. But jealousy, pride, and lethargy stayed men's hands. So, also, did over-rigid adherence to political tenets, and morbid fear of what might evolve from opening the door to a change in the form of national government.

In Massachusetts, the seven years' contest had spelled increased prosperity for a considerable number of individuals: for some merchants; for many inhabitants of the coast communities which profited from privateering; for speculators with cheaply purchased soldiers' certificates or other claims; for army contractors. But for a much greater number—and they included particularly the small farmers, artisans, and laborers of the inland counties—it had in general meant the laying of heavy additional burdens on their always meager resources.

Peace and independence had come, but important sources of Massachusetts' pre-war prosperity were held closed by English orders which barred American ships from the British West Indies and forbade the importation into them of American-caught fish, placed an excessive duty on whale oil, and in other ways obstructed efforts to revive American commerce. France and Spain also, though to minor effect, raised impeding barriers.

This crippling of the fishing, shipping, and ship-building industries imposed a serious handicap on Massachusetts. It delayed the return of the privateersmen to their peacetime callings and affected the value of every farmer's crop—in many cases, added to the other troubles of the times, resulting in its lying unused and unmarketable in his barn.

Most successful had been the national outcome of the contest with Great Britain, but its initial legacy was an oppressive weight of continental, state, and town indebtedness, and an excessively disordered condition of individual finances.

The alarming aggregate of private indebtedness represented the accumulations of several years—their normal totals enhanced both by the inflation resulting from cheap paper money and by war's claims on men's time and services.

Many causes had operated to delay the payment of debts: the lack of an adequate circulating medium, and the unsettled condition of trade; the individual unrest, and the lessened individual industry inevitable under conditions of abnormal excitement; the (also inevitable) looseness of thought, and —where possible—extravagance of living.

During much of the time preceding, and also during the first years of, the Revolution, a majority had practised self-denial, but later had come the reaction so severely censured by contemporary writers and legislators. The epidemic of self-indulgence was a natural result of war conditions. The excessive severity of its punishment was due, largely, to the lack of a national currency.

An emission of continental-state paper money had followed the expiration of the continental paper money in 1781, but it enjoyed only a short life.

For a while its place was generously filled by specie flowing in through various channels: from the disbursements of the British and French armies; from trade with Havana and other points under the protection of the French fleet; from prize ships, etc.

In eastern Massachusetts the atmosphere of prosperity had been further stimulated by the expenditures of the French fleet during its visit to Boston after the battle of Yorktown.

Soon, however, this foreign specie began to disappear. Large amounts were shipped to England and elsewhere to pay for the great quantities of goods imported—goods which filled merchants' shelves to overflowing, bought at prices with which the smaller American industries could not compete; and much of the remainder was gathered into the coffers of the "money-holders"—and by them closely hoarded.

In the central and western counties of Massachusetts, trade came to a paralytic halt, labor could find no employment, and entire communities found themselves reduced to the level of barter.

Vehement demands arose for paper money to make people prosperous again.

It was the natural desire of private creditors to realize on their claims—many of them long deferred—which finally raised class antagonism to the highest point. There were not wanting creditors keen to take the fullest advantage of the abnormal conditions, just as in the earlier legal-tender paper-money days there had not been lacking debtors endeavoring to evade a just settlement of their indebtedness.

The flood of suits that had set in soon after the opening of the courts under the state constitution, reached a great height in 1783, 1784, and 1785, continuing on into 1786. In many hundreds of cases, decisive action had been deferred as a result of the Tender Act and by court extensions, and by agreement; but such deferments could prove of only temporary service, and one after the other they broke down, leaving a large part of the population of Massachusetts almost hopelessly entangled in debt and legislation.

Very precarious, in truth, was then the position of a debtor in Massachusetts.

A debt contracted when money was cheap and plentiful, gained hugely in burden if to be paid when currency was nearly extinct. As cash was almost unobtainable, a judgment was quickly translated into execution; and execution meant the seizure of any or all property that a man might have—there was then no "homestead" or any other exemption, save only, by common law, a man's tools and absolutely essential clothing and household furniture. As the next step, the debtor would see his belongings publicly sold at ruinous prices, for few, save the creditors, were financially able to bid at the sales.

As a final weapon, the barbarous laws permitted imprisonment for debt (or for unpaid taxes)—even for a small balance unrealized by the sale of all a man's possessions; and the abominable jails were quickly filled—were crowded to the very roofs—with debtors.

Especially hard hit were the returned soldiers. Their farms, or their other private affairs, had suffered in their absence and many of them were in debt for necessaries for their families. For their back pay, they had received certificates which they had been obliged to sell at heavy discount.

They had no money to show for their services or to apply upon their obligations.

In Worcester County, 104 prisoners were committed during 1785. Ten of them had been sentenced on criminal counts—the other 94 were jailed for debt.[1] They were all herded together in a building rotten and fetid with age—the poorest of them crowded "fifteen into one small room."[2]

The propertyless debtor was utterly at the mercy of his creditor. His creditor, by paying a small charge for board (only four shillings and sixpence a week), could keep him in jail as long as he liked. A judgment, with the threat of incarceration in such a pest-hole as the Worcester County jail of 1785, could, in many cases, be used to control a man's labor as effectively as if he were a slave.

To parallel today the Massachusetts conditions of 1785, imagine that, of the population of New York City, 10,000 men—none of them guilty of any crime except that of being in debt—had been stripped of all their possessions and thrown into crowded dungeons to be kept there at the will and whim of their creditors; and that the threat of similar calamity swung over the heads of a hundred thousand men of the city! To gauge the emotions that would be aroused, know also that a majority of the men thus imprisoned are debtors because of economic conditions which they had been powerless to control; that many of them have seen possessions worth much more than the sum of their debts sold for a mere fraction of those debts because money had almost disappeared; and that a great number of them are ex-soldiers returned from a victorious war. Broaden the view by spreading the same conditions over a large part of the country, and heighten the tension by a vigorous community of feeling—for the men thus jailed in Massachusetts, and the men threatened with jail, were not of large cities where neighborliness is little

[1] These figures are drawn from a contemporary register preserved in the Worcester County jail. Study of the register suggests that a complete total, if obtainable, would give a still higher number of debtors jailed.

[2] Report of a committee of the Court of General Sessions, March 28, 1786.

known, but chiefly of small towns where (in those days) blood ties were strong and neighborly fellowship was a living creed.

The pressure was kept at full by the hungry competition of creditors—each one beset by the fear that some other might forestall him. There were no insolvency laws to guard the distribution of a living debtor's estate: the first man to obtain an execution might swallow it all.

These serious flaws in the social system gaped into chasms under the financial stress of the times and imperiled the structure of the commonwealth.

The people of Massachusetts had brought themselves to believe that the end of the war would mean the end of their troubles. Instead, especially in the central and western counties, their burdens were heavier than ever and their condition much more onerous than when under the "tyranny" of Great Britain.

Who was to blame for this? How should they relieve themselves from the pressure of their loads?

The taverns—and wherever else men congregated—again heard the excited arguments and angry accusations that had preceded the outbreak of the Revolution.

Those who had complained and protested in 1782—and later—now held many new grievances. And those of tory inclination—open or concealed—eagerly swayed backward to the hope of renewed allegiance to England.

Lawyers were denounced as public enemies and as unfit to serve in the assembly. The legislature was upbraided for the weight of taxation, and it was charged that the additional taxes laid in July, 1784, and March, 1786, to take up the notes given to the soldiers for back pay, had been promoted by speculators who had purchased the notes at excessive discounts. The lower courts were held to be instruments of oppression and an unnecessary expense. Merchants, as encouraging extravagance and damaging domestic trade by their importations, were assailed as the root of economic troubles.

There was an undercurrent of suspicion that the "rich men" of Boston were planning "to bring the state into lordships" and that to obtain their end they had deliberately brought about "a tax so heavy on the people that there was not sufficient money in circulation to pay for it."[3]

Equally dangerous to the peace of the state were charges or insinuations that the burdens under which it suffered were made heavier by the monopolizing of power and position by family cliques.[4] People began to wonder if they had merely cast off one set of undesired rulers for the privilege of being weighed down by others yet more self-seeking.

[3] *Memoirs of "Billy" Hibbard, Minister of the Gospel,* 50.

[4] Below is an article published in the *Massachusetts Spy,* April 14, 1784:

"Before the revolution, Mr. Hutchinson was Lieutenant Governor, Mr. Oliver was Secretary of the Province, Peter Oliver and Foster Hutchinson Esqrs. were Judges of the Superior Court: The people were alarmed at that accumulation of power in one family and connection—they very justly considered it a source of corrupt influence dangerous to publick liberty; and accordingly exerted every effort in their power to dissolve the combination—but unhappily their means were not adequate to their security. Since the revolution, the offices of Lieutenant Governor, Secretary of the Commonwealth, Justice of the Peace for the County of Suffolk, Chief Justice of the Supreme Judicial Court, Clerk of that Court by a brother of the Chief Justice, and another of the Judges, Judge of the Maritime Court, and one of the Council of the Commonwealth, and a Judge of Probate, are held by one family and connection, without any apprehension from the influence and power.

"Is publick virtue now so universally prevalent that there is no necessity for adverting to circumstances of this nature? Or are the extraordinary merits of this family sufficient to justify the inattention? I will not inquire what they were in the beginning of the contest with Great Britain, or whether their conduct was so uniform and vigorous in the cause of their country as to justify the present confidence, and predilection in their favour. —I leave these questions to the discussion of others, and only observe that it appears to me, the combination is strong, that the conclusion is obvious, unless the integrity and ability of these men, secure us from danger, or their incapacity renders them harmless."

A host of readers also approvingly read "A Shorter Catechism," widely distributed at about the same time. It was printed in the *New York Packet,* February 5, 1784, the *Massachusetts Gazette,* February 17, 1784, and elsewhere. It includes the following *Questions* and *Answers:*

"*Question.* What is law?	*Answer.* A servant to the rich and task master to the poor.
Q. What are Courts of Justice?	*A.* Executioners of the law.
Q. What are lawyers?	*A.* Rods of correction.
Q. What is independence?	*A.* Dependence on nothing.
Q. Do we enjoy it?	*A.* Yes.
Q. Who gain'd it for us?	*A.* The army.
Q. How shall we reward them?	*A.* Cheat 'em.
Q. What is gratitude?	*A.* Disposition to repay benefactors.
Q. What is public gratitude?	*A.* Forgetfulness of benefits.
Q. What is public credit?	*A.* Soldiers' notes at 30 per cent discount."

Carrying the tide higher was the swelling restlessness of the young men back from camp with no settled prospects and, many of them, impelled by the doctrine that those who had fought for their country should have a full share in all its property and resources, no matter how or by whom held.[5]

And surging upward again were the chronically discontented who see only that others are more prosperous than they and who bear an ever-present resentment of that fact and an ever-ready hatred toward those thus favored. The laboring of communities in the aftermath of the war gave this class both opportunity and many temporary allies.

The breaking point came in 1786. The spring elections had placed in the House a number of Representatives who leaned toward the debtors' side, but they produced no relief, and when the legislature adjourned on July 8, reliance on constitutional methods suddenly vanished—legislative process appeared too slow for the thousands of men caught in the quicksands of the times. As an evil background, prison conditions became continuously more revolting—by June 30 the Worcester County jail was so choked with debtors that twenty-six were confined in one small garret.[6] Debtors yet free, and the relatives and friends of debtors both free and imprisoned, turned angrily from talk and argument to the determination to prevent any further court procedure until aid should come from, or be forced from, the legislature—or until a new legislature could be elected.

The debtors' reasoning was simple. If the courts and present legal processes continue uninterrupted, we shall lose our property, be in danger of jail for debt, and be disfranchised.[7] If we prevent the courts sitting, we shall,

[5] "Their creed is that the property of the United States has been protected from the confiscations of Britain by the joint exertions of all, and therefore ought to be the common property of all." Knox to Washington, October 23, 1786. Brooks, *Henry Knox*, 194; Drake, *Life and Correspondence of Henry Knox*, 91–92.

[6] Report of a committee of the Court of General Sessions, June 13, 1786.

[7] The new constitution contained a property qualification restricting the votes for Governor, Senators, and Representatives. It was half as high again as the qualification required of electors of Representatives under the Province charter.

for a time at least, keep both our possessions and our votes; and perhaps a new legislature will devise a way out of our troubles.

The fallacy of the plan, as many discovered later, was the impossibility of continued obstruction of the courts without incurring the responsibility and dangers of armed opposition to both the state and the national governments, but its apparent promise served to unite those in distress—and to their standard flocked all the restless and disloyal.

In the year preceding the Revolution, people had learned the political strength of county conventions, and now township after township turned toward the same panacea.

The first gathering to make its resolutions felt was that of Worcester County at Leicester on August 15.

Delegates from thirty-seven towns came together to discuss grievances and debate remedies.

They recorded their objection to the sitting of the legislature in Boston: they felt that in the capital it was too much under the influence or the domination of the wealthier classes; they wanted it to meet elsewhere, believing that it would then be more responsive to the needs of the state in general. They emphasized next the need for a circulating medium. And they continued with complaints of "abuses in the practice of the law, and the exorbitance of the fee-table"; the existence of the Courts of Common Pleas "in their present mode of administration"; the appropriation of the impost and excise revenue for the payment of the interest of the state securities; the "unreasonable and unnecessary grants" made by the General Court "to the Attorney General and others"; the government employees "being too numerous and having too great salaries"; and the state "granting aid or paying moneys to Congress, while our Public accounts remain unsettled."

Ward's influence with the discontented of his fellow citizens, even with those of his home town, was this time unavailing.

Shrewsbury had elected him Representative in 1785 and

1786, and he had been made Speaker of the House (first, February 3, 1786, for the concluding weeks of 1785–1786 by a vote of fifty-two out of eighty-one; and then by reëlection for 1786–1787 by ninety-nine out of a hundred[8]), but in this new revolt against conditions it turned suddenly from his leadership. As Speaker of the House of Representatives and Chief Justice of the Court of Common Pleas for Worcester County, he stood as too conspicuous a figure of the government which the discontented held responsible for their troubles.

Also there were, probably, many to declare that he had become prosperous, and therefore anathema, because he had during 1784 and 1785 enlarged his house by the addition of the "New Part," thus changing it from a seven-room home to a more imposing dwelling of eleven rooms. In truth, Ward never acquired the gift of money-making, and his modest investments were the result of rigid personal economy. The "New Part" had not been built because of overflowing prosperity but because more space was needed to house together his own family and that of his son, Thomas Walter, who on its completion came to live under the same roof, bringing with him his wife and two babies. General Ward's repeated absences—in Boston and Philadelphia—made this arrangement very desirable, especially as his wife's health was failing.[9]

The Leicester gathering was succeeded by a Hampshire County convention at Hatfield; and that was followed by the insurgents' forcible closing of the Court of Common Pleas at Northampton on August 29.

Bowdoin—governor now, for his second term—met the Northampton outbreak with a proclamation (September 2)

[8] On the afternoon of the same day that gave him this all but unanimous election as Speaker, the House for the second time elected him Senator, but he again declined.

There were four sessions in the critical legislative year of 1786–7: May 31, 1786, to July 8, 1786; September 27, 1786, to November 18, 1786; January 31, 1787, to March 10, 1787; April 25, 1787, to May 3, 1787. Ward was present every day.

[9] After several years of ill health, General Ward's wife died December 13, 1788.

calling upon all officers, civil and military, and the public in general "to unite in preventing and suppressing all such treasonable proceedings," but the proclamation had little effect and the insurgent leaders pressed their plans with complete disregard of it.

Two men had by this time attained prominence in the movement—Daniel Shays of Pelham and Luke Day of West Springfield. Both had served as captains in the Revolutionary army. It is said that Day was the stronger character, but the insurrection is indelibly stamped with Shays' name.

The insurgents' next purpose was the closing of the Worcester County Courts of Common Pleas and General Sessions to be held commencing September 5. Five hundred cases were to come before the justices of the Common Pleas—a large grist—fewer than at preceding sessions but equal to the average of an entire year prior to the Revolution.

Bowdoin had followed his proclamation by orders both to the sheriff of Worcester County and to Major-General Warner of the county militia to protect the courts, but this precaution had no more efficacy than the proclamation. Popular sentiment paralyzed authority, and on the night of September 4 a body of armed men, commanded by Captain Adam Wheeler of Hubbardston, entered Worcester and found no difficulty in taking possession of the court-house.

Early the next morning Wheeler's company was joined by new contingents under several other insurgent leaders.

Shortly before noon Ward left the house of Joseph Allen[10] and walked toward the court-house[11] to open court. He was

[10] Clerk of the courts and a nephew of Samuel Adams.

[11] This was the "Second Court House," a wooden structure about 42 feet front by 33 feet in depth, built 1751–1754 near the site of the north wing of the present court-house. In 1803, soon to be succeeded by the "Old Brick Court House," it was rolled along Main Street and thence down Franklin Street, twenty yoke of oxen hauling, to the locality now known as Trumbull Square (then a beautiful rural section), there to serve as a residence for four generations of the Trumbull family.

In 1886, shortly after the death of Mrs. George A. (Louisa Clap) Trumbull (December 5, 1885), the house was rented to Dr. Joseph H. Kelley, who used part of it himself (building an addition for a waiting room) and sublet the remainder.

On June 1, 1892, the building was sold by the Trumbull heirs to Dr. Kelley and

THE ARTEMAS WARD HOUSE, SHREWSBURY, MASS.
As enlarged in 1784–1785

accompanied by the other justices of the Common Pleas, a number of the justices of the Sessions, the clerk, the sheriff, court attendants, and members of the bar.

Court-house Hill was thronged with men. On the outskirts of the crowd stood a sentry, and he challenged the judges as they approached. Ward sharply ordered him to "present arms"; and the man, formerly a subaltern in Ward's own regiment, instinctively obeyed, saluted, and stepped aside to let his old commander pass. With the first honors thus readily won, Ward and the other members of his party resumed their progress, and the insurgents, following the example of the sentry, fell back to left and right and let them through.

A curious repetition of that other walk through the ranks of armed men to the same court-house, staged in that same month twelve years before, when Ward, setting himself in opposition to his associates on the bench, had become marked as a leader of the people in the dangerous road to rebellion. Now, as Chief Justice, surrounded by a riotous mob of armed men, he as undauntedly faced them in opposition to their revolt against the authority of the state which he and they together had helped to erect.

The judges reached the court-house, but at its doors they were brought to a sudden stop by a row of men with fixed bayonets.

Dr. William J. Delahanty (whose office was across the street), and in the spring of the following year it was again moved—though this time only a few feet—to make room for a brick apartment house, The Trumbull, No. 5 Trumbull Square.

In 1899 its owners were about to demolish it in order to use its site for the construction of another apartment house, No. 15 Trumbull Square, adjoining The Trumbull, but Miss Susan Trumbull came to the rescue, purchased it, and with infinite care supervised its taking down and rebuilding, restoring it to dignity as a residence again on its present site at No. 6 Massachusetts Avenue, near the home of the American Antiquarian Society.

In this restoration, the style and dimensions of the original building were carefully followed, and the old material utilized where possible. The only modifications in exterior appearance are the added porches, side terrace, and rear extension. One cannot speak with the same certainty of the interior divisions because of the many changes that the building has undergone—from court-house to mansion, from mansion to tenement, and back again to mansion, but the court-room (about 31 feet by 18 feet 8 inches), occupying the entire southerly side of the second floor, is said to be an exact reproduction of the days of Shays' Rebellion, and its doors, mantels, and most of the wainscoting are from the original structure.

Ward sternly asked "who commanded the people there; by what authority, and for what purpose, they had met in hostile array?"

"[Captain] Wheeler at length replied. After disclaiming the rank of leader, he stated, that they had come to relieve the distresses of the country, by preventing the sittings of courts until they could obtain redress of grievances."

Ward answered "that he would satisfy them their complaints were without just foundation." He demanded that they "take away their bayonets and give him some position where he could be heard by his fellow citizens, and not by the leaders alone who had deceived and deluded them. . . ."

"The insurgent officers, fearful of the effect of his determined manner on the minds of their followers, interrupted. They did not come there, they said, to listen to long speeches, but to resist oppression: they had the power to compel submission: and they demanded, an adjournment without day."[12]

Ward peremptorily refused to reply to any proposition thus delivered.

They then told him to "fall back." "The drum was beat, and the guard ordered to charge. The soldiers advanced, until the points of their bayonets pressed hard upon his breast," penetrating his robe, but he "stood as immoveable as a statue, without stirring a limb, or yielding an inch."[13]

He told the men that he did not fear their bayonets, that "he was in the way of his duty" and that he was determined to do it: they might plunge their bayonets into his heart; that when opposed to his duty his life was of little consequence.[14]

His intrepidity prevailed. The men lowered their bayonets; and Ward turned and addressed the insurgent crowd.

Then happened a strange thing—a minor miracle!

Ward's public career had brought him many distinctions.

[12] Lincoln, *History of Worcester, Mass.,* First edition, 135–136; 1862 edition, 119.

[13] *Ibid.,* First edition, 136; 1862 edition, 119.

[14] *Massachusetts Gazette,* September 8, 1786; *Massachusetts Centinel,* September 9, 1786.

He had commanded a regiment, and then an army; had presided as judge and as Chief Justice; had headed the Council of Massachusetts, and served as Speaker of its House of Representatives—but he had never possessed the gift of ready speech. No orator he, but, on the contrary, inclined to stumble in public utterance.

But now at this moment—when he saw the fruits of the long labors of a generation of Massachusetts patriots imperiled by assaults within the temple—the gift which had been denied him as a young man and through his middle age came to him as he stood there, a man close upon his threescore years.

In "clear and forcible argument" he pleaded the insurgents' own cause against themselves and opposed their attempts at political self-destruction. He "explained the dangerous tendency of their rash measures; admonished them that they were placing in peril the liberty acquired by the efforts and sufferings of years, plunging the country in civil war, and involving themselves and their families in misery; that the measures they had taken must defeat their own wishes; for the government would never yield that to force, which would be readily accorded to respectful representations; and warned them that the majesty of the laws, would be vindicated, and their resistance of its power avenged."[15]

For nearly two hours he spoke, frequently interrupted, but ready with retort and reply. Finally, turning to Captain Wheeler, he told him "that he had better take his men away; that they were waging war, which was treason; and that the consequence would be (here he made a short pause, and then added in a strong voice) the Gallows."[16, 17]

[15] Lincoln, *History of Worcester, Mass.,* First edition, 136; 1862 edition, 119–120.

[16] *Massachusetts Centinel,* September 9, 1786.

[17] George Allen in his "Reminiscences" (*Reminiscences of the Reverend George Allen of Worcester,* 41–42) endeavored to rob Ward of the credit of his speech on the courthouse steps September 5, 1786. "General Ward of Shrewsbury," he wrote, "frequently visited my father. He had no command of language—was hesitating in his speech. The address to the insurgents in Worcester during Shays's Rebellion, which Lincoln prints in

Ward made no further attempt to enter the court-house. Instead, as he ceased talking, he stepped down among the insurgents. One of their officers ordered the men to open ranks, and he walked slowly through, followed by the other members of his party, and made his way to the United States Arms tavern.[18]

Court was formally opened in the tavern, and messengers were dispatched calling upon the militia to come in for its protection. Adjournment was then taken until the following morning.

The insurgents meantime continued their garrison of the court-house and patroled the town.

The following day brought a large addition to their forces, but no aid or protection for the court. Instead of the militia-men, came word that their officers could not marshal them to oppose the insurgents: "for they were too generally in favor of the peoples measures."[19]

To attempt any further court procedure would have been futile. The Court of Common Pleas was adjourned sine die, all cases being continued to the next term (December 5). The Court of General Sessions was put over to November 21.

The insurgents had won their point and prevented the county courts sitting to any effect, but Ward's firm stand for law and order, and his impassioned harangue on the court-house steps, shone as a beacon-light over the troubled seas. The little newspapers of those days all told the story. Its

his History as having been made by Ward, is purely fictitious. He was incapable of such an effort."

Allen's contention is upset by the fact that Lincoln based his narration on a contemporary account—written on the evening of the very day on which Ward made this, the longest speech of his life, and published in the newspapers of the period—*Massachusetts Centinel,* September 9; *American Herald,* September 11; *New York Packet,* September 18; and others.

[18] Also known as "Patch's Tavern." Then a new and pretentious establishment, and the resort of visitors of consequence. Later, under Colonel Sikes (famous as a stage-coach proprietor), it became the center of stage-coach travel to, from, and through Worcester. Its third story was added by Sikes in 1813. In the generations that have passed since the days of Shays' Rebellion, it has seen numerous changes of ownership, and some in construction, and borne several different names, its last being that of the Exchange Hotel. It still stands (1921), but uncouth and dilapidated, an eyesore to the neighborhood.

[19] *Massachusetts Archives,* CXC, 233.

moral strength persisted and fructified long after Shays had fled and the rebellion had subsided. It still lives as one of the finest traditions of the county.

Next to sit in Worcester was the Supreme Judicial Court—the old Superior Court under a new title. The insurgents, apprehensive of the result of carrying their opposition too high, kept themselves well in hand and made no attempt to interfere with its proceedings. Nor, on their part, did the justices take cognizance of the obstruction of the county court fourteen days earlier. They did, however, affirm judgments against debtors in almost all the cases (more than 250) brought before them on appeal from the county court, and thus turned upon themselves the wrath that had been withheld.

From Worcester the justices went to Springfield. Their arrival found excitement running high and the insurgents gathering to prevent their holding court—the temper of the people growing steadily more violent from anxiety concerning the court's action on appeals in civil cases and, among the more prominent insurgents, from perturbation lest they be indicted for the blocking of the lower courts, despite the pacific attitude of the justices at their Worcester session.[20]

The court opened on September 26 under the protection of several hundred militiamen commanded by General Shepard, but insurgent officers mustered a large enough force to render judicial procedure impossible and the court was adjourned on its third day without any cases coming before it.

All eyes were now turned on the legislature, which had convened in special session on September 27. The gravity of the political situation was undeniable, but there was much difference of opinion in the House on the course to be adopted,

[20] Historians give only the second reason—the insurgent leaders' fear of indictment—as the cause of the forcible closing of the Supreme Judicial Court at Springfield. That was a lesser cause. Its chief aim was to prevent the issuance of further judgments and executions, for—as the debtors of Worcester County had discovered—it was largely futile to close the Court of Common Pleas unless the Supreme Judicial Court also was blocked. To obstruct the Supreme Judicial Court with the sole intent of protecting insurgent leaders would have been a poorly considered aim, for they would still remain liable to arrest and imprisonment by the General Court.

and insurgent sympathizers were loath to cast their votes for punitive, or even suppressive, measures. Agreement was, nevertheless, finally reached on a number of acts designed both to strengthen the hands of authority and to alleviate some of the grievances complained of.

For the first purpose, the General Court effected (October 28) a new law, with very severe penalties,[21] against the assembling of armed persons, or of "riotous" or "tumultuous" assemblies whether armed or not; and (November 10) suspended the privilege of the writ of habeas corpus, at the same time empowering the governor and Council to bring about the arrest and imprisonment without bail of any one whom they considered dangerous to the commonwealth.

For the second purpose, it provided (November 8) for the payment of back taxes in kind; and a week later adopted a measure to lower the cost of many civil cases, passed a new Tender Act, and offered full pardon to those who should desist from illegal activities and take the oath of allegiance.

It also (November 14) adopted an address to the people summarizing the state's indebtedness and explaining the necessity of the taxes that had been laid. It demonstrated that some of the grievances complained of were unfounded and that the state officials were by no means overpaid; and it blamed the people for unnecessary extravagance—for wasting money on "gewgaws imported from Europe & the more pernicious produce of the West Indies" (*i.e.,* rum, and molasses for conversion into rum), and for indulgence "in fantastical and expensive Fashions, and intemperate living"—but it admitted that "the taxes have indeed been very great." Biblical comparisons, so familiar to the Massachusetts of those days, added vividness to the address.

Meantime, the successes achieved in the closing of the

[21] The full penalty decreed for offenders was that they should forfeit all "lands, tenements, goods and chattels" and should further "be whipped thirty-nine stripes on the naked back, at the public whipping-post, and suffer imprisonment for a term not exceeding twelve months nor less than six months; and once every three months during the said imprisonment receive the same number of stripes on the naked back, at the public whipping-post as aforesaid."

courts, and the government's hesitancy to take effective action, increased the boldness of the insurgent leaders. While the General Court sat, insurgent circulars went out (October 23) to the towns of Hampshire County, instructing them to assemble their men, to see that they were all "well armed and equipped with sixty rounds each man, and to be ready to turn out at a minute's warning."

As the disorders spread they raised two widely differing classes of political extremists: among the propertyless, some who planned for the state's plunge into the communism of land;[22] and among the well-to-do of Revolutionary patriots, some—shocked into reactionism by the sight of the country floundering in political quagmires—who hoped for a monarchy to set it again on its feet.[23]

The insurgent movement held the attention of the entire nation. It was feared that sinister forces were magnifying the grievances and playing upon the passions of the people. There were many who believed the disturbances in Massachusetts (and elsewhere in New England) were encouraged by English emissaries and tory agents, and feared that their growth might disrupt the republic before it was out of its swaddling clothes.

This dangerous possibility was felt in the breasts of those highest in the land. "What is the cause of all these commotions?" asked Washington in a letter to Colonel Humphreys. "Do they proceed from licentiousness, British influence disseminated by the tories, or real grievances which admit of redress?"[24]

And Humphreys replied, "From all the information I have been able to obtain . . . I should attribute them to all the three causes which you have suggested."[25]

[22] Knox to Washington, October 23, 1786.—Brooks, *Henry Knox,* 195; Drake, *Henry Knox,* 92.

[23] Minot, *History of the Insurrections in Massachusetts,* First edition, 62–63; Second edition, 61–62.

[24] October 22, 1786.—Ford, *Writings of Washington,* XI, 77, note.

[25] Marshall, *Life of Washington,* First American edition, V, 113–114 (different page numbers in other editions).

As the weeks passed, Washington's suspicions increased. He declared that he felt no doubt that Great Britain was "sowing the seeds of jealousy and discontent among the various tribes of Indians on our frontiers" and that she would "improve every opportunity to foment the spirit of turbulence within the bowels of the United States."[26]

Ward held the same opinion. A few days after the closing of the Worcester Court of Common Pleas he had written to Governor Bowdoin his belief that the disturbances in Hampshire and Worcester did not originate in those counties but were "the effects of British emissaries . . . employed . . . to stimulate the unwary to acts of disorder & violence, [and] to poison the minds of others with unreasonable jealousies of their rulers—suggesting they are oppressed by them unnecessarily."

"It is my opinion," he continued, "the plan is deeper laid than many are aware of. Why such care in a British Governor to strengthen the out Posts with such dispatch? Have we not great reason to suppose they are waiting for an opportunity to take advantage of these States who are at this time as inattentive to their real interest as the beasts that perish."[27]

Some modern writers have minimized the dangers of the uprising, but that is to disregard or contradict the observation and impressions of the best informed of the men who lived through the period.

Worcester was on November 21 again occupied by insurgents—coming from Princeton, Hubbardston, Shrewsbury, and other adjacent towns to prevent the adjourned sitting of the Court of General Sessions.

As the government had made no move to back its legislation with force, they easily accomplished their purpose.

The capital was, indeed, troubled by reports that the insur-

[26] To Knox, December 26, 1786.—Ford, *Writings of Washington,* XI, 106.

[27] Original letter, September 12, 1786, *Charles Roberts Autograph Letter Collection of Haverford College.*

gents, growing in confidence and strength, planned a march eastward to stop the sitting of the Court of Common Pleas in Cambridge on November 28—this to be followed by a demonstration in Boston and the coercion of the General Court itself.

On the twenty-third an insurgent convention, held in Worcester, published an address calling upon the people to stand together and asserting their right to "examine, censure, and condemn the conduct of their rulers," adding that, as many of the rulers of Massachusetts had been "born to affluence," and "perhaps the whole in easy circumstances," they were not "under advantages of feeling for the less wealthy."

The address deprecated the closing of the courts as unwise policy, but this admonition was not taken seriously, for in the following week insurgents from Hampshire and Worcester counties gathered to prevent the opening of the Court of Common Pleas at Worcester on December 5.

Their first rendezvous was at Shrewsbury, and their headquarters "in the large yard in front of the Baldwin Tavern directly opposite Judge Ward's house."[28] Later, they centered at other towns nearby.

General Warner issued orders to the militia of his division to hold themselves in readiness to march to Worcester, but he found insurgent sympathy so wide-spread that he dispatched an express to Bowdoin warning him that it might be impossible to muster enough loyal Worcester County militia to be effective, and that to ensure the protection of the court it would "be necessary to send on a formidable force from the Lower Counties and Perhaps some Pieces of Artillery, as I am credibly informed the Insurgents have obtained some."[29]

Bowdoin immediately gave Warner's message to the Council, but it voted against aiding him with militiamen from the

[28] Elizabeth Ward, *Old Times in Shrewsbury,* 185. It was in this house, before it became the Baldwin Tavern, that Ward had been brought up (as noted also on page 4).

[29] December 1, 1786.—Original letter, *Massachusetts Archives,* CLXXXIX, 46.

eastern counties. The councilors feared to detach any men that might be needed for the defense of the capital.

Bowdoin returned word to Warner that no reinforcements could be sent, but urged him—and also the sheriff of the county—to every means to prevent interference.

On the same day (December 2) he wrote warning Ward that reports had been received in Boston that the insurgent chiefs had decided, "in consultation this or last week, that in case Government took up any of them, they would retaliate on the friends of Government—And that you & Judge Gill were agreed on."[30]

Overnight, the governor and Council decided against any attempt to meet the issue in Worcester. On the third (Sunday) Bowdoin dispatched another express, countermanding Warner's orders and notifying the judges that the Council advised adjournment to January 23 if they should find themselves unable to sit without molestation.

That same evening a party of insurgents entered Worcester and took possession of the court-house, their ranks being strengthened during the night and the day following by the arrival of numerous reinforcements.

A violent snowstorm set in Monday evening and raged all next day, but the insurgents continued to gather, numbering five or six hundred by the time appointed for the opening of the court.

To have attempted to transact court business would have brought fresh indignities upon the judiciary, but Ward and Samuel Baker—the only two of the four judges who had arrived—went through the formality of opening court[31] and then adjourned it by proclamation[32] to January 23.

[30] Original letter (by John Avery, Jr.), *Artemas Ward MSS.*

[31] As the United States Arms tavern was in the possession of the insurgents, court was this time opened in the Sun Tavern. The Sun, also known as "Mower's Tavern," had prior to the Revolution been the residence of the loyalist judge John Chandler. It was in 1818 replaced by a new building, known first as the Worcester Hotel, or Hovey's, and later as the United States Hotel. Its site (the southeast corner of Main and Mechanic streets) has for many years been covered by the Walker Building.

[32] The original is among the *Artemas Ward MSS.*

The judges held the Council's advice to adjourn if opposition was offered to their sitting, but they were able to avoid public acknowledgment of this new interruption of justice by having another reason for adjournment in the absence of the two judges who had been "providentially detained."

Ward remained in Worcester Tuesday night, virtually a prisoner, for the insurgents placed a guard around the house where he was staying, but he was permitted to return to Shrewsbury the following day.

Meantime, an insurgent council of war declared for a march on Boston to liberate insurgent prisoners as soon as a large enough force had collected.

In anticipation of such a move, the governor and Council prepared for the defense of the capital—"guards were mounted at the prison, and at the entrances of the town; and all things seemed to carry the shew of a garrison." Outside the town, Major-General Brooks held "the Middlesex militia contiguous to the road, in readiness for action."[33]

Wednesday morning the insurgents received additional reinforcements and during the day paraded to meet Shays, who came in from Hampshire County with about 350 men. This was Shays' highest moment. His column of a full thousand men[34] made an imposing appearance marching through the streets. "The companies included many who had learned their tactics from Steuben, and served an apprenticeship of discipline in the ranks of the revolution: war worn veterans, who in a good cause, would have been invincible. The pine tuft supplied the place of plume in their hats. Shays, with his aid, mounted on white horses, led the van. They displayed into line before the Court House, where they were reviewed and inspected."

The possession of the town was complete, and Shays took every precaution against surprise. "Chains of sentinels were

[33] Minot, *History of the Insurrections in Massachusetts,* First edition, 88, 87; Second edition, 87, 86. *Council Records,* December 7, 1786.

[34] *Worcester Magazine,* first week in December, 1786, says "about 800,"—but the next week's continuation of the account has it as 1000.

stretched along the streets; planted in every avenue of approach, and on the neighboring hills, examining all who passed."[35]

Fortunately for Massachusetts the excessively severe weather made the roads so nearly impassable that the full insurgent strength could not gather. Short by many hundreds of their expected numbers and unable to bring in sufficient supplies over the snow-choked roads, the plan for a descent upon Boston faded to impossibility. Nor even could Shays subsist his men in Worcester except by levying on the inhabitants—which (to his credit be it told) he did not attempt—so on December 7 he marched a large detachment out of the town and two days later the remainder were temporarily disbanded.

On December 14 Bowdoin wrote to Ward advising that the Council would meet on the twentieth, "when the means of effectually suppressing the insurgents will be taken into serious consideration," and asking his suggestions and advice. His letter in facsimile is on the page opposite.

Ward, replying, estimated 1500 as the strength that the insurgents would be able to muster at Worcester for the next court sitting—that of the Court of Common Pleas, January 23—and he strongly advocated the government's putting into the field a "decided superiority" of numbers as "the most likely way to prevent the shedding of blood." He advised that a force double that of the insurgents be drawn from the "lower counties"—this would "serve as a stimulus to the militia in this county to turn out in support of Government," and would "convince the insurgents that they are not the people, as they affect to call themselves."[36]

On December 26 Shays' men closed the Springfield Courts of Common Pleas and General Sessions. The news reached Boston the following Sunday, and coupled with it was word

[35] Lincoln, *History of Worcester, Mass.*, First edition, 146; 1862 edition, 127.

[36] Bowdoin and Temple Papers, II, 118.—*Massachusetts Historical Society Collections*, 7th, VI.

Boston Decem.r 14th 1786

Sir,

The Council will meet the 20th instant, when the means of effectually suppressing the insurgents will be taken into serious consideration.

Please to let me have your ideas of the best plan for that purpose: extending it from the first outset to the completion of the business: beginning with the support of the Worcester Court, which by adjournment is to sit the 23d of January next: particularizing what force (if any should be necessary) should be sent from the lower Counties: what can be depended on from Worcester, Hampshire & Berkshire: how long the Militia will be content to be in the Service, if the business should not be speedily accomplished: what resources and regular supplies of Provisions &ca can be depended on from those three Counties and every other information necessary to be had.

Be as full and particular as may be.

Not having time to enlarge, I am very respectfully ~~Your~~ Sir,

Your most Obed.t hble Serv.t

James Bowdoin

Hon.ble Artemas Ward Esq.r

From the original (7⅞ × 12⅝) in the *Artemas Ward MSS.*

GOVERNOR BOWDOIN'S LETTER ASKING WARD'S ADVICE ON THE SUPPRESSION OF SHAYS' REBELLION

that the insurgents were already preparing to prevent the sitting of the Worcester court.

The Council was at last aroused to the necessity of effective action. On January 4, acting on Ward's advice, an army of 4400 men was ordered raised, and its command was entrusted to General Benjamin Lincoln. 3200 men were to form the army with which Lincoln was to march to Worcester to uphold the court; 1200 were to rendezvous at Springfield. There was no money in the treasury to supply the troops, but a sufficient fund was quickly raised by loans from private citizens.

On January 12 Ward wrote to Bowdoin telling of a conference of insurgent officers to be held at Rutland on January 16, and suggested an attempt "to cast the net over them."[37] Bowdoin passed the letter on to Lincoln, but the latter's preparations were not sufficiently advanced to make the plan feasible.

Lincoln and his troops reached Worcester on January 22 and were joined there by loyal militia units. They encountered no opposition and the court sat uninterruptedly, for the insurgents had shifted their aim and were gathering their forces for an attempt on the continental arsenal at Springfield, planning to strike for its capture before the main government army could be thrown into the scale against them.

The insurgents had suffered from the lack not only of competent leaders, but also of firearms and ammunition. Possession of the arsenal would greatly increase both their military strength and their political power.

The court completed its labors on Thursday, January 25. On the same day, Shays attempted a descent on the arsenal. He was easily repulsed, but General Shepard was nevertheless much perturbed by the strength of the insurgent bodies encamped around him. He feared for the safety both of the arsenal and of Springfield itself, and he sent expresses to

[37] *Worcester, Original Papers,* III, 14, American Antiquarian Society.

Worcester calling for help. Lincoln immediately responded, throwing one regiment of foot and a small detachment of cavalry into the arsenal camp on the night of the twenty-sixth,[38] and following them next morning with his full command.

Ward, meanwhile, returned to Shrewsbury and thence to Boston.

The opening of the General Court had been scheduled for January 31 and Ward was present on that day, but it was February 3 before a quorum gathered.

Governor Bowdoin's opening speech urged vigorous action to restore order. And both branches of the legislature promptly responded.

"The plans for the session seem to have been prearranged by some guiding minds; for there was a concert of action between the two branches as well as with the Governor, unknown since the outbreak. To Bowdoin's patriotic address, urging a determined suppression of the rebellion, the Senate [February 4] replied by the hand of Samuel Adams, declaring a rebellion to exist, and promising to support him in all his measures to restore the supremacy of the law. The House immediately concurred."[39]

The very day that a state of rebellion was thus declared, the rebellion received its death blow.

The insurgents had retreated as Lincoln advanced upon them after reaching Springfield, and soon after had come their dispersal—and the breaking of the backbone of the insurrection—at Petersham on February 4, following Lincoln's famous pursuit in a forced march of thirty miles through a driving snow-storm.

Small bodies of insurgents continued in arms for a while, essaying guerilla tactics, but they were for the most part of the element lawless by nature. Among the people gener-

[38] Lincoln to Washington, February 22, 1787, *Sparks MSS.*, LVII, f. 10, Harvard College Library.

[39] Wells, *Life of Samuel Adams*, III, 236.

ally, there was little appetite left for armed protest. "Shays' Rebellion" was no longer a menace to the institutions of the commonwealth.

The strength of the insurgency had, even at its height, rested much less in the half-armed forces which represented it on the march or in the field than in their background of a public sentiment aflame with anger at the legal pitfalls besetting scores of communities. And public sentiment, perceiving the futility of insurrection, had withdrawn its support. Hundreds of the men whom circumstances had swept from the well-traveled highway of political protest into the whirlpool of rebellion, were at heart fully loyal to both their state and the Confederacy, and they rejoiced when the rebellion subsided and their feet were once again on solid ground—though they were perhaps not regretful of their sudden plunge if it should have opened the eyes of their fellows to the needs and grievances of so many of the people of the state.

And very soon—so soon indeed that the embers of the insurrection were barely cold—one sees dissolve the worst features of the economic and legal tangle which had imperiled the commonwealth. No great constitutional change took place, but several causes united to set its life currents coursing more healthfully. Judges held creditors to some degree in check; and creditors in general had been shocked into a more careful consideration. Further, in the following November the General Court struck the shackles from propertyless debtors by a new law which permitted them to step out of the gloom of the jails into the sunshine of freedom. The creditor could still pursue without restriction for any property that his debtor might have or might acquire, but he could no longer condemn him indefinitely to the dungeon.

Then, too, commerce found new outlets—and regained some old ones—and, before long, prosperity, in at least tolerable measure, flowed again through the highways, helping to wipe out both old debts and old grievances.

In national affairs, also, the rebellion had served a purpose as a warning that could not be ignored by any thoughtful man. Despite their handicaps, the insurgents had shaken the government of one of the strongest states in the Confederacy. And, as Washington testifies, there were "combustibles in every state, which a spark might set fire to."[40]

If a new and greater conflagration should break out, where could be found the power to quench the flames? There could be little reliance in a national government so weak that—even while recording its belief that its aid was necessary for the support of the government of Massachusetts in order to save the United States from "the calamities of a civil war"—it confessed itself afraid of the "perilous step" of arming its ex-soldiers had it not received assurances that "the money holders in the state of Massachusetts and the other states" would fill the loans to pay the soldiers' wages.[41] It was high time for an abatement of personal jealousies and grudges, of personal absorption in pursuit of gain, of state rivalries and selfishness. Time too for statesmen, hard set on political theories, to learn to bend or shape them to meet the needs of the nation.

Old objections to a change in the form of national government had weakened under the pressure, and every state but Rhode Island was represented in the Constitutional Convention which on September 17, 1787, after four months' labor and debate, adopted the present Constitution of the United States and submitted it for ratification.

Then followed a series of stirring—frequently bitter—factional fights within the states. Victory was won by the advocates of the constitution, and the young republic thus took another and a firm step forward on the road to its future greatness. It accepted the strong national government of the "Federalists" instead of the League of States of which the "Anti-Federalists" were enamored.

[40] To Knox, December 26, 1786.—Ford, *Writings of Washington,* XI, 104.

[41] *Secret Journals of the Congress of the Confederation, Domestick Affairs,* October 21, 1786, I, 268–270 (1821).

There was much opposition in Massachusetts to the restrictions and sacrifices of state sovereignty which the Constitution embodied—the Worcester County delegates voted forty-three for rejection and only seven for acceptance—but public opinion gradually veered toward it and Massachusetts became the stronghold of the "Federal" party.

With that change of heart came Ward's vindication among his townsmen. It had been against an overwhelming majority that he had maintained his stand for the political integrity of the commonwealth, but in after years there were many who contritely asked his pardon for the abuse they had poured on him for refusing to join with them in revolt.[42]

And the clemency extended to the insurgents, both leaders and rank and file, must have been satisfactory even to Thomas Jefferson, who had expressed hope that no severity would be exercised in punishment. Jefferson believed that an occasional spirit of revolt was beneficial—even if wrongly directed, it was better than none at all! "I like a little rebellion now and then," he declared. "It is like a storm in the atmosphere."[43]

[42] Silvanus Billings petition, Henry Baldwin acknowledgment, etc.—*Artemas Ward MSS.*

[43] To Abigail Adams, February 22, 1787.—Paul Leicester Ford, *Writings of Thomas Jefferson,* IV, 370.

CHAPTER XV

1787–1800: Age 59–72

After Shays' Rebellion to 1800. General Ward as a "Federalist" in the Second and Third United States Congresses. His political views. The break with Samuel Adams. His death.

DURING the legislative year commencing May 30, 1787, Ward took no part in the Massachusetts government, but on June 4, 1788, he was elected one of the nine councilors provided by the new state constitution to advise and assist the governor.

In December of the same year he was a candidate to represent the Worcester district in the first United States congress under the new national constitution. He was handicapped by the "insurgent" vote—which was not yet fully reconciled to the part he had taken in opposing the Shays movement—and he ran third in a hotly contested election. The two leading contestants were Colonel Jonathan Grout and Timothy Paine. On the third vote Grout was elected.[1]

[1] Rice, *The Worcester District in Congress*, 4.—"Grout, although a lawyer, had sympathized with the insurgents, during the Shays Rebellion, and was known as a pronounced Antifederalist. Paine had been a tory of the mild stripe in the Revolution but had readily regained the favor of the community in which he lived by his cheerful acquiescence in the new order. He was a man of wealth and influence, and was supported by the Federalists.

"Three trials were necessary before a choice was effected. [On the first, Grout received a plurality.] On the second Paine received a plurality. . . . Artemas Ward appearing as a candidate of some strength, and drawing from both sides. [This is inaccurate, as the Ward vote was approximately the same on each ballot—and was a little higher on the first than on the second and third.] These failures prolonged the contest through the winter, with increasing excitement and ill feeling. The merits and demerits of the candidates were set forth with earnestness in the public print, and discussed in private with acrimony. Paine was denounced as a tory, an aristocrat, and an enemy to the common people. The objections to Grout were, that in education and ability he was Paine's inferior, and that he had large property interests in Vermont and New Hampshire. A third attempt on the 2d of March, 1789, resulted in Grout's election by a small majority."

Time was, however, correcting the vision of the men of Shrewsbury and in the following spring (1789) they elected Ward as Moderator—the chief office of the township; and thereafter twice reëlected him.

It was in the fall of the same year that Washington as the first President of the United States visited New England: everywhere to be received with the highest respect and greatest acclaim. He arrived in Worcester on the morning of October 23, escorted into the town by a party of prominent citizens. He breakfasted at the United States Arms and then set out again on the road for Boston, passing Ward's house on his way; but Ward was not there to greet him, nor had he taken any part in the Worcester reception—so deep-seated and lasting had proved the estrangement of the two men.

Ward spent the greater part of 1789 and 1790 in semi-retirement on his Shrewsbury farm, but in the fall of the latter year he was again a candidate to represent the Worcester district in the United States House of Representatives, and again the election was close and hotly contested.

Grout ran for reëlection, and the fight this time was between him and Ward, a third candidate running well behind both.

On the first vote (October 4) neither Ward nor Grout obtained the requisite number (1123) of votes: Ward receiving 798 and Grout 800. In the second contest, November 26, Ward made the goal, his vote running up to 1248, and Grout's reaching only 1081.

Ward set out for Philadelphia in the following October (1791), traveling this time by stage coach instead of on horseback as eleven years earlier he had ridden to the same town to attend the Continental Congress. He arrived October 22,[2] two days before the opening of the first session of

[2] *Philadelphia,* October 22: " . . . Artemas Ward, Representative in Congress from Massachusetts, is arrived in this city. To that state and to this officer, American liberty is particularly indebted. In that gloomy year, viz 1775, when Boston was in the pos-

the Second Congress. And he was equally punctual at the other three sessions of his two terms.

The United States Congress then was a small assemblage compared with that of today. The total enrolment of Representatives in the Second Congress was only sixty-nine; and only thirty-eight were present when it was called to order.

Ward aligned himself with the "Federalists" (or "Nationalists," as they had better been called), who supported Washington and Alexander Hamilton and John Adams in their stand for a strong central government exercising the fullest possible power that could be assumed under the Constitution; and many of whom inclined toward a social system akin to that of England. Of opposing views were the "Anti-Federalists": those of states' rights and individualistic views, who objected to the national government's reaching out for power and authority, and who looked askance at the almost regal ceremonials of Washington's administration. Sectionalism and variance of agrarian and commercial interests also provided reasons for cleavage.[3]

Political parties did not in those first years attain strong cohesion, but the outstanding testimony of the recorded votes of the House of Representatives of the Second Congress is that New England, led by Massachusetts, supported Washington's administration in nearly every important vote, and that the South, led by Virginia, opposed it; that New

session of a regular and well appointed British force, inimical to liberty, before the other colonies had fully taken the alarm, the sons of Massachusetts dared to assert their rights, and this gentleman was appointed by them to conduct their enterprises. To have mentioned resistance in the field, would have been acknowledged a proof of temerity, in some parts, at the period to which we allude. But Ward and his followers thought and acted otherwise. Scantily supplied with arms and ammunition, they kept in awe the flower of the British troops. To him therefore and to them the praise of firmness and conduct are due—They gallantly began to effect that revolution, which was afterwards gloriously completed by confederated America, under the auspices of a Washington, to whom the patriotick Ward, in obedience to Congress, resigned the command of the army, and continued to act as first Major General."—*Massachusetts Spy,* November 3, 1791.

[3] The issue which gave rise to the party names of "Federalist" and "Anti-Federalist" had been banished by the acceptance of the constitution, but the names continued with changed, and changing, significance as party labels.

England was generally Federal, and that the South was generally Anti-Federal.[4]

Ward had full confidence in the honesty and intelligence of the people and their ability to decide correctly on subjects familiar to them, but during the years of the Revolutionary War, and those succeeding it, he had witnessed so many instances of the populace acting upon subjects of which it had little understanding that he felt that the public weal was best served by a government with balance-wheels set beyond its direct control.

As early as March 13, 1781, he had written to Samuel Osgood: "You say that which comports with the general sentiments of the people is political justice. If you mean to have them first well informed I shall not differ much about the matter; but if you mean the general sentiment of the people made up without due consideration I must beg leave to dissent."[5] Again, two years later (April 23, 1783), to General Lincoln: "When I see the methods that are taken by some & the inattention of others, to their Rights and Priviledges, I am almost ready to say, that the choice of the first magistrate [*i.e.*, the choice of the governor of the state] ought by no means, be committed to the People at large. I apprehend the inattention of the people is so great that there is danger of their being undone before they are aware of it."[6]

Thus feeling and believing, Ward was a whole-souled Federalist. He was proud to belong to the party whose strong constructive work is the most remarkable feature of the first years under the United States Constitution. The Federal policies were to him the true *New England Politics* (that was his favorite way of referring to them), as Congregationalism

[4] An interesting tabulation of a number of the votes of the first four United States congresses is given in Libby's "Political Factions in Washington's Administration," *Quarterly Journal of the University of North Dakota*, III, 293-318. I cannot, though, agree with the deductions that Professor Libby draws. An important inaccuracy in the votes of the Third Congress, Table VI, is corrected on page 311, note 17, of this chapter.

[5] MS. draft in the possession (1921) of Ward Dix Kerlin, Camden, N. J.

[6] Original letter, *Fogg Collection*, Maine Historical Society.

was to him the *New England Religion*. As such he upheld them both in his adjurations to his sons.[7]

Ward was an appointee on numerous military committees. Among them—only eight days after his first attendance—was one (November 1, 1791) to prepare and bring in a bill for the establishment of a militia, and competent magazines, arsenals, and fortifications.[8]

Faithful attention to duty marked him as in his younger days. On January 23, 1792, he notes, "I have had an ill turn for one day whereby I was prevented from attending my duty in Congress"; but he proudly adds, "saving that, I have not been absent one hour."[9]

His body was, however, weaker than his will, for the following month (February 18) he was obliged to write that he had been prevented from attending his "duty in Congress about ten days by reason of Indisposition. I was first taken with the Gravel. As soon as I had got well of that difficulty, I was taken with the Gout in my feet. Have been much exercised with pain in them. They are now become quite easy but much swollen. I am not able to put on my shoes. I hope by the Blessing of a kind Providence in a few days to be able to attend Congress again."[9]

Four days later (February 22) he wrote, "I am still detained from attending Congress on account of the gout. I

[7] To his youngest son, Henry Dana, then living in Orangeburgh, S. C., Ward wrote, February 25, 1795, "I wish to have you obtain the esteem of the people among whom you dwell; but to obtain that, I would not have you renounce the New-England Politics nor Religion"; and again on March 3 of the same year, "I hope you will endeavor to get the good will of the people among whom you reside, but in order to obtain that I hope you will not sacrifice your Political principles, nor your religion, as too many have done. A steady firm adherence to right principles is more likely to raise a man in the opinion of others than shifting & turning about like a wethercock with every breth of wind." The originals of both these letters are in the possession (1921) of Maria Whittelsey Norris, Grand Rapids, Mich.

[8] The membership of the committee is not given in the generally consulted "Annals of Congress" (Gales and Seaton, *Debates and Proceedings in the Congress of the United States*, 1849), but it may be found in the first (1792) edition of the House Journal, the Gales and Seaton reprint of 1826, and (incorrectly dated October 31) in [John Agg's] *History of Congress exhibiting a classification of the proceedings . . . the first term of the Administration of General Washington*, 489.

[9] To his son, Thomas Walter Ward.—Original letters, *Artemas Ward MSS.*

have but little pain, but my left foot, ankle & small of my leg is very much swollen. I can't get on my shoe, and the Streats are so damp & wet that it's not safe to go out unless I could wear my shoe. Hope in a short time to be able to attend my duty in Congress."[9]

One consolation he found in his sickness was that it afforded him an excuse for not taking part in the celebration of Washington's birthday. "This day" (February 22), he wrote, "is the President's birthday & there is a mighty fuss in this City on that account. Being unwell I am excused from taking any part therein, & that gives me no pain, but rather pleasure."

Ward supported many Washington policies, but he never attained a personal liking for the Virginian.

His interest in the welfare of his constituents is ever present. He writes (in his letter of January 23, already quoted), "there are matters before Congress of very great importance, such as the Indian war,[10] representation in Congress whether one for every thirty thousand, &c, militia law &c. I wish they may all be determined in such manner as will be most for the benefit of the people at large."

He dwelt (February 22) on the danger of too many Representatives: "I fear the next choice of Representatives for Congress will give too many members for the benefit of the people at large; Congress having determined there shall be one for every thirty thousand persons in the United States, so that Massachusetts will have fifteen members instead of eight. It will make the expence of Government much greater and the business not done any better, and I think the people be in more danger of having their Rights incroached upon; for an Individual in a large assembly will not look upon himself so much accountable to his constituents for what is done,

[9] See note 9 on preceding page.

[10] The intermittent warfare with the Indians—chiefly at this period in western Ohio and Indiana (both Indiana and Ohio then being part of the Northwest Territory),—had temporarily assumed a serious aspect by the complete rout of St. Clair's force on November 4, 1791.

—he will hide himself in the multitude and say I was not present when this & that thing was transacted. I wish many things were different from what they are at present."

He never held a high opinion of the chronic speechmaker. On March 1 he writes: "There is more business that ought to be done before we rise, than we have hitherto done. There are so many that have so high a favor for speechafying that they hinder business amasingly, and one half of it is nothing to the purpose. If there were fewer speakers & more independent men we should do much better."

He found the life in Philadelphia "Very unpleasant and irksome," and he declared that he wished "never to be reelected."[11]

March 10, there came up a resolution which reads interestingly in the light of the startling events which followed:

"*Resolved,* That this House hath received, with sentiments of high satisfaction, the notification of the King of the French, of his acceptance of the Constitution presented to him in the name of the Nation: And that the President of the United States be requested, in his answer to the said notification, to express the sincere participation of the House in the interests of the French Nation, on this great and important event;

"And their wish, that the wisdom and magnanimity displayed in the formation and acceptance of the Constitution, may be rewarded by the most perfect attainment of its object, the permanent happiness of so great a people."

Ward voted for the first section, but against the second. He perhaps did not believe in the "magnanimity" of Louis XVI, and he saw further than some of his colleagues, for it was only five months later that Louis fled to the Assembly for protection, and a mob sacked the Tuileries—young Captain Napoleon Bonaparte being an interested observer; and it was less than a year before he was condemned to the guillotine for "conspiracy against the liberty of the nation and criminal attacks upon the safety of the state."

[11] To Thomas Walter Ward.—Original letter, *Artemas Ward MSS.*

A few weeks after the House vote on the congratulatory resolutions to Louis XVI, Congress (May 8) adjourned to November 5, and Ward returned to Shrewsbury.

The journey to and from Philadelphia every year by stage over the broken, eroded route of the eighteenth century was a severe strain upon a man of his age and condition. Of that to the second session of the Second Congress he wrote (November 13), "I arrived at this place on the first instant much unwell by the fatiguing journey I had," and again, on December 28, "I have been unwell a great part of the time I have been here, . . . I have at times been exercised with excrutiating pain. That is now abated and I hope through Divine goodness I may enjoy better health."[12]

In his letter of November 13, he spoke of the hope of terminating the Indian war, "which has cost us millions of dollars." The English government was suspected of aiding the Indians with supplies and ammunition, but English traders had become "sick of the war, because the Indians have nothing to trade with; they having spent so much time in Counsels & war."

In his letter of December 28, he approvingly noted the reëlection of John Adams as Vice-President "by a much greater majority than he was first chosen by, to the great mortification of those who have been endeavouring to prevent his being chosen." Washington had again been unanimously elected President.

Ward rejoiced also at the victories of the French revolutionists. "I congratulate you," he wrote, "on the success of the French armes against the combined Armies. They have drove them out of France, killed and taken many thousands of them with large quantities of Ordnance & Stores and were pursuing them in the beginning of October last, which is the latest accounts we have from France."

He added the hope that "the French may have wisdom to make a right improvement of the advantage they have ob-

[12] To Thomas Walter Ward.—Original letters, *Artemas Ward MSS.*

tained over their enemies,"—for on November 13 he had noted "from France they appear to be in a very disagreeable situation, not knowing how to use their rights & turn their rage against their best friends."

But no one could yet foresee the distortions and deformities which the European turmoil was to breed in the American body politic!

Ward had declared himself as opposed to a second term, but he was nevertheless reëlected—this time on the first vote and by a handsome majority—to the Third Congress.

The Second Congress closed on March 2, 1793, and the Third Congress did not meet until December 2.

Between those two dates lies a spectacularly feverish period of American history, for domestic divergencies split wide open upon the rock of the French Revolution. The upheaval in France had shaken the entire civilized world and the waves rolled high upon the American shore, all but wrecking the government with the extreme violence of the emotions it roused.

France, in her desperate defiance of the monarchical powers of Europe, claimed the aid of the United States, and thousands of Americans—blind to, or disregarding, the vulnerability of their own so newly established country—were eagerly willing that she should respond immediately and in full to the French demands upon her.

By the early summer, sympathy with the French revolutionists had mounted to the point of passion. "Democratic Societies," modeled on the Jacobins Club of Paris, were organized by the extreme "French Party" of the Democratic-Republicans—a new name for the Anti-Federalists. Politics boiled as a veritable orgy of factional discord, dissension, and abuse.

America's clash would be with England—and this added zest instead of exciting caution, for the old Revolutionary antagonism, continued and nursed by years of unsettled grievances, had been heightened by the depredations on American merchantmen which followed England's entry into the European conflict. "Ten thousand people in the streets of Philadelphia, day after day, threatened to drag Washington out of his house, and effect a revolution in the government, or compel it to declare war in favor of the French revolution and against England."[13]

Washington held firm for neutrality. His stand drove the "French Party" to frenzy, but it saved—just barely saved—the country from being drawn into the European maelstrom.

The swiftly moving current of events heightened differences of opinion and viewpoint, and strengthened new lines of demarcation. Ward stood firm with Washington: sheerly opposite to the sentiments of his old friend Samuel Adams. Ward and Samuel Adams had been drifting apart, and the acrimony over the American policy toward England and France severed the ties of a generation of intimate political fellowship.

It was the same practical bent which had directed Ward's support of so many Federal measures that enlisted him also for neutrality.

He was thoroughly imbued with the belief that self-government is an inherent right, and his sympathies were with all those struggling for political freedom,[14] but it was solely and specifically for the political liberty of his own province of Massachusetts, that, nineteen years before, he had risked life and honor by heading a revolutionary army—not for the general theory of human rights; and he was not willing to endanger the triumphant result, an independent American re-

[13] *Works of John Adams*, X, 47.

[14] On the news of the Polish triumphs of the spring and summer of 1794, he wrote (November 20, 1794) to his daughter Sarah and her husband, Elijah Brigham: "The King of Prussia does not succeed to his wish against the Poles. He will it is hoped have more to do to suppress the insurrections in his own dominions than he will be able to accomplish. The spirit of liberty appears to be kindling in Europe, & will it is thought burst forth into a mighty flame. Then Emperors & Kings must hide their heads or lose them."—Original letter owned (1921) by the Reverend Francis E. Clark, Boston. (Poland's success was short-lived. She had been crushed at Maciejowice and Praga during the October preceding the date of Ward's letter.)

public, on so unsatisfactory a hazard as a naval war with Great Britain: neither to aid revolutionary France, nor in retaliation for commercial losses, while there existed the possibility of peaceful adjustment.

Samuel Adams, on the other hand, stood as the Massachusetts leader of the "Antis," the Democratic-Republicans or "Republicans"—of the sentiment of the Democratic Societies —or the "Jacobins," as they came to be known.

The hectic excitement had subsided before the Third Congress met—the pro-French exhilaration had been damped both by the fearful epidemic of yellow fever which scourged the capital and by the political excesses of Citizen Genet, the French minister—but there remained the strong rancor against England, and early in 1794 the war spirit began mounting again as Congress and the country dwelt upon the ruin that English activities were bringing upon American maritime commerce.

With the world in convulsion, a host of vessels—British, French, and Spanish—and both the English and French Admiralties—were preying upon American ships,[15] but England's greater fleet gave her more numerous opportunities and much the largest list of victims. English warships and privateers had fallen with overwhelming force upon hundreds of American vessels which had swarmed to the French West Indies to enjoy the advantage of the French Declaration placing American ships trading with French colonies on a full equality with French ships.[16] Further, England's impressment of American seamen whipped rage to a keener edge.

The Democratic-Republicans now found allies among the Federalists, and both Congress and the country began to prepare for war. Resolutions passed for coast fortifications, and the purchase of artillery; plans were submitted for the raising of an army; and citizens volunteered for work on the defenses.

[15] *American State Papers, Foreign,* I, 424.

[16] February 19, 1793, *American State Papers, Foreign,* I, 147.

On April 7 there appeared again the favorite weapon of the Revolution—a resolution prohibiting commercial intercourse with British subjects—and it found quick support in both House and Senate.

The outlook was even more dangerous than it had been the preceding summer. War with England was being demanded for the protection of American shipping; yet at that time war could only have meant its annihilation without the possibility of adequate reprisal. Above all else, the new United States required peace: time in which to develop its resources, and tranquillity so that its people might devote themselves to industry instead of to conflict.

Measures for military preparation were justifiable—were indeed imperatively demanded by the world turmoil—but the situation was rapidly getting out of hand.

Ward voted five times against the resolution prohibiting (or, as finally amended, severely restricting) commercial intercourse with British subjects, but united Republican and Federal votes passed it in the House of Representatives. It received less than majority support on the second reading in the Senate, but only John Adams' vote as president of the Senate stopped its passing to a third reading and possible acceptance.[17]

[17] Several histories incorrectly report, or convey an incorrect impression of, this incident of John Adams' vote. They state that the non-intercourse bill was "defeated in the Senate only by the casting vote of Vice president Adams."—Avery, *History of the United States*, VII, 127; that "it was lost in the Senate only by the casting of the vote of the vice-president."—Bassett, *The Federalist System*, 125 (Volume XI of *The American Nation*), and so forth. The history of the bill in the Senate is, instead, briefly as follows: It was read the first time on April 25 and ordered to a second reading. It was read the second time on April 28 and put to a vote, but was rejected (the leading section by a vote of 14 nays against 11 yeas). Next came the vote on a motion to pass it for a third reading. The loss of the motion meant the loss of the bill; to carry the motion would give another opportunity to endeavor to carry the bill. Its advocates mustered two additional votes, and one of its opponents failed to vote, thus bringing about the tie of 13 and 13 which was ended by John Adams. Under the circumstances one can only speculate on the outcome if the bill had passed to a third reading.

On page 303, note 4, this chapter, reference is made to a tabulation of votes of the first four United States congresses in Colby's "Political Factions in Washington's Administration." One of the seemingly inevitable inaccuracies of such tabulations unfortunately reversed the record and significance of all the votes on this proposed "Non-intercourse with Great Britain." The Nays are listed as *Anti*-Administration, whereas the opposite

The need for an understanding with England had become urgent, and Washington, with the consent of the Senate (obtained while the non-intercourse resolution was hatching in the House), sent John Jay across the ocean to negotiate it.

The year following was a most difficult and trying period. The harassing of American commerce was maintained to an extent which kept the country in hysterical anger. The Washington-John Adams Federalists held the helm steady awaiting the result of Jay's efforts in England, but under a continuous fire of insult from the "French Party"—which charged toryism and monarchical tendencies, subservience to England and English gold—ignoring the fact that France to the best of her lesser ability was almost equally culpable with her foe across the channel.

In Ward's case at all events his stand was not suggested or influenced by any partiality toward England. Despite the excesses and atheism of the French revolutionists, their offenses against American commerce, and the political methods of their chief protagonists in this country, his sympathies were still for France in her conflict with England and her other enemies. He was strongly gratified by the defeat of the Duke of York and the other allied commanders at the battle of Tourcoing—"By accounts arrived here," he wrote, "the French still continue to conquer. The Duke of York has met with a sad rebuff. I wish he may meet with more of the like kind."[18]

The Democratic Societies nevertheless burrowed desperately in their efforts further to undermine the Federal Party, and Ward and the other strict Federalists were, using the words of an indignant writer in the *Columbian Centinel* (October 25, 1794), "vilified worse than Robbers and even Dev-

is the truth. The error involves between one-fifth and one-sixth of all the Third Congress votes considered.

[18] November 20, 1794, to his daughter Sarah and her husband, Elijah Brigham. This letter is quoted also on page 309, note 14.

ils would be, and charged with crimes that Men are not capable of committing."

The conditions were a severe strain upon the general, whose health was again poor, but he stood to his post despite the remonstrances of his family. Henry Dana, writing to his brother Thomas Walter (June 30, 1794), said he feared that their father would "be called to take his seat in Heaven at least four years sooner for his having holden on in Congress."[19]

The summer and fall were further perturbed by the "Whiskey Insurrection"[20] in western Pennsylvania. The disturbances which bear that title arose from efforts to enforce the payment of United States excise fees and the resentment of the inhabitants at government interference with, and taxation of, their whiskey distilling—an industry of high importance to them because it afforded the easiest and most profitable method of marketing their surplus corn. Riotous defiances of government revenue officers mounted finally to the brink of armed rebellion, with several thousand men gathering in opposition to the government. Grave fears were aroused that their action might stimulate uprisings in other parts of the country; and that English agents were responsible for the spread of disaffection.

The insurrection died down at the (intentionally) leisurely approach of a government army of 15,000 men, but it fed the flames of party animosity. Washington, in a formal message to Congress, November 19, charged the serious character of the disturbances to the Democratic Societies—referring to them by the peculiar euphemism of "certain self-created societies"; and members of the Democratic Societies retorted that the insurrection had been grossly exaggerated by Alexander Hamilton—the most monarchical of the Fed-

[19] Original letter, *Artemas Ward MSS.*

[20] At the time also known as "Gallatin's Insurrection" because, until it verged to arms, opposition to the excise had been led by Senator Albert Gallatin, the young Swiss, already well on his way to political leadership and high government position.

eralists—for the express purpose of staging an example and proof of the strength of the authority of the national government.

In the preparation by the House of Representatives of its address in response to the President's message, Ward voted in the affirmative to so amend a proposed clause as to specifically endorse Washington's charge against the "self-created societies." Thus amended, the clause read: "In tracing the origin and progress of the insurrection, we can entertain no doubt that certain self-created societies and combinations of men, careless of consequences and disregarding the truth, by disseminating suspicions, jealousies, and accusations of the government; have had all the agency you ascribe to them, in fomenting this daring outrage against social order and the authority of the laws."

Ward voted against the majority which as an afterthought modified the charge by limiting it to "certain self-created societies and combinations of men in the four Western counties of Pennsylvania, and parts adjacent"; and again against the majority by his vote to restore most of the original significance of the clause by supplementing the limiting sentence with the words "countenanced by self-created societies elsewhere."

On yet another vote the entire clause was defeated, and direct reference to "self-created societies" was avoided in the address adopted (November 28), but the record of the debate is valuable as an indication of the thought and trend of the times.[21]

The Third Congress dissolved on March 3, 1795, and General Ward welcomed its end as the self-appointed termination of his political career. "This day the Session of Con-

[21] In the Senate, the Federalists defeated an effort to expunge reference to the "self-created societies" in its reply to the President's message. The Senate address declared that "our anxiety arising from the licentious and open resistance to the laws in the Western counties of Pennsylvania has been increased by the proceedings of certain self-created societies, relative to the laws and administration of the Government; proceedings, in our apprehension, founded in political error, calculated, if not intended, to disorganize our Government, and which, by inspiring delusive hopes of support, have been influential in misleading our fellow citizens in the scene of insurrection."

gress closeth," he wrote to his son Henry Dana, "and this day finisheth my public political life. I shall now return to the private walks of life, and spend the few remaining days of my Pilgrimage . . . in solitude; I have spent many of my days, I may say years, in the bustles of this transitory world; I hope not altogether unprofitably to my constituents, myself, & those that shall hereafter come on the stage of life."[22]

On his way home from Philadelphia he stopped off at Middletown, Conn., to visit his daughter Maria (Tracy). Of his journey he wrote thence, March 17, to his son Thomas Walter, "the travelling is excessive bad, I never saw it worse, nor more dangerous."[23]

Only four days after the Third Congress had closed its labors, Jay's treaty with Great Britain was placed in Washington's hands. With the greatest care he guarded it from the public eye and called the Senate in special session. The Senate gathered June 8, debated behind closed doors, and gave their ratification (excepting only one article). It also endeavored to continue Washington's policy of secrecy concerning the provisions of the treaty, but its caution was without avail, for one Senator rebelled and the full text became public property on July 1.

The Democratic Societies immediately raised a storm of protest. The treaty was denounced as grossly inadequate, as a proof of the Federal Party's truckling to England, as a betrayal of American rights. There were wild scenes in many places. Alexander Hamilton was stoned by a New York mob.

Washington ratified the treaty in August, and then the anti-English wrath turned upon him and he was reviled in terms which he bitterly complained could scarcely be applied "even to a common pick-pocket."[24]

[22] Original letter owned (1921) by Maria Whittelsey Norris, Grand Rapids, Mich.

[23] Original letter in the possession (1921) of Ward Dix Kerlin, Camden, N. J.

[24] To Thomas Jefferson, July 6, 1796.—Ford, *Writings of Washington,* XIII, 231.

Abuse and political tirades continued for months, and the uproar intensified Ward's aversion for the Democratic-Republican following. "I hope," he wrote to his son Henry Dana (in South Carolina), "that you will shun the Southern politics as you would the poison of an asp, and indeavour to enlighten the dark minds of your legislators so far as you can with prudence. It's my opinion you may in time do much good in that way. It's through ignorance they do as they at this time do."

In the same letter he earnestly defended the treaty. "Let them," he said, "compare the treaty made with Great Britain with the treaties made with other Nations, particularly with that made with France. They will find privileges in the British treaty that are not in the French treaty, particularly the trade to the East Indias. Before the treaty, it was all upon sufferance in the British East Indias, and is now so in the French East Indias. I readily allow there are things in the treaty I could wish were otherwise, but at the same time I must say we had it not in power to have them otherways. Upon the whole I think we had best be easy with it as it is, it's not to last always. What makes many uneasy with it is they are plague loth to pay the debts they owe to Great Britain."[25]

He also noted that the country towns of Massachusetts held themselves steadier than the capital—"those restless mortals in the metropolis have used every art to make the people uneasy in the Country, but have pretty generally failed."

His viewpoint was justified by the results. The treaty, despite its defects, proved of substantial value. Trade improved and a fair degree of prosperity returned.

France, though, was seriously disgruntled by the concordance of England and the United States and by the provisions of the treaty.

[25] Original letter, February 1, 1796, owned (1921) by Maria Whittelsey Norris, Grand Rapids, Mich.

Increasing age compelled Ward, this time, to adhere to his resolution to retire from the stress of political life, but for another three years he continued to preside as chief justice of the Worcester County Court of Common Pleas.

His interest in affairs remained keen and his convictions were by no means softened.

By correspondence with Dwight Foster, who had succeeded him as United States Representative, he kept himself informed on the political sentiments of the Fourth Congress.

On January 15, 1796, shortly after it convened, he wrote asking "for a list of your house, the States they come from, with a mark for Federalists and one for Jacobins if any such there be." Those marked by Foster as Federal were not as numerous as Ward had hoped. Acknowledging the list, he says (March 1, 1796), "I wish you had been able to have dotted more of the new members"; and he adds as postscript, "I hope Congress will do no mischief."

He termed "a peculiar smile in Providence" the interception of a letter written by Joseph Fauchet, French minister to the United States, which, with an earlier communication it dragged into the light, charged that at the time of the "Whiskey Insurrection" Edmund Randolph, Secretary of State—a strong opponent of the treaty with England—had solicited some thousands of dollars of French money on the plea that it was urgently needed to pay the debts of four men whose talents, influence, and energies might avail to fend off civil war in the United States, but who, as debtors, could make no move for fear of being thrown into prison by their English creditors.[26]

"In my opinion," Ward continued, "it has had a tendency to silence the Jacobins who were forever declaiming against the Federalists, saying they were influenced by British Gold.

[26] *A translation of Citizen Fauchet's Intercepted Letter No. 10; to which are added Extracts of Nos. 3 and 6,* published in Philadelphia, 1795. Fauchet's explanation and qualified retraction appeared shortly after in *A Vindication of Mr. Randolph's Resignation* [of his office of Secretary of State on being confronted with Fauchet's letter]. The subject is treated at length in Conway's *Edmund Randolph.*

Now we may conjecture with a good degree of certainty who would receive foreign bribes."[27]

The second presidential term was drawing to a close. Washington declined to be a candidate for a third term, and so in the fall of the year there came the first real presidential contest—John Adams, the Federalist, against Thomas Jefferson, chief of the Democratic-Republicans.

"There will be a great struggle," writes Ward, October 10. "John Adams will I trust have the votes for President in New England & I trust some more. . . . Some talk of Thos. Pinckney for Vice President. I wish they may be chosen. It is of great importance we should have federal men in those places.

"I hope we shall not have in either of those places a person so frenchified as some of the characters to the southward are. It seams some are so attached to the French they would do nothing without their leave. We are an Independant nation & we ought to act independently."[28]

Ward had the satisfaction of seeing John Adams elected to the presidency, but had to be content with Jefferson for Vice-President. (It will be remembered that in those days prior to the Twelfth Amendment a possible result of the vote of the electoral college was the election of a defeated presidential candidate as vice to his victorious opponent.)

A little later, he saw the European conflict again drawing the United States toward war, this time through the depredations of French privateers; and it was not long before he was to read the famous X, Y, Z dispatches—the demands of agents of the French Directory for bribes and a large national loan—for "money, a great deal of money"—as the price of peace, and to see the country reverse its pro-French attitude and howl for war with France, using as their slogan Charles Cotesworth Pinckney's "millions for defense, but not one cent for tribute."

[27] Original letter owned (1921) by Charles P. Greenough, Brookline, Mass.

[28] Original letter owned (1921) by Maria Whittelsey Norris, Grand Rapids, Mich.

By the summer of 1797 General Ward had begun to feel that his strength was unequal to his judicial duties. On June 12, writing to his daughter Maria and her husband, Dr. Ebenezer Tracy, he says: "the lawyers in the general court are endeavoring to demolish the Courts of Common Pleas in this Commonwealth & to establish a circuit court in lieu thereof, and it is probable they will effect it. It don't affect me much for I shall soon leave that Court and confine myself at home. I am old & infirm, it is time for me to quit the theatre of action, and while I remain here live a domestic life."[29]

He sat in court for the last time during the session of December, 1797, and soon after terminated his long career as a judge.[30]

He spent the remaining two years of his life in quiet retirement in his home, the now famous old Artemas Ward House.

"His grandchildren lived to tell their grandchildren about the handsome old man, with his erect and portly figure set off with his ruffles and shoe-buckles and all the touches of the old time costume—how he would rise from his straight-backed chair and take from a shelf of a tall cupboard in his room, crackers, or raisins or some other dainty (as they were then) and give them as a reward for some little service they had done."[31]

His letters show him, in his old age, as in his younger years, full of kindly love for his children and the members of their families—condoling with them in their afflictions, and rejoicing in their happiness, always keeping in the foreground the God he had served so conscientiously all his life, and inculcating the same reliance in, and acceptance of, divine decrees. For himself, he was expecting the end and praying that he might be "prepared."

[29] MS. copy, *Artemas Ward MSS.*

[30] On March 20, 1798, writing to the Tracys, he says, "I have resigned the office of Judge in the Court of Common Pleas, it being too hard service for me to perform under my difficulties. I shall attend these courts no more."—Original letter owned (1921) by Frank C. Whittelsey, Flushing, N. Y.

[31] Elizabeth Ward, *Old Times in Shrewsbury,* 186.

His health became precarious in 1798. On July 18, in a letter to the Tracys, he writes: "I have been much unwell. For four months I have not been one hundred rods from my house: in which time I longed to see you & for your advice. Through Divine goodness I am much better on some accounts, although far from being well. I am an old man upwards of seventy years of age, so that I have no right to expect to injoye perfect ease & comfort. We are told in scripture that threescore and ten years is the age of man; beyond that *is grief and pain.*"[32]

There is much the same story in the spring following. On March 6, 1799, again to the Tracys, he wrote: "My health is no better than when you saw me last, I have not been one hundred rods from my own house for more than twelve months. I have just recovered from a verry ill turn."[33]

In November he suffered a paralytic stroke and his life was despaired of, "but through divine goodness I was restored in a merciful degree."[34] He was very weak though, unable to dress or undress without aid.

His faithful correspondent, Dwight Foster, still kept him informed on national politics. On December 28 Foster sent him "a List of the two Houses [of the Sixth Congress] marked . . . to note the political Character by the Terms *Federal, antifederal* and *doubtful,*" and wrote him that there was "little doubt" that the Federalists could muster "a respectable majority in the House of Representatives"; and that in the Senate there was "a majority as large, as respectable and as decided as there was previous to last March when one third were either re-elected or returned as new members."[35]

[32] Original letter owned (1921) by Frank C. Whittelsey, Flushing, N. Y.

[33] Original letter owned (1921) by Mary Clap Wooster Chapter, D.A.R., New Haven, Conn.

[34] To the Tracys, June 12, 1800.—Original letter owned (1921) by Frank C. Whittelsey, Flushing, N. Y.

[35] Original letter, *Artemas Ward MSS.*

The Federal Party was nevertheless nearing the end of its tenure.

On the twentieth of March Ward suffered a second paralytic stroke, but it was lighter than the first and did not immediately affect his general condition to any marked extent.

In the fall he failed rapidly, and on Tuesday, October 28, he lay dying. His son Thomas Walter wrote to Maria Tracy, telling her of the approaching end—"there has been a great alteration in the good old gentleman for the worse. He is past speaking or taking anything unless it be a little water to wet his mouth." For twenty-four hours he had appeared almost unconscious of his surroundings. "I have no doubt he will make a happy change when he changes time for eternity. I shall feel the loss more than any one of my brothers or sisters, for I always have lived with him & it is hard to part with so good a Father, but it is the wish of God & we must not murmur nor complain."

He died a little before seven of the evening of that day. He was occasionally "exercised with the same distressing pain" in his last hours that he had been troubled with "for months and years past," but he passed away easily with "scarce a struggle in death."[36]

He was buried on the afternoon of the following Friday, October 31—a "cloudy day with an easterly wind." A long procession of carriages formed his funeral cortège[37] and an impressive address marked the last rites.

Thus closed the career of Artemas Ward, one of the worthiest of Massachusetts' many noble sons. He had played a prominent part in the generation which founded the great republic of the United States. He had stood in the forefront of revolution when the challenge was thrown down to

[36] Thomas Walter Ward to Maria Tracy, October 28 and November 6, 1800.—Original letters owned (1921) by Frank C. Whittelsey, Flushing, N. Y.

[37] Ruth Henshaw Bascom (original) diary.—Owned (1921) by Caroline Thurston, Leicester, Mass.

the might of the British Empire, and had held equally resolute against the wrath of compatriots when it ran counter to the best interests of the state or nation. His had been a character of strength and stability which could be swayed neither by favor nor by fear; and a life of continuous industry from youth to old age. A character and a life well deserving a high place in the annals of Massachusetts.

As he passed on, there closed not only the calendar years of the eighteenth century but also a well defined period of the history of the United States. Washington had died the year before. The Federal Party lost the fourth presidential election and never again achieved importance. A new chapter, embodying new thoughts and new conceptions, opened with the nineteenth century and the presidency of Thomas Jefferson.

THE ARTEMAS WARD MEMORIAL ENTRANCE, MOUNTAIN VIEW CEMETERY, SHREWSBURY, MASS.

Erected in 1918 by his great-grandson, Artemas Ward, New York

INDEX

INDEX